MODERN HOMELESSNESS

Selected Titles in ABC-CLIO's
CONTEMPORARY WORLD ISSUES
Series

Animal Rights, Clifford J. Sherry
Autism Spectrum Disorders, Raphael Bernier and Jennifer Gerdts
Climate Change, David L. Downie, Kate Brash, and Catherine Vaughan
DNA Technology, David E. Newton
Domestic Violence, Margi Laird McCue
Education in Crisis, Judith A. Gouwens
Environmental Justice, David E. Newton
Gay and Lesbian Rights, David E. Newton
Genocide, Howard Ball
Global Organized Crime, Mitchel P. Roth
Global Refugee Crisis, Mark Gibney
Identity Theft, Sandra K. Hoffman and Tracy G. McGinley
Lobbying in America, Ronald J. Hrebenar and Bryson B. Morgan
Modern Piracy, David F. Marley
Modern Sports Ethics, Angela Lumpkin
Obesity, Judith Stern and Alexandra Kazaks
Same-Sex Marriage, David E. Newton
Sentencing, Dean John Champion
Sexual Crime, Caryn E. Neumann
Sexual Health, David E. Newton
Substance Abuse, David E. Newton
U.S. Border Security, Judith A. Warner
U.S. Space Policy, Peter L. Hays, PhD
U.S. Trade Issues, Alfred E. Eckes Jr.
Women in Combat, Rosemarie Skaine

For a complete list of titles in this series, please visit
www.abc-clio.com.

Books in the Contemporary World Issues series address vital issues in today's society, such as genetic engineering, pollution, and biodiversity. Written by professional writers, scholars, and nonacademic experts, these books are authoritative, clearly written, up-to-date, and objective. They provide a good starting point for research by high school and college students, scholars, and general readers as well as by legislators, businesspeople, activists, and others.

Each book, carefully organized and easy to use, contains an overview of the subject, a detailed chronology, biographical sketches, facts and data and/or documents and other primary-source material, a directory of organizations and agencies, annotated lists of print and nonprint resources, and an index.

Readers of books in the Contemporary World Issues series will find the information they need to have a better understanding of the social, political, environmental, and economic issues facing the world today.

MODERN HOMELESSNESS

A Reference Handbook

Mary Ellen Hombs

Foreword by Philip F. Mangano

CONTEMPORARY WORLD ISSUES

ABC-CLIO

Santa Barbara, California • Denver, Colorado • Oxford, England

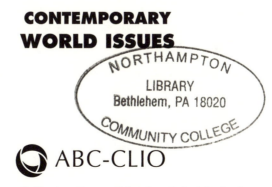

Library of Congress Cataloging-in-Publication Data

Hombs, Mary Ellen.
Modern homelessness: a reference handbook / Mary Ellen Hombs ; foreword by Philip F. Mangano.
p. cm. — (Contemporary world issues)
Includes bibliographical references and index.
ISBN 978-1-59884-536-5 (alk. paper) — ISBN 978-1-59884-537-2 (ebook)
1. Homelessness. 2. Homelessness—Government policy. 3. Homelessness—Prevention. I. Title.
HV4493.H63 2011
362.5—dc22 2011008474

ISBN: 978-1-59884-536-5
EISBN: 978-1-59884-537-2

15 14 13 12 11 1 2 3 4 5

This book is also available on the World Wide Web as an eBook.
Visit www.abc-clio.com for details.

ABC-CLIO, LLC
130 Cremona Drive, P.O. Box 1911
Santa Barbara, California 93116-1911

This book is printed on acid-free paper ∞
Manufactured in the United States of America

Contents

Foreword

A decade into the 21st century, homelessness is yielding to solutions. Even as the United States and countries around the world struggle with the effects of an ongoing economic downturn, governments at every level across the Atlantic and Pacific Oceans have acted in unprecedented ways in unprecedented partnerships with unprecedented results to prevent and end homelessness.

Having served as the point person of the federal effort on homelessness from 2002 to 2009 under President Bush and in the first 100 days of the Obama administration, I saw firsthand that we made progress in increasing resources and decreasing numbers. During those years we more than doubled federal investment and reduced street and long-term homelessness. In the years 2005–2009 the number of homeless living on our streets and languishing in our shelters dropped by 36 percent. That outcome was the first sustained decrease in street and shelter homelessness in our nation's history documented by data and research.

During those years we left behind much that had not worked, moving beyond compassion fatigue and frustration and policy détente. Belatedly we learned that if good intentions, well-meaning programs, and humanitarian gestures could end homelessness, it would have been history decades ago. They don't, and it isn't.

We shaped a new approach to homelessness based on what works: a strategy that emphasized local political and civic leadership, business principles and practices, and field-tested and evidence-based innovative initiatives in engagement, housing, employment, and services.

The new approach resulted in more than 1,000 mayors and county officials partnering in 10-year plans to prevent and end street and chronic homelessness. That worked. All across the country, cities and counties began to report reductions on the streets and in shelters. Those reports continue. From 2005 to 2009, the decrease in street and chronic homelessness was documented by data and research in communities across the nation. The average 9 percent annual decrease signaled that we are on track to accomplish the 10-year goal.

The long-term street homelessness of the most disabled individuals continues to yield to innovative solutions fashioned in the United States and now adopted internationally.

What elements of that strategy and success should be sustained? What changes were made to secure the unprecedented reductions? What can we learn from the innovations and new results?

First, on this issue of homelessness, partnership trumps partisanship. On this issue there is no D or R. We are simply Americans partnered to end the disgrace. There can be no partisan divide that undermines our most vulnerable neighbors. The Bush and Obama administrations and the Congress all ensured increased resources for the past nine consecutive years.

Second, local planning fueled by the political will of jurisdictional CEOs —mayors and county officials—can create and sustain policy and resources that reduce homelessness. Local leadership informed by national innovation—our practice was always the rapid dissemination of innovation—offers the ingredients of solutions. Local plans, led by elected officials convening all of the stakeholders, created reductions.

Third, the new political will is inspired and fueled by cost studies that reveal the economics of homelessness and the expense of ad hoc, uncoordinated responses. Street homeless people are expensive to the public purse. The cost of doing nothing for them is very expensive—in hospitals, emergency rooms, acute mental health and addiction programs, police lockups, courtrooms, and jail cells.

More than 65 cost studies across the nation revealed that this random ricocheting costs between $35,000 and $150,000 per person, per year in expensive health and law-enforcement systems and simply maintains people in their homelessness. But the cost of the supported housing intervention for these vulnerable individuals ranges from $13,000 to $25,000 a year and literally ends their homelessness. You don't need to be a hedge fund manager to know which is the better investment.

Fourth, as a result of these cost studies, we recognize that the stakeholders of homelessness are a much more expansive group than once thought. Not only are they well-intentioned homeless providers and faith communities on the front lines, but the issue also impacts hospital administrators, businesses, police, judges, jailers, chambers of commerce, pedestrians, and librarians. Self-interest as a motivator for cost efficiency and results makes sense—common sense and dollars and sense—for many of these stakeholders.

Our mission is clear and unambiguous. Our intent is to move beyond managing the crisis to ending the disgrace. We know we have more work to do. Our research and data-driven strategies, when applied to families and youth, will lead us to the field-tested and evidence-based innovations that will reduce those populations of homeless people as well.

The new business mindset requires us to prioritize consumer preferences, develop relevant metrics, and invest only in quantifiable results. Our new focus moves us away from process, inputs, and funding to performance, outcomes, and investments.

The good news is that we can speak of investment in innovative ideas that end the long misery of our homeless neighbors—ideas that are proven in the field and in the research. Initiatives focused on housing, engagement, and employment—Pathways to Housing, Assertive Community Treatment Teams, Street to Home, Ready, Willing & Able, and Project Homeless Connect. These innovations engage our homeless neighbors wherever they are, house them, and support them with services and employment.

Of these innovations, Housing First is the most significant. After all, the central antidote to homelessness is a place to live. Consumers know that. Now it's our turn to connect our execution to their aspirations. In doing so, we change the equation of homelessness and create a trajectory toward safety, recovery, and upward mobility.

Through our focus on solutions, results, and sustained political will we achieve a public policy trifecta: good for homeless people; good for the community; good for the taxpayer.

In this comprehensive volume, the remarkable story of a public policy mindset change is chronicled. Political leaders, researchers, and innovators are named and their impact analyzed. The results of their leadership are made available to the reader, and their investment in innovation challenges the policy maker.

More importantly the achievements and strategies detailed here offer, for our era, a template of strategic response for other social wrongs. For those societal ills that seem intractable, here is a roadmap to abolition.

Philip F. Mangano
President and CEO of the American Round Table to Abolish Homelessness

1

Background and History

Introduction

Fundamental change occurred on the issue of homelessness over the past decade in the United States and other countries with comparable socioeconomic conditions. Both the problem of homelessness and other issues (such as the worldwide economic crisis) became more widely understood through research and data. New strategies and solutions emerged and yielded international dialogue about preventing and ending homelessness. In the last decade, the problem of modern homelessness seemed to be growing and irreversible—"intractable" was a common characterization. The last decade, however, brought key developments in research, policy, housing strategies, and service delivery that were shown through data to decrease homelessness. Active partnerships among governments of the United States, Canada, England, and Australia moved the issue and its remedy in a new direction.

This chapter provides a brief history of the contemporary issue of homelessness as well as insight into changes at work in research and policy during the last decade. Homelessness itself has not been new for over 25 years. In the 1980s, the problem was perceived at epidemic proportions, and frontline local crisis response became visible in soup kitchens and shelters nationwide. Many of those local programs endure today.

As the numbers of those experiencing homelessness continued to increase, service providers and public officials alike recognized that the problem was often complex. That perceived complexity also made solutions difficult for elected leaders to craft and made meal programs and shelters the most visible response in communities. For different profiles of people experiencing homelessness, achieving stability touches on many issues of poverty such as public assistance, wage levels, addiction, mental illness, education, and housing costs. The commonality in all homelessness is a lack of housing.

The unique safety net and welfare-state programs of national governments once seemed to define what government response was possible, making international comparisons of policy initiatives and budget investments speculative at best. But larger global economic issues are not confined by national borders, as evidenced most recently in the worldwide downturn. Peers in policy making from several national governments came to see that they had much to convey about strategies and investments targeting homelessness. Insight could be mined in peer-to-peer settings for the larger lessons that were changing the historic response in nations toward one of targeted investment and an expectation of reducing and ending homelessness.

In addition to economic crisis, natural disaster, in the form of hurricanes Katrina and Rita in the United States in 2004, provided valuable lessons on new ways to organize community response for those in need. The ongoing wars in Iraq and Afghanistan made addressing homelessness for service members a key priority.

A significant portion of the story told here starts with the initiatives of the federal government in the United States. The events of the last decade provide a basis for this approach. It is not the case that the response to homelessness begins and ends with national government anywhere. But the degree of change in the United States during this period was driven by concrete goals, strong leadership from the public and private sectors, new investment, and consistent effort to disseminate new ideas to the field and identify those innovations that were being developed locally. Not since the first legislative response in Congress in 1987 has the federal government made such a major contribution to change on the issue.

What Changed in the United States?

The unprecedented change that occurred in the United States on the issue of homelessness—which itself resulted in never-before-seen reductions first announced in 2007—resulted from several crucial shifts in strategy, investment, and results, which will be highlighted throughout this book. The dramatic changes in policy and investment strategies of the last decade can be analyzed for the factors that proved to be most effective in changing the nature of the national and local dialogue, response, and results.

In 2002, the new Bush administration established through language in the annual federal budget a goal to end chronic homelessness within a decade (OMB, 2002). For those who asked, "Why chronic homelessness?" the federal goal drew on new research data that showed this most long-term homeless adult population as finite (estimated at 150,000), expensive, and with deep levels of disability (Kuhn and Culhane, 1998). Critics challenged the notion of such a targeted goal coming at the expense of others in need, including homeless families (NPACH, 2005). Debate over the definition of the chronic population and its targeting was unabated and eventually was reflected in legislative changes to the homeless programs in 2009 (HEARTH, 2009).

While the federal government in 2002 had 15 years of history in administering homeless programs, the new federal goal was surprising in its details. First, federal homeless appropriations had steadily increased over those 15 years, yet there was little expectation that the existing investment would end homelessness in the nation. There was likely less expectation by policy advocates and service providers that a new Republican administration would set such a target or follow through to demonstrate its consistent support for meeting the goal. The federal budget increased investment in homelessness initiatives every year from 2001 on, yielding unprecedented resources for the new strategies it was identifying and supporting (USICH, 2008c).

At almost the same time as the administration's new policy announcement, several more resources had become available to support strategies to accomplish the federal goal. The federal Interagency Council on Homelessness, composed of 20 federal agencies, was created by federal legislation in 1987 but was dormant and unfunded in the several years prior to the Bush administration (1994–2000) (USICH, 2010b). The council was revitalized in 2002 with U.S. Department of Housing and Urban Development secretary Mel Martinez serving as chair. The agency was put under the strong leadership of Philip Mangano, an entrepreneurial advocate on the issue for more than two decades. Mangano identified several emerging elements for a federal strategy and partnership for the newly independent agency. One was the new data that offered quantifiable insight into the needs of homeless adults who were the most disabled and long-term homeless on the streets and in shelters, the "chronically homeless." Another was the commitment and political will of state and local jurisdictional officials.

The new federal goal and its strategies drew directly on the lessons of the Rough Sleepers Initiative in England. In 1999, British prime minister Tony Blair issued a new plan for addressing the needs of the country's "rough sleepers," or people living outside. The government's initial report recommended setting up the Rough Sleepers Unit, with the target of reducing rough sleeping in England to as near to zero as possible, and by at least two-thirds, by 2002.

Coming in from the Cold: The Government's Strategy on Rough Sleeping in 1999 noted that "a steady population of long-term rough sleepers who have not been helped effectively by previous initiatives" needed to be the focus of new "braver" approaches and that "some services have in practice sustained people in a street lifestyle, rather than helping them off the streets." The report concluded: "The balance in the system must be tipped towards the most vulnerable rather than making the streets a fast track for the most able." Blair further noted: "Government will provide the tools, and the funding. But we know that this approach will only succeed as part of a genuine partnership—between central and local government, the voluntary sector, statutory bodies, businesses, community groups and rough sleepers themselves" (ODPM, 1999).

The government policy peers of the Rough Sleepers Initiative were a resource to the new direction of U.S. policy makers focused on chronic homelessness, giving rise to what became a new and regular series of exchanges between counterparts that expanded to include Canadian and Australian initiatives.

Developing Policy and Investment with Data

The new federal policy target was based on research data that clearly identified the chronic population and some of its dynamics and informed strategy. Data had been a missing ingredient to the development of policy and investment on homelessness, but the Bush administration's management agenda required all investments to be data driven, performance based, results oriented, and consumer focused.

One key problem in crafting responses to homelessness had historically been the lack of data about who is homeless and why and what is needed to end their homelessness. Prior to the last decade, very little data was available to guide public investment or policy in the United States. Anecdotes and information on inputs (meals served, beds filled) characterized the issue of homelessness. This was both a practical problem and a cultural one for social services programs, which were more focused on assisting individual and families than on collecting or analyzing data. There was no expectation that homelessness was being prevented or ended for those in contact with such programs. Thus, ending homelessness as an expected outcome of resources being invested was not a part of the dialogue on the issue.

An important new development during the last decade in the United States was the shift of public policy development and budget investment on homelessness to data-driven initiatives and an increased expectation of measurable results. While national data collection efforts in the federal homeless programs were directed by the U.S. Congress, new academic research also emerged to reshape public and policy debate. The new developments included data on specific populations (such as veterans, youth, and the long-term or chronically homeless), on the quantifiable outcomes of new strategies, and on the costs and results of new approaches.

Research on Chronic Homelessness

Research, especially cost and cost-benefit research about the underlying cost of the status quo response to homelessness—for public systems such as police, fire, EMTs, hospital emergency rooms, libraries, and more—emerged as a new component of policy. Cost data demonstrated that communities of all sizes that faced the challenge of homelessness—whether visibly on downtown streets, in encampments along rivers or in parks, in winter shelters, or in other settings—could quantify their problem, its costs to public systems and taxpayers, and more effective solutions.

Until the late 1990s in the United States, public policy for homeless adults (not families) was largely based on stereotypes of visibly homeless individuals on the streets as unreachable, isolated, and untreatable. These individuals, viewed as the majority of homeless adults, were often seen as a nuisance, asking for change on the streets or publicly suffering the effects of alcohol, drugs, and/or mental illness. Volunteers and outreach workers brought blankets, coffee, soup, and more, with little expectation that more could be done for individuals who had often been on the same streets for years. Their situation was viewed as frustrating and not changeable. If they used shelter or mission programs periodically to escape the weather or access food, clothing, and showers, they were likely expected to participate in treatment or other programs. Their continued homelessness, albeit accompanied by disability, was a choice in the eyes of many.

The research of Dr. Dennis Culhane of the University of Pennsylvania was key to changing how shelter use and individual need was understood. Dr. Culhane looked at shelter beds as a system of resources through which people with distinct needs came and went, with bed turnover as a crucial and measurable component, much as hospital beds would be analyzed (Kuhn and Culhane, 1998). This view of emergency shelter as a resource that could be tailored to specific profiles of greater or lesser need changed the view of the adult population from one that was static and homogenous to a dynamic one with distinct subpopulations. The data changed the idea of what factors were important in policy and investment.

Dr. Culhane's data revealed that the single adult homeless population is made up of three distinct groups or clusters. The largest group (80 percent) is transitional in nature, staying only a brief time in shelter and never returning. These individuals are helped by access to permanent housing and income through jobs. A second group (10 percent) stays in shelter and then returns, often using other public systems between episodes. They experience medical, mental health, and substance abuse problems and chronic unemployment, using costly services in hospitals, jails, and detoxification programs (Kuhn and Culhane, 1998).

The third group, highly visible and inaccurately perceived as the largest group of homeless adults, in fact turned out to be a small percentage of the population—the chronically homeless (10 percent) (Kuhn and Culhane, 1998). Their stays in shelter (and on the street) are long and virtually unbroken, their levels of disability from mental illness and substance abuse are deeper, and their almost permanent residence in emergency programs absorbs 50 percent of available homeless resources. The nearly constant presence of this third group in homelessness was the basis of the expectation that they were the largest number of homeless adults with the least connection to services and the least potential to end their homelessness. Both of these assumptions were soundly challenged and disproven by the results of policy and investment changes that followed Dr. Culhane's research. Subsequent research by Culhane that focused only on costs for chronically homeless individuals in psychiatric care, addiction treatment, and incarceration (but not in law enforcement, courts, EMS, and general health care) demonstrated that 20 percent of those with the highest service costs represented 60 percent of total annual costs (Poulin et al., 2010).

While consuming most of the homeless resources, this small group—on the streets and in shelters—was offered little to end their homelessness; they were seen as the manifestation of the intractability of the problem. There was no perceived "win" in directing public policy or investment to these visible individuals. Yet, during the last decade, new strategies for this population emerged and were proven to end homelessness. Rather than a sequence of programs, ready access to cost-effective housing solutions worked. Against most expectations, the long-term, disabled homeless adult population showed a high rate of success in supported housing programs that combine appropriate services with housing subsidies.

Collecting Data Nationally

The U.S. Congress understood the need for more data on homelessness, both to understand the problem and to examine the incrementally increasing investment of federal budget resources in homeless programs. During the last decade, the U.S. Congress was newly interested in what data revealed about homelessness. In 1998, Congress through the annual budget process directed the U.S. Department of Housing and Urban Development (HUD)—the federal agency where the key McKinney-Vento homeless programs have historically been administered—to develop a standard process for collecting data about people experiencing homelessness across the nation.

Specifically, Congress indicated that HUD should collect an unduplicated count of people who were homeless; characteristics (such as age, race, sex, disability status, health status, and income); types of services that homeless clients received; and client outcomes (such as length of stay in transitional programs, success in acquiring permanent housing, and employment status). Congress concluded that this information would allow HUD to better assess the quality of programs supported with federal funds.

In 2001, HUD began to implement what is called the Homeless Management Information System (HMIS). HMIS established standard pieces of information or data definitions to be collected from people seeking shelter or services, created a means to aggregate this information within communities, and provided the opportunity to social services agencies to coordinate their work with individuals by using electronic data. Communities must undertake a biennial one-night count of streets, shelters, and other sites during a late-January time frame.

Congress directed that data be reported from HUD annually. In 2007, HUD released the first analysis of data from a sample of communities participating in HMIS in a report called the *Annual Homeless Assessment Report (AHAR)*. An overview of key data from the 2009 AHAR is included in chapter 6, and a summary is provided here (HUD, 2010c).

Data from the 2009 report reflect 334 communities as they are grouped geographically to apply for federal homeless funds. Together they represent 2,988 counties and 1,056 cities reporting data. The 2009 report includes 2007 and 2008 data, allowing for comparison as well as information from personal interviews in 9 cities.

According to the report, on the night of the January count across the nation, there were an estimated 643,067 people experiencing homelessness (including both sheltered and unsheltered people). More than 60 percent were in shelter or transitional programs, and 37 percent were living on the streets (HUD, 2010c).

Individuals accounted for 63 percent of the population, and 37 percent were in a family. Just 21 percent of family members were without shelter, compared to almost half of all homeless individuals. The estimate of people experiencing chronic homelessness was 110,917, demonstrating over a 10 percent decrease from the 2008 count of 124,135 chronically homeless people and a total 36 percent drop in chronic homelessness since 2005. All of the 2009 decrease was among unsheltered chronically homeless people (HUD, 2010c).

The data that make up the AHAR are limited by the time lag of local communities reporting their annual data centrally for aggregation. In 2009, HUD announced that it would begin another data initiative, called the "Homelessness Pulse Project," to collect quarterly data on sheltered families and individuals that were more timely from nine localities. According to HUD's announcement, the agency's goal is "to help gauge whether rising unemployment, increased foreclosures, and a struggling economy are leading to marked increases in homelessness in these nine communities. The up-to-date information enhances HUD's ability to respond to the economic crisis and inform public policy. . . . Its contents should be taken as suggestive—not definitive—of how homelessness may be changing during these uncertain economic times" (HUD, 2010a).

Partnership, Investment, and Innovation

Jurisdictional Partnership with State and Local Government

Many of the new solutions that emerged during the decade were the result of the leadership of government at every level—national, state and provincial, and local—and locally tested innovations whose results were documented through data. Engagement of other levels of government was a centerpiece of the federal strategy in the United States.

The decade brought increased focus on strategic planning using business principles, inclusive community partnerships that established the participation and leadership of business and civic figures alongside front-line social services providers, and a new expectation of results in reducing and ending homelessness. This major shift in partnership and strategy was characterized by Philip Mangano, the leading policy maker at the federal level in his role as the appointed executive director of the federal U.S. Interagency Council on Homelessness from 2002 to 2009, as "changing the national mindset from *managing* homelessness to *ending* homelessness" (Mangano, 2002).

The council had an existing legislative mandate to encourage the development of state interagency councils on homelessness that mirrored the federal council in its membership and mission of coordination and partnership. Such state councils assemble a broad partnership of state agencies, legislative representatives, business and civic leaders, and social service providers and advocates to focus on the unique role of states, state resources, and federal resources provided directly to states.

Every state governor was contacted by the federal council to take this step or revitalize an existing state-level entity in order to provide state partnership with federal and local government. State after state convened new councils, created state plans, and engaged local government to coordinate investment and solutions.

Additionally, a concept paper on local planning had been outlined in 2000 by the National Alliance to End Homelessness (NAEH). The alliance had developed a conceptual approach to four ideas: planning for outcomes, closing the "front door" of homelessness by increasing accountability in mainstream programs, opening the "back door" out of homelessness by increasing housing opportunity, and building infrastructure in housing, services, and income supports (NAEH, 2000).

With a set of sophisticated and proven strategies and a continuing commitment to jurisdictional leaders to deliver evidence of "what works," the Interagency Council adopted 10-year plans as a key tool for new business-oriented planning and strategy. Plans were developed with the consistent guidance and support of the council based on jurisdictional leadership, business principles, and inclusive partnership. From a handful of early plans in 2002, over 350 plans involving partnerships of over 1,000 elected mayors and county officials had been recorded by 2009 (USICH, 2009d).

Ten-year plans became the primary tool to enlist elected jurisdictional officials at the state, county, and city level to become partners in ending homelessness, a role that would expand partnership, provide accountable leadership, and draw other sectors to the new dialogue. Local jurisdictional leaders who committed to create and implement business-oriented plans frequently appointed a "community champion," a local business, civic, or political leader who could give a higher profile to the plan and help attract the resources needed for implementation. Champions were another planning innovation that emerged.

When Council Director Mangano first presented the U.S. Conference of Mayors with the challenge to develop plans in 100 cities in January 2003, the mayors demonstrated their support by passing a unanimous resolution. When Director Mangano reported back to the mayors the next year, over 115 mayors had committed to plans. From New York, Chicago, Miami, and Denver to Atlanta, San Francisco, St. Louis, and Washington, D.C., to Norfolk, Virginia, Springfield, Massachusetts, Chattanooga, Tennessee, and Asheville, North Carolina, mayors moved forward with 10-year plans. Also in 2003, both the National League of Cities and the National Association of Counties passed resolutions endorsing the goal of ending chronic homelessness and 10-year plans. The mayors' resolution is included in chapter 6.

In a 2007 homelessness summit of mayors and county officials convened in Denver, local jurisdictional officials signed a statement of commitment that demonstrated the evolution of key principles and innovations through planning and partnership titled "America's Road Home." The new statement was signed by more than 300 city and county officials by 2009 (USICH, 2009a).

The council also developed toolkits and other resources to support officials in moving forward. The key components of the 10-year plan strategy were laid out: committing the jurisdiction to developing a plan; identifying stakeholders; convening a working group; gathering research and data on homelessness; defining the community's homeless problem; developing strategies to address these problems; soliciting stakeholder feedback and finalizing a strategic plan; creating an action plan to implement strategies; announcing and publicizing the strategy; and implementing the plan (USICH, 2009e).

Emerging strategies in implementation included regular public "report cards" on progress and subsequent "recalibration" of plans to incorporate new ideas and innovations.

The Economic Argument to End Homelessness

Business thinker and writer Malcolm Gladwell also influenced change on homelessness. Gladwell's popular book *The Tipping Point* demonstrated the value of investing modest new resources in the most visible expression of a social problem. "Concentrate, don't dissipate" was the lesson for investing against the goal. This argument took on the prevailing expectation that every resource should be expended equally over all need. It countered with an expectation that concentration would show results, which would then attract more resources (Gladwell, 2002).

Gladwell contributed another vital resource to the national effort with a February 2006 essay in the *New Yorker* magazine titled "Million-Dollar Murray: Why Problems like Homelessness May Be Easier to Solve than to Manage." The cost of what was seen as "managing" homelessness through an individual's frequent use of public services (including hospitalization, incarceration, detox treatments, and ambulance rides) was demonstrated for a Reno man, Murray Barr, whose street homelessness cost an estimated $1 million in public resources (Gladwell, 2006).

The magazine article caught and kept the attention of policy makers, media, and local partners, who embarked on their own cost studies to provide the economic argument for ending the expensive chronic homelessness of their neighbors. No city could afford the costs being revealed. Soon, local planning efforts were seen as incomplete without a cost analysis of heavy users of public services. Those very vulnerable individuals who lived on the streets and sidewalks turned out to be very expensive to emergency medical services, ambulances, EMTs, primary health care, behavioral health care, psychiatric treatment, detox facilities, and the justice system, police, law enforcement, corrections, and the courts.

Local Cost-Analysis Studies

The cost-benefit research many local officials conducted on homelessness with the Interagency Council's encouragement became the convincing economic argument in 10-year plans. While data published in the early 1990s had demonstrated that hospitalization costs were higher for individuals who were homeless, with their homelessness accounting for the increased expense, data also indicated that their hospitalizations for substance abuse and mental illness were far higher than for other patients (Salit et al., 1998).

Other data that gave direction to research and practice had emerged from the Boston Health Care for the Homeless Program. Some 119 chronically homeless individuals were tracked through data that showed that they had 18,000 emergency room visits in five years, each estimated at a cost of $1,000 per visit (O'Connell et al., 2005).

In the early 1990s Dr. James O'Connell of the Boston Health Care for the Homeless Program had examined the street deaths of 13 individuals in downtown Boston in six months. He identified factors ranging from the day and week of death to key individual characteristics. He found that those who died were chronically homeless, lived on the streets and avoided shelters, and were very vulnerable to injury, trauma, and hypothermia. They showed a high utilization of emergency services and detox. Importantly they each had multiple major medical issues, including mental illness, alcohol abuse, dual diagnosis, and several major medical illnesses, constituting so-called trimorbidity (O'Connell et al., 2005).

Dr. O'Connell applied this profile of risk to identify those most in danger of death on the streets. His research is now at the core of the "Vulnerability Index," a tool to register those in critical need of intervention and housing placement now in use in numerous cities globally.

More than 65 cost studies emerged around the country, from jurisdictions large and small. Three of the most often cited are summarized here. In San Diego, California, the University of California at San Diego followed 15 chronically homeless street people for 18 months, tracking their use of behavioral health acute systems, mental health and substance abuse services, law-enforcement interventions on the streets, and temporary periods of incarceration. Their total cost was $3 million, or $200,000 per person.

In Seattle/King County, a $4 million savings to public systems through the 1811 Eastlake Housing First initiative was documented. The project, for 75 chronic inebriates, was reported in the *Journal of the American Medical Association* in 2009. "Providing housing and support services for homeless alcoholics costs taxpayers less than leaving them on the street, where taxpayer money goes towards police and emergency health care. Stable housing also results in reduced drinking among homeless alcoholics." The reduced costs included 41 percent in Medicaid costs, 19 percent in EMS paramedic interventions, and 42 percent fewer jail days (Larimer et al., 2009).

In Denver, a Housing First study examined emergency room, inpatient medical, psychiatric, outpatient medical, detox services, incarceration, and shelter costs and utilization for two years pre- and post housing placement for a group of chronically homeless individuals with an average of eight years of homelessness per person. Over 80 percent housing retention was reported at six months, with a 73 percent reduction in emergency costs, or nearly $600,000, in the two years post placement compared to two years while homeless. There was a 66 percent decrease in inpatient costs, 40 percent fewer inpatient visits, and 82 percent fewer detox visits (Perlman and Parvensky, 2006).

The Denver results in 2008 led to an announcement by Mayor John Hickenlooper that the city would reinvest $20 million in savings in public systems to create 200 new units of housing for persons who are chronically homeless. This reinvestment strategy was the first of its kind in the nation (USICH, 2008a).

New Federal Funding Approaches

With new data, new budget resources, and new partners focused on chronic homelessness, the federal government in early 2003 undertook an unprecedented joint-funding initiative on homelessness involving the U.S Interagency Council on Homelessness and the Departments of Housing and Urban Development, Health and Human Services, and Veterans Affairs. Practitioners in the field had long sought federal funding opportunities that combined the resources of multiple agencies in the same time frame so that they could compete for dollars that would blend effectively and holistically for local needs. More than 100 applications were filed for what would be 11 local awards (HUD, 2003).

The joint-funding announcement, published in the *Federal Register* on January 27, 2003, and which eventually awarded $55 million, summarized the research basis for the focused initiative and concluded: "Research indicates that these individuals consume more than half of all homeless services. As such, there are significantly fewer resources available for 90 percent of the homeless—including families—who, with a little assistance, could often exit homelessness relatively quickly. By addressing the housing and service needs of persons who are chronically homeless, we will have more resources available to meet the needs of other homeless people. When persons who are chronically homeless have access to basic assistance like housing and treatment, they have fewer problems and are less likely to need expensive emergency interventions. The research makes it clear that one of our best hopes for ending homelessness of every sort depends on addressing chronic homelessness. We are setting policy and taking action based on that research."

The goals of the new initiative were to increase the effectiveness of integrated systems of care for persons experiencing chronic homelessness by providing comprehensive services and treatment and linking them to housing; create additional permanent housing for persons experiencing chronic homelessness; increase the use of mainstream resources (e.g., Medicaid, Temporary Assistance for Needy Families, Food Stamps, Substance Abuse Prevention and Treatment Block Grants, Mental Health Block Grants, Social Services Block Grants, State Children's Health Insurance Program) that pay for services and treatment; replicate service, treatment, and housing models that have proven to be effective based on sound evidence; and support the development of infrastructures that sustain the housing, services, treatments, and interorganizational partnerships beyond the federal initiative.

HUD subsequently awarded 12 demonstration grants totaling $10 million to sites focusing on chronic street alcoholics. The second initiative was designed to identify unique needs and successful housing strategies for the over 500 individuals in the "serial inebriate" population (HUD, 2005).

Identifying and Adopting Innovation

Other new and innovative approaches were tested during the decade, displacing established thinking and practice to achieve new results. Whether in housing, employment, engagement of the most difficult to reach on the streets, or accessing benefits, innovations surfaced and were propelled back to the local level to be adopted by more communities through organized efforts to infuse new ideas into the field. The federal Interagency Council took as its goal the identification and "rapid dissemination" of emerging innovations that were being tested locally and evaluated through data, promoting "the art of legitimate larceny" among communities that tailored and adopted what was working elsewhere (Mangano, 2005).

One new approach was Housing First, a housing strategy that has now been recognized as an evidence-based practice with a more than 85 percent success rate. Seeing that "business as usual" was not working for the homeless individuals he was supporting through street outreach and other services, Dr. Sam Tsemberis in New York City listened harder to what they told him they wanted. It was not a sequence of programs that required them to maintain sobriety or treatment and succeed at each step until they were judged ready for housing. Instead, his clients wanted housing and choice about the services they used. In other words, their expressed desire was for housing "first."

Just as many found the Bush administration commitment on homelessness counterintuitive to expectations of a Republican president, the trajectory of Housing First seemed unlikely. As characterized by Dr. Tsemberis, "Fifteen years ago, who would have imagined that the most humane and effective solution for ending homelessness would come directly from the people who were living on the streets—people who were, by all accounts, helpless, disoriented, and vulnerable?" What would happen if you offered the person who slept on the sidewalk the key to an apartment? How could someone who might have spent years on the streets, who might be mentally ill or addicted, who had not lived independently, sustain housing? Thousands of vulnerable individuals—formerly living at great risk on the streets and costing communities disproportionate expense in resources—now show the stabilizing effect of housing itself and how the model succeeds in cities around the globe that have adopted it as a central strategy (Pathways to Housing, 2007).

Another innovation was Project Homeless Connect, which gained global traction after being developed in San Francisco, adopted in more than 250 U.S. cities, and then migrating to Canada and Australia. Again, business as usual was challenged by this innovative "one-day, one-stop" model in delivering easy and expedited access to services, benefits, and "quality of life" resources, such as haircuts and clean clothes. Connect drew on the need to make access easy and choice available for people living on the streets who were often distrustful of their prior experiences in seeking services (PHC, n.d.).

Connect took lessons from the one-stop centers that were spontaneously organized in many welcoming communities after hurricanes Katrina and Rita and from veterans' "Stand Down" events, which were typically outdoor, multi-day encampments. Those displaced by natural disaster had not been stigmatized by their status or need. Communities welcomed families and individuals with expedited and simplified resources ranging from identification to health care to clothing, setting up one-stops in armories and convention centers. The same consumer-focused approach was modeled by Connect with events in nonhomeless locations such as civic centers, hotels, and sports arenas. Connect events were convened for families and youth to specialize resources for these populations.

All of these factors worked together to change the way all sectors—government, business, faith communities, social services agencies, law enforcement, health care, and more—were thinking about homelessness and responding to it. After 20 years of crisis response and increased federal funding but no decline in numbers or development of strategies that could be applied broadly, the last decade was a time of unprecedented change.

Unprecedented Reductions in Homelessness

The changed approach delivered unprecedented news in November 2007 when, for the first time in the history of contemporary homelessness in the United States, the federal government released national data that had been reported by over 3,900 local communities showing a "nearly 12 percent decrease in the number of chronically homeless persons living on the nation's streets. HUD's analysis found that more than 20,000 persons moved from the streets into transitional and permanent supportive housing between 2005 and 2006." According to HUD data, the 175,914 individuals reported in 2005 decreased to 155,623 in 2006. (HUD, 2007) A November 7, 2007, statement released by the White House on the announcement noted that the new results demonstrated that "targeted, focused resources can achieve measurable results" (White House, 2007).

When a 36 percent reduction in chronic homelessness for the years 2005 to 2009 was announced in 2010, it underscored the effectiveness of the new strategies underway and highlighted the needed progress to meet the 10-year goal. As noted in a national editorial, "The Bush administration focused mainly on the chronically homeless, whose numbers have dropped 30 percent since 2006. An Obama plan wisely builds on that foundation to help more of the homeless, such as families and veterans" ("Obama," 2010).

Research and Resources for Homeless Populations

The *2009 Annual Homeless Assessment Report* from HUD to Congress noted several key facts about the data from local communities that had been aggregated nationally in the annual report. According to the 2009 report, almost 1.56 million people used either emergency shelter or a transitional program during the year (October 1, 2008, through September 30, 2009). Two-thirds of those reported were individuals, and one-third were members of families (HUD, 2010c).

While adult males make up just over 40 percent of the general population, they represent 63.7 percent of the homeless adults. The profile for a shelter user is an adult male, a member of a minority group, middle-aged, and unaccompanied. Slightly over two-thirds have a disability. The number of sheltered homeless families increased for the second year, and, similarly to 2008, the number of sheltered homeless individuals decreased. Most families have a female head of household under age 31. Sixty percent of those in families are children, and more than 50 percent of the children are under age six.

Homeless Families

With new research emerging on chronic homelessness, there was a parallel federal strategy building to develop a research base to address family homelessness and other issues. The U.S. Department of Health and Human Services (HHS) convened a national research conference and commissioned papers to look at many homeless populations and strategies. Dr. Debra Rog, a leading researcher on homeless families, reviewed what was known from prior family research. She found that most homeless families are headed by a single woman in her late twenties with an average of two children, one or both under six years of age. Those at most risk of homelessness are also from ethnic minority groups. Families are very poor and lack assets in education and employment. Families demonstrated a high level of housing instability, living "doubled up" with others and moving frequently. Dr. Rog found that partner violence and childhood abuse were strongly present in these families. Mothers exhibited poorer health than housed mothers and comparable levels of mental health problems but self-reported higher levels of substance abuse (Rog and Bruckner, 2007).

Dr. Rog also found that, while homelessness had an impact on children's health and well-being, including on education, there was little research on long-term effects and evidence that impact declined over time, with exposure to violence being a more significant factor that homelessness.

Dr. Rog pointed to the role of housing affordability—variable across markets—and the lack of research data on common models in use for families. No studies had compared transitional programs (the longer-stay model emphasized in federal homeless spending), permanent supported housing, or permanent housing for homeless families or identified the right mix of housing and services that was cost effective and stabilizing. The idea of rapid rehousing strategies for families was not yet visible.

A subsequent 2007 research study by Dr. Dennis Culhane sought to apply the same "cluster" analysis he used on single adults to the family population. Analyzing data from several jurisdictions, Dr. Culhane found that the majority of families fell into the temporary stay category. "In terms of the relative use of shelter system resources, the groups again exhibit fairly comparable results across sites. In all four jurisdictions, approximately half of the total bed days are used by the roughly one-fifth of family households in the long-stay category" (Culhane et al., 2007).

The lack of a research basis for new initiatives for families demonstrated the need for additional strategies and research. The federal Interagency Council in 2008 published the results of a federal survey of programs that could serve homeless families with children, an inventory of 73 programs in 11 federal agencies. Just as the federal investment in chronic homelessness had yielded insights into "what works" to house and stabilize individuals, HUD sought to learn more about family rapid rehousing strategies. In 2009, it awarded over $23 million to support and evaluate 23 pilot projects across the country (USICH, 2009c). Subsequent new resources under the Recovery Act (ARRA) yielded a new $1.2 billion for the Homelessness Prevention and Rapid Re-Housing Program (HPRP) (USICH, 2009b).

HUD undertook a study of transitional programs to address the gap in knowledge identified by Dr. Rog and determine if length of stay was a factor in program benefits. In 2010, HUD released findings from a five-city study that showed that "while transitional housing programs produced increasingly positive outcomes for families with longer stays, HUD found the number of barriers facing families did not impact outcomes. Given the significant costs associated with service-intensive transitional housing programs, HUD's report brings into question whether this housing model is the most appropriate intervention for those families who do not have significant barriers to housing" (HUD, 2010b).

Veterans

In November 2009, the U.S. Department of Veterans Affairs (VA) announced a five-year plan to end homelessness among veterans. When the federal Interagency Council released its new strategy in mid-2010, the VA noted that homelessness among veterans had been reduced from 195,000 to 107,000 over six years (VA, 2010b). AHAR data estimated veterans to represent about 13 percent of persons in shelter (HUD, 2010c). AHAR also reported that veterans are slightly more likely to be represented in the sheltered homeless population than the general population but are a much smaller share of the adult poverty population (5.1 percent) than the homeless population, in part because the adult poverty population includes fewer adult men who are the most likely to be veterans. The estimated number of homeless veterans will be a focus as the number of veterans returning from Iraq and Afghanistan increases during the next few years (HUD, 2009).

Women veterans now number approximately 1.8 million, according to the VA. This number has steadily increased, up from 1.2 million in 1990. Representing 6 percent of veterans in 2000 data, women are estimated at 8 percent of all veterans in 2010. At median age 47, they are also younger than the average male veteran at 61 years of age (VA, 2010a).

The VA plan includes preventive measures such as discharge planning for incarcerated veterans, supportive services for low-income veterans and their families, and a national referral center to link veterans to local service providers. The plan calls for expanded efforts for education, jobs, health care, and housing. VA partners with more than 600 community organizations to provide transitional housing to 20,000 veterans. It also works with 240 public housing authorities to provide subsidized permanent housing to homeless veterans and their families under a partnership with the Department of Housing and Urban Development. The VA/HUD partnership will provide permanent housing to more than 20,000 veterans and their families.

Young Adults

Homeless young adults reflect several specific background issues, though there is little data to determine how much overlap exists. Young people—and there is no commonly agreed on age range—may have aged out of foster care at age 18 or left the child welfare system even earlier, be runaways or throwaways from family difficulties or sexual, physical, or other abuse or neglect, or have left the juvenile justice system.

The federal Runaway and Homeless Youth Act, the key federal legislation for the population, created programs that are operated by the U.S. Department of Health and Human Services (HHS). The legislation defines the population as "individuals under age 18 who are unable to live in a safe environment with a relative and lack safe alternative living arrangements, as well as individuals aged 18 to 21 without shelter" (HHS/HCF, 2001).

The Office of Juvenile Justice and Delinquency Prevention (OJJDP) of the U.S. Department of Justice (DOJ) distinguishes runaways and throwaways by looking at young people who left home without permission and stayed away for specified periods of time, young people who left at the direction of an adult without adequate alternatives, and young people prevented from returning by an adult.

Numbers have been difficult to establish, and little is known about costs of youth homelessness. Causes are several from the description above, but there has more recently been attention focused on the needs of this population. The 2010 federal homeless strategy, *Opening Doors,* which set a goal to prevent and end youth homelessness in five years, called for targeted outreach and improved access to health care, housing, and supports to "Advance Health and Housing Stability for Youth Aging Out of Systems such as Foster Care and Juvenile Justice" (USICH, 2010a).

A short list of federal resources for the young adult population would include the Chafee Foster Care Independence Act; the Runaway and Homeless Youth Act (HHS); other federal programs, such as the Workforce Investment Act (WIA), Temporary Assistance for Needy Families (TANF), and Medicaid, which provide states flexibility to use various funding streams to help youth transition out of foster care; the Department of Labor's Re-integration of Ex-Offenders program (REXO) for youth and juvenile justice cases; DOL's YouthBuild program; and the DOL Job Corps/Foster care recruiting initiative.

Homeless Children

The homeless young adult population is not the same population as that of homeless children, who generally are defined as being part of a family household that has become homeless or is at risk of homelessness. This group, including those who are living doubled up, has long had protections under the federal education laws.

Data on the number of children are reported to the U.S. Department of Education under the McKinney-Vento Act education provisions. The National Center for Homeless Education reported in 2010 on data from the 2008–2009 federal data collection of state reports that require that all children have access to a free, appropriate education, including children who are homeless (NCHE, 2010).

Homeless children and youth are considered enrolled if they are attending classes and participating fully in school activities. In the school year 2008–2009, local education agencies (who are required to have a designated liaison for homeless children) reported a total of over 956,000 homeless students. Some 66 percent of those reported, or more than 600,000 children, were reported living doubled up. This figure represents an increase over 2006–2007 figures of 420,995 (NCHE, 2010).

The report suggests that the increase may be due to one or more factors, including improved data collection, the nation's economic downturn, and displacement of students by disasters such as hurricanes Katrina and Rita.

Domestic Violence and Homelessness

Domestic and family violence contribute to homelessness, but the safety and confidentiality concerns for victims and their families means that programs and services operate in an arena that is frequently set apart from other homeless resources. Domestic violence programs include shelters, rape crisis centers, battered women's shelters, transitional housing programs, and other resources for victims of domestic violence, dating violence, sexual assault, or stalking. The separateness of this network also generally means that locations of services and shelters are kept confidential. While victims of domestic violence using homeless programs were reported in the 2008 Annual Homeless Assessment Report (AHAR) as representing almost 13 percent of those in shelter, domestic violence providers do not enter their client information in the HMIS system. This prohibition was established by the Violence against Women and Department of Justice Reauthorization Act of 2005 (HUD, 2010c).

Rural Homelessness

Little data has been available to focus on the needs of rural areas. A 1996 U.S. Department of Agriculture report, *Focusing on the Needs of the Rural Homeless,* was used by the federal Interagency Council to convene a panel of experts to identify gaps in the report and emerging needs. The USDA reported key findings from rural homelessness conferences conducted by USDA's Office of Rural Economic and Community Development (RCED): the invisibility of rural homelessness including lack of shelters; isolation from services due to distance and lack of transportation options; the need for increased networking and training opportunities for community providers to learn more effective service methods; the need for more flexibility in federal program requirements; recognition that housing quality in rural areas is as much a problem as housing affordability; and support for reinforcing existing network of community agencies and faith-based organizations that traditionally help people in their community in lieu of creating separate systems of care for homeless people. Participants also noted the role of technology in bridging rural geography.

New 2009 legislation for the federal homeless programs added a new rural homelessness funding category for the Rural Housing Stability Assistance Program at HUD, designed for rehousing or improving the housing situations of individuals and families who are homeless or in the worst housing situations; stabilizing the housing of individuals and families who are in imminent danger of losing housing; and improving the ability of the lowest-income residents of the community to afford stable housing (HEARTH, 2009).

A 2010 federal report called for by the HEARTH Act found that both targeted and nontargeted federal programs can meet the needs of people who are homeless in rural areas. However, GAO identified that federal agencies do not have important data on rural resources awarded in these programs, which would make comparisons with other areas more possible. In its focus on areas in six states

(Arizona, Kentucky, Maine, Minnesota, New Mexico, and Texas), GAO found similar barriers to those identified in 1996: large areas with low population density, lack of transportation, shortages of housing, and gaps in collaboration (GAO, 2010).

Background to the Early Response to Homelessness

Beginning in the early 1980s, the problem of homelessness in the United States received increasing attention across the country. In 1980, then congressman Ron Dellums, the chair of the House Committee on the District of Columbia and subsequently mayor of Oakland, California, convened the committee for the first contemporary congressional hearing to focus on homelessness, with specific attention to the District of Columbia (House District Committee, 1980).

As the problem of homelessness grew through the 1980s, the sheer visibility of contemporary homelessness was perhaps its most identifiable attribute. Whether it was the sight of a person begging on the corner, a family living in a car, or the countless homeless people in the streets and subways of big cities, striking images of this utmost poverty were inescapable for most Americans. Little was known about homelessness outside cities, in suburbs or even rural areas. Over time, communities of all sizes discovered within their own borders a version of a problem many Americans previously associated only with the Depression years or with certain stereotypes of hobos and tramps of another era.

Ultimately replacing the heavy media coverage of the mid-1980s were the more intermittent and less sympathetic stories of the "truth" about homelessness, including the reported incidence of alcohol and drug use and mental illness among adults, especially those living on the streets. Gone—except for the traditional Thanksgiving and Christmas press coverage—were the stories asserting that "homeless people are just like the rest of us except they've had a few bad breaks."

Throughout this period, a pair of policy and budget debates continued. Are there homeless and very poor people who are simply victims of bad luck and deserve help and support? Are there people whose own personal behavior—whether alcohol or drug related, whether laziness or lack of thrift—could be rectified by their own efforts and contribute to their more stable, more "normal" future? In other words, as the dilemma was more usually phrased, aren't some of the poor deserving of help and some not? Second and more simply stated was the question, what are the dimensions of the homelessness problem?

During the same period, more communities passed new laws or undertook punitive enforcement campaigns of existing laws to regulate the behavior of homeless people in public spaces. Laws prohibited acts such as sleeping, camping, storing belongings, or distributing food. There were also documented acts of violence against people on the streets. These actions also brought new and increased press coverage, though seldom of a sympathetic nature when it came to panhandling or public inebriates.

The nation faced a significant challenge: not only did people continue to be pushed to the streets and shelters, but for some of them, escape from homelessness seemed nearly impossible, the problem intractable. Nonprofit social services agencies and the faith community provided emergency response. Few states or cities invested or directed policy aimed at solutions.

Early Advocacy and Federal Response in the United States

The federal government had tried to respond to homelessness beginning in the late 1980s. Federal policy and funding for homelessness in the United States was driven largely by the 1987 passage of the Stewart B. McKinney Homeless Assistance Act (P.L. 100-77), subsequently renamed the McKinney-Vento Act to recognize two key U.S. House of Representatives leaders who oversaw its passage and implementation. Originally the McKinney-Vento Act was introduced in January 1987 as the Urgent Relief for the Homeless Act and was passed quickly by the U.S. Congress to show concern about the growing problem of homelessness. The act was passed by overwhelming bipartisan majorities in both houses and signed by President Ronald Reagan on July 22, 1987 (Pear, 1987).

Twenty Years of Federal McKinney-Vento Homeless Programs

McKinney-Vento, which originally included 20 programs in 7 federal agencies (U.S. departments of Education, Health and Human Services, Housing and Urban Development, Labor, and Veterans Affairs, General Services Administration, and Federal Emergency Management Agency) and created the new entity of the Interagency Council on the Homeless, was a major component of the federal response to homelessness as the problem grew in the 1980s (GAO, 1992).

The McKinney-Vento programs and other federal initiatives on homelessness reflected the multiple elements of the emergency response to homelessness as well as the variety of populations (families, youth, veterans, people with disabilities) and systems of care and treatment (drug treatment, mental health, primary health care, education) and resources (rental subsidies) that interacted with the lives of homeless individuals and families. Funds were designated primarily for emergency food and shelter programs, transitional programs, supportive services, and some permanent housing. Funds were distributed by formula to all eligible entities or by competitive grants.

The first targeted federal funding response to homelessness had been the creation in 1983 of the Emergency Food and Shelter Program (EFSP), a component of the Federal Emergency Management Agency (FEMA), now part of the U.S. Department of Homeland Security. EFSP remains in operation today. Originally $50 million was appropriated to assist hungry and homeless people with food and shelter through formula awards to local boards at the community level. Since its creation, the program has disbursed over $3.4 billion to over 12,000 local providers in more than 2,500 counties and cities. Local boards include the same organizational representatives as well as a homeless or formerly homeless person (EFSP, 2010).

By the early 1990s, when the McKinney-Vento programs underwent major reauthorization (a legislative term for revising and updating existing programs), key constituencies concerned with homelessness attached some importance to revising the federal programs on which most communities rely. There was an emerging understanding of the problem, the availability of new data, and the opportunity to concentrate resources locally. Housing, and especially permanent supported housing for persons with disabilities, had emerged as a new solution to homelessness.

The federal government continued to try to break through the growing problem, both through policy and personal commitment. News coverage actually began to increase in the early 1990s, due to several factors. Shortly after U.S. secretary of Housing and Urban Development Henry Cisneros declared homelessness to be his agency's top priority in 1993, a homeless woman died at a bus stop outside the federal agency. Her death was highly publicized and analyzed as a symbol of a larger social problem (Cisneros, 1993). Just a few months later came the release of a federal strategy on homelessness, prepared as a result of President Clinton's 1993 executive order. While federal funds for these programs grew incrementally, there were no breakthroughs on the issue (HUD, 1994).

Some key references from prior to the last decade are included in background sections of chapter 8.

Recent Issues in Federal Programs

Passage and Implementation of the HEARTH Act

Reauthorization of the HUD McKinney-Vento programs and fundamental change to their structure and approach occurred with passage of the Homeless Emergency Assistance and Rapid Transition to Housing (HEARTH) Act of 2009. With both House and Senate leadership, new legislation passed in early 2009. The legislation was incorporated in the Helping Families Save Their Homes Act, signed into law by President Barack Obama on May 20, 2009 (HEARTH, 2009).

Reauthorization had been an ongoing process for the HUD programs, as multiple versions of the legislation were brought close to passage over several years, reflecting a common understanding that emerging new themes and strategies should be incorporated in the federal programs.

The HEARTH legislation was also the vehicle for more controversial issues, including the expansion of the definition of homelessness used by HUD. The expansion to include people defined as homeless by other federal programs and those living doubled up with friends and families had been controversial among advocates and policy makers.

The impact of the expansion, even for steadily increasing resources, could not be estimated with credible data. One national advocacy organization looked at U.S. Census data in 2007 and published its analysis, which estimated, "Approximately 744,313 people on a given night currently meet the HUD definition of homeless. Expanding the definition by including the 3.8 million people who are doubled up for economic reasons would increase the size of the homeless population by a factor of five. The current funding for homeless assistance grants funds only enough shelter for 56 percent of those who are currently defined as homeless. The amount that would have to be appropriated so that the amount of funding per homeless or doubled up person matched the actual amount of funding per homeless person in 2005 is $7.725 billion instead of the $1.241 billion that was actually available" (NAEH, 2008). More detail on the definitions is provided in chapter 6.

As passed and signed by the president, the purposes of the HEARTH Act are to consolidate the existing McKinney-Vento homeless assistance programs, which had grown in 2009 to represent 6,445 individual renewal awards to existing local projects and more than 450 local, regional, or statewide groups preparing applications (HUD, 2009). The new law codified this continuum of care process in use since the 1990s as the local provider process for developing projects and preparing funding applications and to establish a goal that families who become homeless return to permanent housing within 30 days. Performance and outcomes will be emphasized in funding applications, including reducing the lengths of homeless episodes, reducing the number of people who become homeless, and reducing the number of those who return to homelessness. Rapid rehousing strategies are emphasized, as is prevention and continuing results in ending chronic homelessness (HEARTH, 2009).

Legal Issues

Language sought by national organizations and accompanying the HEARTH Act requires the U.S. Interagency Council on Homelessness to devise constructive alternatives to criminalization measures that can be used by cities around the country to "develop constructive alternatives to criminalizing homelessness and eliminate laws and policies that prohibit sleeping, feeding, sitting, resting, or lying in public spaces when there are no suitable alternatives, result in the destruction of a homeless person's property without due process, or are selectively enforced against homeless persons" (HEARTH, 2009).

Punitive measures, such as laws against sleeping, camping, food distribution, storing belongings, and more, had never proven successful in reducing the street presence of individuals. Given the limited power of federal agencies to change local law, the inclusive partnerships of stakeholders to homelessness convened for 10-year plans had been seen by both the federal and local jurisdictional partners as an affirmative strategy focused on outcomes. A defense of civil rights for people on the streets assumes their continuing presence there, while results-oriented planning was focused on ending their homelessness. In fact, many Housing First initiatives focused on the availability of an actual door key in reaching out to those experiencing chronic homelessness, saying: here is the key to your new apartment, if you want to come—as many did. There was no denying, however, that physical danger was also present as long as people lived outdoors. Attacks were reported in cities of all sizes.

Legal advocates for people who are homeless and living outside emphasized protection of the rights of individuals but seldom gave concrete support to the work of 10-year plans or measures that placed people in housing. According to the American Bar Association Commission on Homelessness & Poverty, many shared the view that it was an individual's choice to stay out. Ensuring protections of person and property was vital where so-called banishment practices were instituted by officials, and addressing homelessness without addressing poverty was futile. There was little affirmation of the interests or insights of the business or law-enforcement partners key to many plans (ABA, 2010). More details on legal issues and civil rights initiatives are provided in chapter 2.

The Role of Mainstream Resources

The use of federal mainstream resources to prevent and end homelessness and stabilize those who have moved out of homelessness has remained a concern. A 1999 government report observed that "homeless people can be served by two types of federal programs: (1) those targeted to the homeless population, such as the programs authorized under the McKinney Act, and (2) those designed to assist all eligible low income people. As we reported in 1999, 50 key federal programs administered by eight federal agencies provided services to homeless people. Of these 50 programs, 16 were specifically targeted to homeless people and 34 were mainstream programs designed for low-income people in general. In fiscal year 1997, the federal government obligated about $1.2 billion for targeted programs and about $215 billion for mainstream programs. The deeper resources of mainstream programs needed to be tapped for homeless people" (GAO, 1999).

However, the variety of ways in which mainstream resources reach the local level makes a single set of solutions difficult. Some federal programs are largely administered by the federal agencies, such as Supplemental Security Income (SSI). Others, including the Food Stamp Program (now renamed SNAP), are administered by the states. Another group of resources flows to states as block grants for substance abuse prevention and treatment with choice available to states in using funds. Still other resources, for health care and job training, are awarded competitively to nonprofit providers.

The GAO noted that homelessness itself—a situation of "transience, instability, and a lack of basic resources"—makes it difficult for people to apply, assemble records, travel to government offices, keep appointments, and more. These barriers are greater when programs do not involve providers or outreach workers with experience and expertise in homelessness. Mainstream programs themselves are variable in structure, with differing eligibility and application requirements, making it difficult to know everything that is available or simpler ways of applying for more than one resource (GAO, 1999).

A subsequent 2000 GAO report on barriers to using mainstream resources noted the increases in McKinney Act funding: "Even with this expansion, however, experts generally agree that the McKinney Act programs, by themselves, cannot adequately meet the needs of homeless people and that mainstream programs must be made more accessible to this population" (GAO, 2000).

From 2001 to 2005, the U.S. Department of Health and Human Services, in partnership with the Interagency Council, HUD, VA, the Department of Labor (DOL), and others, convened state teams for a policy academy process focused on access to mainstream resources for both the chronic and family populations. States assembled teams to work with expert faculty who assisted state and local policy makers to develop an action plan intended to improve access to mainstream health, human services, education, and employment and training programs that are coordinated with housing and other existing community programs (HHS/HRSA, 2007).

Key to the process was to create and reinforce relationships among the governor's office, state legislators, key program administrators, and stakeholders from the public, private, and nonprofit sectors. Every state developed an action plan, and many used the process as the launching point for renewed state interagency council initiatives and encouragement of 10-year plans.

Increasing Access to Income

Both the U.S. Department of Labor (DOL) and the Social Security Administration (SSA) offered new resources to secure income for people experiencing chronic homelessness. With the success of the federal chronic homelessness initiative, DOL awarded five grants to combine employment resources with housing and other services for people who are chronically homeless (DOL, 2003). SSA in 2004 awarded multiyear grants to more than 40 sites to increase access to benefits and ensure that applications are completed faster and with higher success rates, thus allowing persons experiencing chronic homelessness to leave the streets, have a source of income, obtain health care coverage, and obtain employment. The SSA awards, titled Homeless Outreach Projects and Evaluation (HOPE), combined with a joint initiative of the U.S. departments of Health and Human Services and Housing and Urban Development to offer training in SOAR (SSI/SSDI Outreach, Access, and Recovery), a best practice in preparing applications. Many enrolled in the HOPE program went on to housing, and the SOAR initiative has assisted both individuals and health care providers (SSA, 2004).

The New Federal Strategy

The HEARTH Act directed the federal Interagency Council on Homelessness to develop a strategy on homelessness and update it annually. The strategy, called *Opening Doors,* was released in mid-2010 and recognized progress in reducing homelessness: "Over the last decade, significant progress has been made in reducing homelessness among specific communities and populations. Communities across the United States—whether it is rural Mankato, Minnesota, to an urban center such as San Francisco—have organized partnerships between local and state agencies with the private and nonprofit sectors to implement plans to prevent, reduce, and end homelessness. By developing the strategy of combining housing and supportive services—delivering permanent supported housing via a targeted pipeline of resources, these communities, in partnership with the Federal Government, have 'moved the needle' on chronic homelessness, reducing the number of chronically ill, long-term homeless by nearly one-third in the last five years" (USICH, 2010a).

The federal strategy focuses on four goals, to (1) finish the job of ending chronic homelessness in 5 years; (2) prevent and end homelessness among veterans in 5 years; (3) prevent and end homelessness for families, youth, and children in 10 years; and (4) set a path to ending all types of homelessness.

The Impact of the Economic Crisis

In February 2009, Congress passed the American Recovery and Reinvestment Act of 2009. Legislation to provide stimulus for the national economy, the new appropriation included $787 billion to create jobs and add to the safety net, including for people experiencing homelessness. The stimulus package included several provisions that were beneficial for preventing and ending homelessness (USICH, 2009b).

A total of $1.5 billion was to be distributed to state and local government through the federal McKinney-Vento Emergency Shelter Grants (ESG) formula as the new Homelessness Prevention and Rapid Rehousing Program (HPRP) for short-term rental assistance, housing relocation, and stabilization services for people who may become homeless. (USICH, 2009b)

Some $70 million was allocated to states to distribute to local school districts to meet the increased needs of children who are homeless as defined by the McKinney-Vento Education for Homeless Youth and Children Program, by ensuring that they are able to enroll in and attend school.

An additional $100 million was distributed through the Federal Emergency Management Agency (FEMA) emergency food and shelter program for rent, mortgage, and/or utility payments, meals or groceries, and shelter or hotel costs.

A second round of the Neighborhood Stabilization Program consisting of $2 billion was provided to assist states, local governments, and nonprofit organizations purchase and rehabilitate foreclosed, vacant properties to create more affordable housing and reduce neighborhood blight. The first round had required that 25 percent of all housing serve people at lower income levels, and the U.S. Department of Housing and Urban Development urged communities to consider rental housing for people with special needs as a way to fulfill this obligation. A third round of funds was released in 2010 (Senate Banking Committee, 2010).

There was $500 million included for the U.S. Department of Agriculture's (USDA) Special Supplemental Nutrition Program for Women, Children, and Infants (WIC) and $19.9 billion for USDA's Supplemental Nutrition Assistance Program (SNAP), formerly Food Stamps, to increase benefit levels by 13.6 percent.

An additional $50 million was included for the U.S. Department of Justice's Violence Against Women Prevention and Prosecution Programs for victims of domestic violence, dating violence, sexual assault, and stalking for services, short-term housing assistance, and transitional programs.

Other measures included an increase in unemployment benefits and a continuation of the extended unemployment benefits program (which provides up to 33 weeks of extended benefits); the creation of a Temporary Assistance For Needy Families (TANF) Contingency Fund through FY 2010 to provide states with relief; one-time payments of $250 to Social Security beneficiaries, SSI recipients, and veterans receiving VA disability compensation and pension benefits; and a temporary increase in the Earned Income Tax Credit (EITC) for working families with three or more children.

International Developments

The Rough Sleepers Unit (RSU) was set up by the Blair government in Britain in 1999 with the aim of reducing the number of people sleeping rough in England by two-thirds by April 2002. The RSU achieved its target by November 2001. Success in the Rough Sleepers Initiative generated broader support to address family homelessness. There were also new insights into other street activities in target areas, such as begging, drinking, and drug use, as well as the development of "street families" who could be identified for special strategies of engagement. Both chapter 3, which focuses on issues outside the United States, and chapter 6, which includes data and documents on modern homelessness, discuss the Blair initiative in more depth.

Other European Action

The emphasis of initiatives on homelessness in Europe has generally been from a perspective of "social inclusion" in society, including through employment and fundamental human rights, such as those recognized by the United Nations. In 1998, the European Federation of National Organisations Working with the Homeless (FEANTSA), a nongovernmental organization, published "Europe against exclusion: HOUSING FOR ALL," which it called "a set of practical policy proposals to promote social inclusion and ensure access to decent housing for all citizens and residents of the European Union." The report was published with the support of the European Commission, with contributions from representatives of FEANTSA member organizations, correspondents of the European Observatory on Homelessness, and selected expert (FEANTSA, 1998).

Since that time, and with the support of international peer-to-peer dialogue among national government representatives, European nations have begun to develop specifics goals and strategies targeted to homeless populations. FEANTSA reported in 2010 that Denmark, Finland, France, Ireland, the Netherlands, Sweden, Scotland, Wales, Hungary, and Norway had national homelessness strategies (FEANTSA, 2010). These approaches are covered in chapter 3.

FEANTSA launched a 2010 campaign to end homelessness in the context of the European Union during the European Year on Combating Poverty and Social Exclusion. A key tool to accompany the effort was FEANTSA's *Ending Homelessness: A Handbook for Policy Makers,* explaining the importance of the entity to their efforts: "The EU is an important arena in which crossnational exchange on homelessness strategies can take place, good practice can be shared, and progress can be monitored. The EU can act as an important source of political momentum to end homelessness. Ending homelessness is now firmly established on the EU agenda as a political priority." The EU's 2010 joint report called on member states to develop integrated policies to tackle homelessness, and in 2008, the European Parliament adopted a written declaration on ending street homelessness (FEANTSA, 2010). More about these measures is covered in chapter 3.

FEANTSA noted that the strategies sought by the EU were to be guided by specific housing-oriented goals and targets based on data, with attention to all policy areas that were relevant. FEANTSA proposed that EU support for member nations should focus on increasing the evidence base available through research and dialogue.

Australia's National Plan

In May 2008, the government of Australian prime minister Kevin Rudd, which had been a partner to prior international dialogue, issued a "green paper" for discussion, noting in his public remarks: "As a nation we have failed to address these issues. Our response to homelessness is not nationally coordinated or strategically focused. While there are excellent programs, many lack sufficient scale or coordination to adequately address the multiple causes and effects of homelessness. The cost of homelessness to individuals and their families is large. The cost to society of our failure to reduce homelessness is even greater. While tackling homelessness involves additional investment, not tackling homelessness will only cost more." The green paper was designed to invite response for the development of the subsequent white paper issued in 2008 (Commonwealth of Australia, 2008a, 2008b). The prime minister appointed a council on homelessness made up of 10 members with a broad range of expertise in the issue of homelessness.

The resulting white paper, *The Road Home: A National Approach to Reducing Homelessness,* identified three strategies for action: "turning off the tap: preventing homelessness, wherever possible, through early intervention and prevention services; improving and expanding services: improving service quality and building better connections between services so clients who are vulnerable to homelessness achieve sustainable housing and improved economic and social participation; and breaking the cycle: ensuring that people who become homeless move quickly through the crisis system to stable housing with the support they need so that homelessness does not recur" (Commonwealth of Australia, 2008a).

Canada's National Partnering Strategy

Canada, also a national partner to international dialogue, launched a national homelessness initiative in 1999 and continued it until 2006, when it announced the new Homelessness Partnering Strategy (HPS), which provided $269.6 million over two years to help prevent and reduce homelessness. This strategy put in place strategic partnerships and structures including long-term housing and stable supports to help homeless persons move toward autonomy and self-sufficiency. In January 2009, the national government announced that it was extending funding two years, from April 2009 to March 2011, and would maintain annual funding for federal housing and homelessness programs until March 31, 2014, as part of its five-year commitment. Funding housing and homelessness programs for a five-year period will provide an opportunity to consider improvements to address housing and homelessness challenges and to ensure that programs continue to effectively respond to the needs of Canadians (HRSDC, 2009).

The Homeless Partnering initiative seeks to prevent and reduce homelessness through investments in transitional programs and supported housing through a Housing First approach; support to community-based efforts to prevent and reduce homelessness; partnerships between the federal government, provinces, and territories; and collaboration with other federal departments and agencies. The funding elements of the strategy are designated communities, outreach communities of smaller cities, rural or outlying areas, aboriginal communities, federal interagency pilot projects, knowledge development funding for communities, not-for-profit organizations, researchers, and scholars; an information management system, and a surplus federal property initiative for municipal, provincial, or territorial governments and community-based organizations.

More details and documents on international strategies are covered in chapter 3.

References

ABA (American Bar Association) Commission on Homelessness & Poverty. *No Such Place As "Away": Why Banishment Is a Wrong Turn on the Path to Better and Safer Cities.* Washington, D.C.: ABA, 2010.

Cisneros, Henry G. "The lonely death on my doorstep; Yetta Adams' story and the new war on homelessness." *Washington Post*, December 5, 1993.

Committee on the District of Columbia, U.S. House of Representatives (House District Committee), Oversight Hearings. "Problems in Urban Centers, Washington, D.C., and the Federal Government Role." Serial No. 996-17 (September 30, 1980).

Commonwealth of Australia. *The Road Home: A National Approach to Reducing Homelessness* (white paper). Canberra, Australia, 2008a.

Commonwealth of Australia. *Which Way Home? A New Approach to Homelessness* (green paper). Canberra, Australia, 2008b.

Culhane, Dennis P., Stephen Metraux, Jung Min Park, Maryanne Schretzman, and Jesse Valente. "Testing a Typology of Family Homelessness Based on Patterns of Public Shelter Utilization in Four U.S. Jurisdictions: Implications for Policy and Program Planning." *Housing Policy Debate*, Volume 18, Issue 1 (May 2007).

DOL (U.S. Department of Labor). Ending Chronic Homelessness through Employment and Housing Projects, 2003. Available at http://www.dol.gov/odep/programs/homeless.htm.

EFSP (Emergency Food and Shelter Program). Alexandria, VA: United Way of America, 2010. Available at http://www.efsp.unitedway.org/.

FEANTSA (European Federation of National Organisations Working with the Homeless). Available at http://www.feantsa.org.

GAO (Government Accountability Office). *Homelessness: McKinney Act Programs and Funding through Fiscal Year 1991.* Washington, D.C., December 1992.

GAO (Government Accountability Office). *Homelessness: Coordination and Evaluation of Programs Are Essential.* Washington, D.C., 1999.

GAO (Government Accountability Office). *Homelessness: Barriers to Using Mainstream Programs.* Washington, D.C., 2000.

GAO (Government Accountability Office). *Rural Homelessness: Better Collaboration by HHS and HUD Could Improve Delivery of Services in Rural Areas.* Washington, D.C., July 2010.

Gladwell, Malcolm. *The Tipping Point: How Little Things Can Make a Big Difference.* Boston: Back Bay Books, 2002.

Gladwell, Malcolm. "Million-Dollar Murray: Why Problems like Homelessness May Be Easier to Solve than to Manage." *New Yorker,* February 13, 2006.

HEARTH (Homeless Emergency Assistance and Rapid Transition to Housing Act), Helping Families Save Their Homes Act, Division B of Public Law 111-22 § 1001, et seq., 123 Stat. 1632, 111th Congress (2009).

HHS/ACF (U.S. Department of Health and Human Services, Administration for Children and Families). Runaway and Homeless Youth Basic Center Program, 2001. Available at http://www.acf.hhs.gov/programs/fbci/progs/fbci_rhyouth.html.

HHS/HRSA (U.S. Department of Health and Human Services, Health Resources and Services Administration). Homeless Policy Academies: Improving Access to Mainstream Resources for People Experiencing Homelessness, 2007. Available at http://www.hrsa.gov/homeless/.

HRSDC (Human Resources and Skills Development Canada). *The Homelessness Partnering Strategy,* 2009. Available at http://www.hrsdc.gc.ca/eng/homelessness/index.shtml.

HUD (U.S. Department of Housing and Urban Development). *Priority Home! The Federal Plan to Break the Cycle of Homelessness.* Washington, D.C.: HUD, 1994.

HUD (U.S. Departments of Housing and Urban Development), Health and Human Services, and Veterans Affairs. Notice of Funding Availability (NOFA) for the Collaborative Initiative to Help End Chronic Homelessness. Federal Register, Volume 68, Number 17 (January 27, 2003).

HUD (U.S. Department of Housing and Urban Development). Housing for People Who Are Homeless and Addicted to Alcohol. Federal Register, Volume 70, Number 5 (March 21, 2005).

HUD (U.S. Department of Housing and Urban Development). "HUD Reports Drop in Number of Chronically Homeless Persons Living on

Nation's Streets: Decrease Largely Attributed to Increase in Supportive Housing" (press statement). Washington, D.C.: HUD, November 7, 2007.

HUD (U.S. Department of Housing and Urban Development). "Obama Administration Awards Nearly $1.4 Billion in Homeless Grants" (press statement). Washington, D.C.: HUD, December 23, 2009. Available at http://portal.hud.gov/portal/page/portal/HUD/press/press_releases_media_advisories.

HUD (U.S. Department of Housing and Urban Development). *The Homelessness Pulse Report: Fifth Quarterly Report.* Washington, D.C.: HUD, 2010a.

HUD (U.S. Department of Housing and Urban Development). *Life after Transitional Housing for Homeless Families.* Washington, D.C.: HUD, 2010b.

HUD (U.S. Department of Housing and Urban Development). *The 2009 Annual Homelessness Assessment Report to Congress (AHAR).* Washington, D.C.: HUD, 2010c.

Kuhn, Randall, and Dennis P. Culhane. "Applying Cluster Analysis to Test a Typology of Homelessness by Pattern of Shelter Utilization: Results from the Analysis of Administrative Data." *American Journal of Community Psychology,* Volume 26, Issue 2 (April 1998).

Larimer, Mary E., Daniel K. Malone, Michelle D. Garner, David C. Atkins, Bonnie Burlingham, Heather S. Lonczak, Kenneth Tanzer, Joshua Ginzler, Seema L. Clifasefi, William G. Hobson, and G. Alan Marlatt. "Health Care and Public Service Use and Costs Before and After Provision of Housing for Chronically Homeless Persons With Severe Alcohol Problems." *Journal of the American Medical Association (JAMA),* Volume 301, Issue 13 (April 1, 2009).

Mangano, Philip F. Remarks at Ohio Dominican University Life of the Mind Series, Columbus, Ohio, October 3, 2002.

Mangano, Philip F. Remarks to the Hartford, CT, Ten-Year Plan to End Chronic Homelessness Event, January 31, 2005.

NAEH (National Alliance to End Homelessness). A Plan: Not a Dream—How to End Homelessness in Ten Years. Washington, D.C.: NAEH, 2000.

NAEH (National Alliance to End Homelessness). *Data Snapshot: Doubled Up in the United States.* Washington, D.C.: NAEH, March 2008.

NCHE (National Center for Homeless Education). Education for Homeless Children and Youth Program: Data Collection Summary 2010. Greensboro, NC: NCHE, 2010.

NPACH (National Policy and Advocacy Council on Homelessness). NPACH Perspective: HUD NOFA Further Restricts Communities and Excludes Populations. Washington, D.C.: NPACH, 2005.

"Obama Builds on Bush Success to Help the Homeless." *Christian Science Monitor,* June 22, 2010.

O'Connell, James J., Shawn Mattison, Christine M. Judge, H. Josiyn Strupp Allen, and Howard K. Koh. "A Public Health Approach to Reducing Morbidity and Mortality Among Homeless People in Boston." *Journal of Public Health Management Practice,* Volume 11, Issue 4 (2005).

ODPM (Office of the Deputy Prime Minister), Government of the United Kingdom, Rough Sleepers Unit (RSU). *Coming in from the Cold: The Government's Strategy on Rough Sleeping.* London, Crown copyright 1999. Available at http://www.communities.gov.uk/archived/publications/housing/cominginfromcold.

OMB (White House Office of Management and Budget). *The Budget for Fiscal Year 2003.* Washington, D.C.: OMB, 2002. Available at http://www.gpoaccess.gov/usbudget/fy03/browse.html.

Pathways to Housing. *Annual Report 2007.* New York City: Pathways to Housing, 2007. Available at http://www.pathwaystohousing.org/files/AnnualReport_2007.pdf.

Pear, Robert. "President Signs $1 Million Bill to Aid Homeless." *New York Times,* July 24, 1987.

Perlman, Jennifer, and John Parvensky. *Denver Housing First Collaborative Cost Benefit Analysis and Program Outcomes Report.* Denver: Colorado Coalition for the Homeless, 2006.

PHC (Project Homeless Connect). Available at http://www.projecthomelessconnect.com/.

Poulin, Stephen R., Marcella Maguire, Stephen Metraux, and Dennis P. Culhane. "Service Use and Costs for Persons Experiencing Chronic Homelessness in Philadelphia: A Population-Based Study." *Psychiatric Services,* Volume 61, Number 11 (November 2010).

Rog, Debra J., and John C. Bruckner. "Homeless Families and Children. National Symposium on Homelessness Research," in *Toward Understanding Homelessness: The 2007 National Symposium on Homelessness Research.* Washington, D.C.: U.S. Departments of Health and Human Services and Housing and Urban Development, September 2007. Available at http://www.hhs.gov/homeless/research/index.html.

Salit, Sharon A., Evelyn M. Kuhn, Arthur J. Hartz, Jade M. Vu, and Andrew L. Mosso. "Hospitalization Costs Associated with Homelessness in New York City." *New England Journal of Medicine,* Volume 338, Issue 24 (1998).

Senate Banking Committee. *Brief Summary of the Dodd-Frank Wall Street Reform and Consumer Protection Act (2010)*. Available at http://banking.senate.gov/.

SSA (Social Security Administration). Social Security Administration (SSA) Service to the Homeless. Washington, D.C.: Social Security Administration, 2004. http://www.ssa.gov/homelessness.

USICH (U.S. Interagency Council on Homelessness). "In the Cities: Denver City Council Approves Reinvestment Strategy to Use Cost Savings for New Housing Investment to End Chronic Homelessness." Washington, D.C.: USICH, 2008a.

USICH (U.S. Interagency Council on Homelessness). *Inventory of Federal Programs That May Assist Homeless Families with Children*. Washington, D.C.: USICH, 2008b. Available at http://www.usich.gov/library/publications/FamilyInventory_Mar2008.pdf.

USICH (U.S. Interagency Council on Homelessness). "President's FY 2009 Budget Proposes a Record Level of More Than $5 Billion in Resources Targeted to the Lives of Homeless People; Eighth Consecutive Year of Record Resources to End Homelessness; Administration Proposes Key Expansions to Intervention and Prevention Resources for Veterans, Housing, Health Care, Treatment, and Employment." Washington, D.C.: USICH, 2008c.

USICH (U.S. Interagency Council on Homelessness). *America's Road Home Statement of Principles and Actions*. Washington, D.C.: USICH, 2009a. Available at http://www.ich.gov/newsletter/Interactive_Statement_Action_Only.pdf.

USICH (U.S. Interagency Council on Homelessness). "In Washington: $787 Billion American Recovery and Reinvestment Act Becomes Law with New Resources to Prevent and End Homelessness as President Obama Calls for Converting Crisis to Opportunity." Washington, D.C.: USICH, 2009b.

USICH (U.S. Interagency Council on Homelessness). "Obama Administration Announces Record $1.6 Billion In Investments to Prevent and End Homelessness, Including 23 New Sites For Rapid Rehousing for Families." Washington, D.C.: USICH, 2009c.

USICH (U.S. Interagency Council on Homelessness). *City and County 10-Year Plan Update, 2009*. Washington, D.C.: USICH, 2009d.

USICH (U.S. Interagency Council on Homelessness). "The 1-Year Planning Process to End Chronic Homelessness in Your Community: A Step-by-Step Guide." Washington, D.C.: USICH, 2009e. Available at http://www.usich.gov/slocal/plans/toolkit.pdf.

USICH (U.S. Interagency Council on Homelessness). *Opening Doors: Federal Strategic Plan to Prevent and End Homelessness.* Washington, D.C.: USICH, 2010a.

USICH (U.S. Interagency Council on Homelessness). *United States Interagency Council on Homelessness Historical Overview.* Washington, D.C.: USICH, 2010b. Available at http://www.usich.gov/PDF/USICH_History.pdf.

VA (U.S. Department of Veterans Affairs) (2010a). *October 2010 Women Veterans Fact Sheet.* Available at http://www1.va.gov/WOMENVET/Women_Vet_Pop_FS_10_10.pdf.

VA (U.S. Department of Veterans Affairs) (2010b). Remarks by Secretary Eric K. Shinseki to the National Coalition for Homeless Veterans, Washington, D.C., June 21, 2010. Available at http://www1.va.gov/opa/speeches/2010/10_0621.asp.

White House. Statement by the White House press secretary, November 7, 2007.

2

Problems, Controversies, and Solutions

Introduction

Over the more than 25 years that modern homelessness has been visible in the United States, a few key issues have consistently been debated in the national dialogue. First among these questions has been the origin of homelessness as a problem. Whenever modern homelessness increases, comparisons to the years of the Great Depression surface rapidly. But this is the 21st century. Is homelessness different?

This chapter highlights key issues and debates that emerged in the last decade, when there was more change in research, policy, investment, and results than at any time since the passage of the 1987 federal legislation of the McKinney Act. Changes included the unprecedented level of engagement of federal, state, and local government officials in an issue that aligned their political will with the historic work of community and faith-based organizations and private charity responding to local homelessness. The content of this chapter represents the range of issues that mark the national debate, touching on enumeration, measures of poverty, modern "messaging" about homelessness that emerged with new electronic tools, and more. The issues presented here also unfold a story about how the seemingly intractable problem of homelessness yielded to new ideas and new outcomes.

Defining and Measuring Homelessness: A New Debate

Are people who are homeless really just like you and me, given a few bad breaks in our personal and economic life? Are you and I really just one paycheck away from homelessness? Or are homeless people individuals and families who made unwise personal choices, used drugs or alcohol, didn't finish school, learn a trade, or hold a job, had children too young and without adequate income to support them, spent instead of saving? Are they veterans who honorably served their country or families and individuals whose disabilities make them vulnerable to instability?

Or are homeless people victims of the global economy in good times and bad—priced out when the economy is robust and off the bottom rung of the economic ladder when bad times hit? Is homelessness more indicative of poverty and the distribution of wealth combined with a frayed safety net? Does it reflect bad public policy choices that leave people at risk? Is it some combination of bad personal and public policy choices? How do the answers affect our ideas about possible remedies?

Another key question is how to identify who is homeless. Clearly, the choice of definition has significant influence when estimating the size of the problem of homelessness. A family or individual may face the circumstances described above, lose their housing, and seek shelter. Having to use a public or community-based shelter or motel may reflect the fact that a person has no social or family network to fall back on in bad times. Or it may reflect shame about the situation or show a desire not to burden available friends or family who may also face difficulties. Or it may mean that the resources of those friends and families—a couch, a spare bed, a makeshift accommodation to keep children from going to a shelter—have been expended. When a mother and her children are sharing the extra bed at a relative's apartment, is that homelessness?

The stigma of homelessness is real, whether for children in the classroom or adults estranged from family or friends through addiction or mental illness, unemployment, or simply years on the streets. The "person-centered" language favored in some public policy discussions (a "person experiencing homelessness" rather than a "homeless person," denoting that homelessness is a circumstance, not a characteristic) is intended to reduce the stigma.

The prevailing federal definition of homelessness as used in the U.S Department of Housing and Urban Development (HUD) McKinney-Vento homeless programs for over 20 years—and by numerous other federal agencies whose programs were established by the same legislation—was in place before more recent debate on expanding the definition. Identifying more people as "homeless" because of "doubled up" and other circumstances was seen by advocates as a reality check for the problem of homelessness writ large, an effort to steer policy away from a history where targeted goals and definitions reflected the reality of scarce public resources and federal executive branch policy making. It was also argued that causing populations to compete for resources was "unethical and ineffective" and that the expansion would recognize all populations and provide local flexibility (NAEHCY, 2006).

National advocacy proponents of the expansion included the American Friends Service Committee, Catholic Charities USA, Child Welfare League of America, Family Promise, National Association for the Education of Homeless Children and Youth, National Center on Family Homelessness, National Coalition Against Domestic Violence, National Coalition for Homeless Veterans, National Coalition for the Homeless, National Health Care for the Homeless Council, National Law Center on Homelessness & Poverty, National Low Income Housing Coalition, National Network for Youth, National Network to End Domestic Violence, National Policy and Advocacy Council on Homelessness (NPACH), and Volunteers of America.

The HUD programs prior to the passage of the 2009 HEARTH Act reflected a more than 20-year history of definition, targeting, and practices that were focused on those individuals perceived as most vulnerable and unsheltered by virtue of living on the streets with mental illness, physical disability, and other issues. Long before the focus on the "chronic" homeless person was supported by data and research—and criticized by advocates for "pathologizing" people—earlier federal McKinney-Vento efforts in several federal agencies (Safe Havens, Shelter Plus Care housing, the PATH mental health outreach program, ACCESS, and more) were intended to focus on those with disabilities and street histories and bring them inside to use the ever-increasing resources of federally funded programs (NCH, 2002). Those who fit the profile were shown by the data, then and now, to be single, unaccompanied adults who were most likely male.

Note that the focus on resources is in the context of federal McKinney-Vento resources. As of 2000, few cities or states were expending their own resources on homelessness, though some did and invested heavily. Some of this spending was driven by legal requirements for shelter. But for many communities, the federal formula and competitive resources, growing each year, were the only available dollars besides local philanthropic and charitable funds. These latter resources are not tracked in an aggregate fashion, whereas the federal investment can be traced across time and through project-specific data.

The more recent debate between government policy makers forwarding the goal of ending chronic homelessness and national organizations representing providers and advocates has focused on the policy target of chronic homelessness (versus other populations). Some commentators question whether any resources should be expended for the chronic population. Cost data showed the public savings from the Housing First innovation and the improved health outcomes and decreased drinking in Seattle's 1811 Eastlake initiative, for example. One media commentator questioned spending anything at all, calling the Seattle housing site "bunks for drunks," adding, "It's a living monument to failed social policy" (Kowal, 2006).

Increasing Resources, Prioritizing Populations

As federal homeless resources grew, advocates critical of the orientation toward single adults with disabilities noted the tilt of the HUD McKinney-Vento housing programs toward that population, including a disproportionate number of veterans. Single-room occupancy units, Shelter Plus Care housing for people with disabilities, and permanent supportive housing all reflected the realities of a specific population. With a shortage of mainstream housing resources such as housing rental vouchers for low-income families and a shortage of public housing units—both of which would provide more housing answers for homeless families—the federal approach and federal homeless funds were seen as falling short for families.

Was vulnerability the right criteria to use to focus resources? Could degrees of vulnerability be compared? Conclusive cost arguments did not begin to surface until after 2002. Are single adults with disabilities on the streets really more vulnerable than homeless children and youth? If public resources will always be limited and policy choices required, is there a way to measure benefit when not everyone is served? Are homeless children and youth reflective of poor families in general, or do they face special risk that should shift the focus of investment?

Children and youth—arguably facing instability and the stress and health risk of living in shelter or unfit housing—do not generally demonstrate the level of "vulnerability" that gave rise to the identification of age, race, gender, and trimorbid medical conditions identified by Dr. James O'Connell of Boston Health Care for the Homeless in chapter 1 and reflecting the greatest documented risk of death for the street population. It is this data-driven profile that is behind the names read annually at memorial services for those who have died while homeless, a national day of remembrance organized by advocacy groups.

If federal resources increased, what should be the strategy to expend them? Should the additional funds be targeted and their effectiveness evaluated for new lessons for specific populations? This was the approach of the HUD-VASH supportive housing voucher program of the 1990s and the federal chronic homelessness and serial inebriate housing initiatives of the last decade. With the goal of ending chronic homelessness set in federal policy, resources were targeted with an expectation of results against the larger goal. The strategies of 10-year plans invoked the economic insights of both *Tipping Point* writer Malcolm Gladwell ("concentrate, don't dissipate") and business thinker and author of *Good to Great* Jim Collins ("results are infectious"), whose findings about what allows good companies to become great companies informed homeless plan strategies. See the biographies of these thinkers in chapter 5 for further details.

Should the increased resources be solely subject to local decision making about priorities or based on larger goals established by the federal funders? This is a basic question, and there are answers from each perspective. There are also associated questions regarding the federal role. What is the federal role and responsibility on the issue of homelessness? Policy maker? Investor? Even national advocates do not agree. More response was sought from the federal government, and certainly in the last decade federal policy and initiatives were made visible to local communities in an unprecedented way.

Recent federal research has demonstrated the costs of first-time homelessness. While the data was not intended to be of national scope, the findings published in 2010 lend themselves to further examination about the variety of responses to homelessness. According to the U.S. Department of Housing and Urban Development (HUD):

- For individuals, overnight emergency shelter has the lowest cost per day (and provides the fewest services and often limited hours).
- For individuals, transitional programs prove more expensive than permanent supported housing, since services for transitional programs were usually offered directly by the homeless system rather than by mainstream service providers.
- For families, emergency shelters are usually equally or more expensive than transitional programs and permanent supported housing, because families are often given private rooms or apartments. Emergency shelters for families are also likely to operate 24 hours, provide supportive services, and have fewer units, yielding higher fixed costs.

HUD found that the average costs for individuals ($1,634 to $2,308) are much lower than those for families ($3,184 to $20,031) (HUD, 2010a).

HUD summarized the research, saying: "In brief, we conclude that communities should explore strategies to (1) prevent homelessness for the majority of families facing first-time homelessness, (2) avoid extensive use of high-cost homeless programs for individuals or families who primarily need permanent housing without supports or those whose service needs can be met by mainstream systems, (3) alter the way their homeless assistance systems respond to households that are unable to remain stably housed and face repeated instances of homelessness, (4) work with mainstream systems to design appropriate discharge planning strategies and ways to identify clients at-risk of homelessness so their homelessness can be prevented."

Federal resources are used to develop data, set policy, and measure results. Not all critics see these as appropriate roles. In addressing the development of the federal strategy in 2010, a national health policy organization stated: "The federal government has a major role to play in addressing the economic and social factors that generate homelessness. The strategy of the previous administration to devolve political responsibility for homelessness to the 'community' level while withdrawing critical federal resources did create new initiatives at state and local levels, but it failed to end homelessness" (NHCHC, 2010). Another organization that characterizes itself as "watchdog and frequent critic" of the Interagency Council revealed new skepticism in a 2010 on-line post: "A plan is not a home—we continue to be skeptical that our government can plan its way to ending homelessness" (NPACH, 2010).

A national homeless education organization urged in its recommendations on homeless families with children that the federal strategy be a proxy for antipoverty efforts "tied closely to, and implemented in conjunction with, a broader plan to address poverty in the United States. Homelessness represents a failure of multiple federal polices: housing, incomes, health care, education, and child welfare. Yet much of the federal response to homelessness over the past decade has been characterized by a separation of homelessness from the larger issues of poverty that underlie it. The most proactive continuum of care is powerless to affect national macro-economic issues, such as the unemployment and foreclosure crises that are driving families from their homes; the most progressive state housing trust fund cannot make up for the lack of federal investment in affordable housing. The FSP must be driven by reforms to, and expansion of, federal mainstream antipoverty programs; it must be grounded in the understanding that targeted homeless assistance programs cannot, by themselves, prevent or end homelessness" (NAEHCY, 2010).

HUD McKinney-Vento dollars are unique in their segregation from other HUD housing and community development resources and other federal homeless resources, which are generally forwarded to state and local government, often by formula and not by annual competition. State and local officials prepare five-year plans and annual updates on their use of these larger HUD dollars. Only the homeless dollars can effectively bypass this process by the setting of priorities in a process that can be driven by social services providers and can be shaped by pressure to renew funding rather than decrease or shift resources in favor of emerging models or engage the larger government plan.

Should the relative size of a population be considered in setting resource priorities? After all, the population with long stays and disabilities was targeted for its finite number—estimated at 150,000 and deemed to be an achievable goal. Within a few years of planning and investment, results were reported. Should a goal have been chosen that was harder to achieve because it required larger resources or would show slower progress? As shown by some of the effective innovations such as Housing First, not all the successful answers for the chronic population were known at the start of the commitment, and some seemed unlikely at first glance. Cities were actively encouraged to visit one another to see innovations in action, to have their skepticism about the viability of solutions confront the results.

The existing targeted federal measures might, in fact, end the homelessness of some, though ending homelessness as a larger goal was not yet on the public policy table for discussion. Targeted measures to engage and move individuals were indeed life-saving work for many. The definition first provided in the McKinney-Vento Act, increasingly under attack as narrow and exclusionary in the 1990s and until the passage of the HEARTH Act to expand it, applied to what data consistently showed were three-quarters of the homeless population: single adults, primarily men. Data showed concretely that single adults, not families with children, were the majority of the homeless population, despite what advocates argued in seeking a HUD definition more "aligned" with other federal agencies. Critics have argued that families, children, and youth were disproportionately excluded by the HUD definition (NPACH, 2007).

Additionally, labeling individuals and families as "hard to serve," "service resistant," "not housing ready," "noncompliant," and "barred" individuals not permitted in programs inevitably leads to discussion about the practices of some social service agencies in "creaming" their clients to choose those with the likely best outcomes.

In the face of the debate over expansion of the definition, the Interagency Council convened federal agencies in 2005 to inventory the federal definitions. The federal inventory revealed that 20 programs across eight federal agencies used a common definition, with just three having an expanded version that linked primarily women and children to health care, education, and domestic violence services. Council director Mangano argued that further expansion would be costly in budget terms, though others asserted that it would provide local flexibility to meet locally identified needs and that "real world" prioritization was needed. Mangano noted that key partners such as mayors understood that resources are often limited and require tough choices to prioritize assistance to help the neediest individuals. "Many would argue that persons who are literally homeless in the streets or in emergency shelters should take precedence over individuals or families that are sharing the housing of others, albeit in an unstable environment, they are nevertheless sheltered," said Mangano (USICH, 2006a).

Establishing a position on the definition question—who is homeless and why—can lead directly to other questions. If homelessness could happen to anyone under the right circumstances, we don't need to label or judge whether an individual or family "deserves" not to be homeless. We may not even debate whether they deserve a specific level of resources in a world of scare resources. But if homelessness happens because of bad public policy and unfair economics, why are local communities expected to pick up the pieces of inadequate and often restrictive government and charitable resources and try to make them work for clients whose personal situations are not likely to change without deeper intervention? Why address homelessness as distinct issue, rather than trying to alleviate the larger problem of poverty?

What about Poverty?

Before examining the issue of numbers, a short look at some poverty issues can help identify why some advocate for rehousing strategies for people experiencing homelessness, to shift the setting of their needs to the stability of housing and not take an "either/or" stance on lifting people out of poverty as a predicate for ending their homelessness. Some communities have gone as far as to continue to count as homeless those placed in housing, on the grounds that they remain at risk of homelessness because of their poverty.

In early 2010, the U.S. Census Bureau issued a statement on work it would begin on a new supplemental measure of poverty. The Supplemental Poverty Measure will be released in late 2011 when the official income and poverty measures for 2010 are released by the Census Bureau (U.S. Census Bureau, 2010). The supplemental measure will look beyond the cash income elements of the existing poverty measure and consider other items that affect family assets, such as tax payments and expenses for work. The new measure will not be used to establish eligibility for federal programs but will offer insight into economic trends.

Several poverty measures and standards have existed at the federal level. Chief among them have been the annual U.S.

Department of Health and Human Services (HHS) figures on what it takes to support a household. HHS releases a new set of income standards each year, and the figures for different size households determine eligibility for many assistance programs. The standards set by the poverty line also determine the federal government's official estimates of how many people are living in poverty (HHS, 2010a).

The 2010 HHS poverty guidelines are as follows: one-person household—$10,830; two-person—$14,570; three-person—$18,310; four-person—$22,050; five-person—$25,790; six-person—$29,530; seven-person—$33,270; and eight-person—$37,010.

One national organization focused on federal and state budget issues for poor and working families found that some key indicators pointed to increased poverty in the nation. The Center on Budget and Policy Priorities (CBPP) reported that there was a significant increase in the number of uninsured people in the nation and that an increase in poverty with a drop in median income in 2008 showed the worst data since 1997. CBPP reported that "the percentage of Americans living in poverty rose from 12.5 percent in 2007 to 13.2 percent in 2008, the highest rate since 1997." Further, the data indicated that poor families were pushed further into poverty—as judged by being below half the poverty line—at the highest rate in 14 years. One in five children were reported below the poverty line, a level not seen in over a decade (Sherman et al., 2009).

Area Median Income (AMI) is the measure used by HUD to determine if individuals and families meet the income guidelines for housing that receives federal assistance. HUD uses data from three years of the American Community Survey, part of the census. "Low-income" is defined as 80 percent of AMI, "very low" as 50 percent, and "extremely low income" as 30 percent or below. By definition, 50 percent of residents earn less than the median or mid-point figure, and 50 percent earn more. AMI differs across geography. Here is just one set of examples of how AMI varies in different regions of the United States: San Francisco—$75,219; Chicago—$60,433; Dallas—$55,263; Boston—$68,488; and Miami—$40,260 (HUD, 2010d).

While people who are literally homeless are not included in the computations, most would fall into the extremely low income category. HUD's annual worst case housing needs data demonstrates the use of this data to show the housing shortage or surplus for each AMI category. The most recent data found that worst case needs are concentrated among extremely low income households. Households where an adult with disabilities is present have the highest risk of such housing needs (HUD, 2010d).

The mismatch of need and housing is significant for extremely low income people, according to HUD: "In 2007, of the 5.91 million households with worst case needs, a majority (4.33 million) fell into the extremely low income group, and a smaller but substantial portion (1.58 million) were in the 30 to 50 percent of area median income group."

When the key factors of affordability, availability (a lower-rent unit not being occupied by a higher-income renter), and physical adequacy are looked at together, the outcome for extremely low income renters is grave: "There are only 76.2 affordable units for every 100 extremely low income households. The ratio of available units is about three-fifths as great, at 44.2 units per 100 households. If physically adequate units are required, only 37.4 are available per 100 extremely low-income households."

What about wages and housing costs? A national housing advocacy organization annually publishes data on the "housing wage," a computation for every locality of how much an earner would need to afford HUD fair market rent levels at no more than 30 percent of income. This figure is then compared to the wage and income levels for every state and local jurisdiction. Data from HUD, the U.S. Census Bureau, the Bureau of Labor Statistics, the Department of Labor, and the Social Security Administration are used (NLIHC, 2010b).

Even factoring in the increase in the minimum wage in 2009, a two-bedroom unit at an average national fair market rent would require $18.44 an hour, or $38,360 annually. The data showed that there was no locality in the United States where a full-time job would provide this income for a renter (NLIHC, 2010b).

How Many People Are Homeless?

Substantial problems of methodology exist in trying to count homeless people, not the least of which is that many homeless people work very hard to obscure their homelessness by location, dress, appearance, and daily schedule. They try to make their homelessness "invisible" to those who might not otherwise recognize it. Others achieve invisibility by sleeping in abandoned buildings, in parked cars, or in a tent in the woods. As revealed by the definitional problem, instability for many others is hidden by precarious housing arrangements with friends or families, circumstances that can be ended in a moment. As previously pointed out, others make do in structures not intended as living quarters, including in rural areas.

Congress directed that new data be collected locally and reported nationally to inform understanding of the problem and to examine the incrementally increasing investment of federal budget resources in the McKinney-Vento programs. Both data collected through the Homeless Management Information System (HMIS) and annual Point-In-Time (PIT) counts conducted in most communities during the last week of January contributed to new insights on sheltered and unsheltered people, use of programs, and homeless in urban and suburban/rural areas.

In the years before standardized data collection, regular counts, and improved methodologies, homelessness was routinely reported to be increasing, and year after year yielded the information that "families are the fastest-growing segment of the population." There was no critique of methodology to arrive at these often-anecdotal conclusions reflecting shelter use but not necessarily homelessness. There was no questioning of headlines announcing record increases. When decreases began to be reported in 2007, the path to those results was deemed to be flawed by advocates and the results achieved through the exclusionary strategies of the focus on chronicity. A fair question seemed to be, if homeless numbers decrease, won't existing and future funds be negatively affected for community providers?

At the same time, the nation's mayors, many of them committed to 10-year plans, began to move their largely anecdotal annual survey of hunger and homelessness in more than 25 of the nation's cities to a basis in data. With the availability of HMIS data, the *Annual Homeless Assessment Report* (AHAR), and other resources, the report that had relied on a question and answer survey since the early 1990s was able to provide more than anecdotes in 2009 and an affirmation of policy direction. In 2009, the mayors reported in the *Hunger and Homelessness Survey* that "most of the cities that experienced drops in individual homelessness attributed the decline to a policy strategy, promoted by federal, state, and local government, of finding permanent housing for chronically homeless disabled adults. Nearly all of the cities on the task force have 10-year plans to end homelessness" (USCM, 2009).

The mayors reported that "despite the recession, 16 cities, 64 percent of respondents, reported a leveling or decrease in the number of homeless *individuals* over the past year. This is an indication of the success of policies aimed at ending chronic homelessness among single adults with disabilities. Nineteen cities, 76 percent of respondents, reported an increase in *family* homelessness. Cities attributed the increase in family homelessness to the recession and a lack of affordable housing."

The U.S. Census has made several efforts to count people who are homeless, dating back to "Transient Night" in 1970, followed by "M Night" in 1980 (rescue missions, all-night movie theatres), and "S Night" (street and shelter) in 1990. Methods continued to change, as the federal agency and local partners examined results and understood homelessness better. In 2000, service-based enumeration was tried. Service-based enumerations were again used in 2010 for emergency shelters, soup kitchens and mobile food vans, and targeted outdoor locations (NAEH, 2010).

Ten-Year Plans: Rhetoric, Restrictions, or Results?

What can't be measured can't be managed, goes the axiom. Setting targets and using quantifiable data to measure progress against benchmarks seemed like a foreign notion when first introduced into the issue of homelessness, where saving a life or serving a meal was the focus. But elected officials prefer solvable problems, and the business-oriented 10-year plans encouraged by the federal Interagency Council on Homelessness brought tools for addressing a problem in large and small communities nationwide. Just as no community had a monopoly on the problem due to size or geography, all had market share in developing innovations and achieving measurable results. And the opportunity was presented to reorient long-standing and institutionalized responses to homelessness.

Researcher Dr. Dennis Culhane of the University of Pennsylvania, whose work on profiling homelessness among adults led to the identification of the chronic population through data, had extended his approach to examine family homelessness. In a policy brief focused on alternatives, Dr. Culhane argued that "services for the homeless have focused on assisting households only when they are literally homeless, and then in a manner that duplicates and often supplants the services of more mainstream social welfare systems like corrections, substance abuse treatment, income maintenance, housing assistance, mental health, and child welfare services" (Culhane and Metraux, 2008).

What has resulted from homeless programs trying to coordinate is "a parallel social welfare system, with an array of health, mental health, employment, legal, dental, homemaking, childcare, and other services, for a select population eligible only by virtue of their temporary housing status, and typically only at the time of their residence in a facility for the homeless." The result, Culhane reports, is that the mainstream systems sending people into homelessness are able to bypass any oversight of the housing status of their clients, reducing accountability and leaving the "front door" into homelessness open.

The existing homeless network cannot reduce homelessness because it has made itself central to an increasing number of people who lack alternatives and remain for longer and longer periods of time. Culhane argues for a reconceived "housing emergency" context to examine resources and responses.

Some national organizations criticized the encouragement of plans that accompanied the Bush administration's commitment to end chronic homelessness in 10 years. Tools and supports did focus on the chronically homeless population where the goal had been set, but many communities for political and practical purposes chose to use their plans to address all forms of homelessness. Many were able to identify innovations and results for other populations, including families. What were also needed were effective strategies to access other investment resources, especially from mainstream programs.

Critics asserted that funding direction adopted by HUD—the federal agency where the McKinney-Vento homeless programs were administered and that was charged to implement the goal along with other federal partners—caused some shifts at the local level, though hard data on this are not available (NPACH, n.d.). Chief among the targets of criticism was the implementation of a congressionally directed 30 percent set-aside of funds for housing and eventually a funding application scoring target to prioritize housing for people who are chronically homeless. Some argued that the need for homeless funds was to replace other fundamental cuts in federal resources, so compelling specific types of applications forced communities to overlook their own priorities and follow HUD's direction. Still, a national survey in 2010 of supportive housing providers published a recommendation that urged policy makers to "make supportive housing a more prominent part of the implementation of Ten Year Plans to End Homelessness" (CSH, 2010).

According to one organization critical of federal direction, "Communities are being forced to overlook the results of their own needs assessments in order to meet federal mandates to serve 'chronically homeless' people. As a result, federal funding is not addressing the service gaps determined by communities. In distributing homeless assistance grants, HUD asks communities to rank local needs and prioritize the gaps in the resources available to meet those needs" (NPACH, n.d.).

Another national organization focused on economic issues for low-income Americans commended the establishment of the policy target on chronic homelessness in an analysis of what works in poverty reduction. Noting that "a target transforms the debate," the Center on Law and Social Policy observed that the identification of solutions plays a key role in reaching a target, which itself must be trackable and transparent. Political will—more in evidence than ever before on the issue of homelessness and at every level of government and with the private sector—is required to move the target to results. The results can leverage additional benefits, as more than one mayor used the lessons learned from 10-year planning to tackle other difficult local issues (Levin-Epstein and Lyons, 2009).

Even before the unprecedented decreases in numbers of people who are homelessness were reported, the new federal direction was receiving media attention. When, in July 2008, the Bush administration announced that between 2005 and 2007 chronic homelessness declined almost 30 percent—from about 176,000 down to 124,000—press attention grew. Further, homelessness overall declined in this period prior to the economic downturn, from over 750,000 on a single night to just more than 665,000. From *American Prospect* headlining "A Major Bush Success" to the *National Review* announcing "Good News on Homelessness," media outlets with little prior interest in the issue recognized the result.

The somewhat predictable story lines about homelessness of the past were now infused with bylines from business and economic reporters and from those who were at far ends of the political spectrum from one another. A sample of excerpts and quotes from the launch of the federal initiative follows.

An Accelerating National Movement Reduces Numbers of Chronically Homeless

Ten-year plans encouraged by the council [are] a burst of effort [that] has buoyed a field long accustomed to futility and part of an accelerating national movement that has reduced the numbers of the chronically homeless.

—*New York Times*, June 2006

Metrics of Business Is the Language of Hope: Targeting the Toughest Customers of All

Here's how hard-headed business practices can help the world's wealthiest nation deal with the hard-core homeless . . .

The market research is done the usual way: asking what they want. The typical response is emphatic. . . . What they want is a room of their own.

As with any business plan, a lot has to go right. But while applying the metrics of business to homelessness may sound icily clinical, ultimately this is the language of hope.

—*Fortune* magazine, 2006

Democrats Say Administration Plan Offers Solutions

A number of big-city Democratic mayors who have often been harshly critical of Bush's domestic policies [say the new approach] offers practical solutions to a problem that has vexed them for decades.

—Bloomberg.com, June 15, 2006

Million-Dollar Murray: Why Problems like Homelessness May Be Easier to Solve than to Manage

By Malcolm Gladwell

Enormous sums of money are already being spent on the chronically homeless, and . . . the kind of money it would take to solve the problem could well be less than the kind of money it took to ignore it.

So far, the Council has convinced more than two hundred cities to radically reevaluate their policy for dealing with the homeless.

—*New Yorker,* February 13, 2006

Solving the Toughest, Most Visible, and Costly Part of the Problem

The mission is to cajole Governors, Mayors and County Executives into not just embracing but owning the elusive goal of ending chronic homelessness.

What matters more than rhetoric and the planning is the new thinking behind it all: focusing on the toughest and most visible part of the problem—the hard-core street homeless, who cost taxpayers dearly in hospital and prison stays.

Abolitionist Apostle: On a mission to end chronic homelessness. Christopher Swope, November 2006

—*Governing*

Something That Works

One factor now motivating local officials is a realization of how much the homeless are costing them. . . . The important thing is that somebody has finally found something that works.

Give 'em Shelter: Good news for the homeless.
William Tucker, July 3, 2006

—*Weekly Standard*

Support also came from experts in the field. The Joint Center for Housing Studies at Harvard published a 2007 report on housing in the nation that included support from former U.S. Department of Housing and Urban Development secretaries Jack Kemp and Henry Cisneros. *Our Communities, Our Homes: Pathways to Housing and Homeownership in America's Cities and States* stated: "Home defines who we are and prepared us for all we can be.

Home should be a source of joy. But for too many people, poor living conditions or the loss of a home engender sorrow. . . . Home at the very least should be shelter from cold and protection from predation. But for the least among us, home is a heating grate or a tarp in the park. It should not be this way."

The secretaries, along with former HUD assistant secretary Nick Retsinas of Harvard and former National Association of Home Builders CEO Kent Colton, introduce the new bipartisan report for state and local jurisdictional leaders on housing strategies and financing, including strategies for ending chronic homelessness (Cisneros et al., 2007).

The report noted that "local officials must lead efforts to end chronic homelessness in their communities using a research-driven approach incorporating the 'housing first' model," further commenting that the targeting of the chronic population can "rally the troops around clear, achievable outcomes that can lead to system changes" and benefit all populations.

The Millennial Housing Commission, charged by Congress in 2000 to report on housing recommendations for the nation, included homelessness in its 2002 report: "Homeless families and individuals generally fall into two categories: the transitionally homeless and the chronically homeless. Transitionally homeless households need adequate housing, first and foremost, while those who are chronically homeless confront health or substance abuse problems in addition to extreme poverty. With its capital subsidy for units targeted exclusively to extremely low-income households and its recommended improvements to public housing, vouchers, and the HOME and Low Income Housing Tax Credit programs, the Commission believes that the tools needed to end transitional homelessness will be available. For the chronically homeless, permanent supportive housing, which combines housing with intensive rehabilitative and other social services, is needed. The Commission recommends the elimination of chronic homelessness over a 10-year period by the creation of additional units of permanent supportive housing and the transfer of renewal funding for such units to HUD's Housing Certificate Fund" (MHC, 2002):

> Targeting resources toward permanent supportive housing for the "chronically homeless," as currently proposed, is unlikely to "free up" emergency resources for families or other populations. The argument that targeting resources toward permanent supportive housing for

the "chronically homeless" will "free up" emergency resources for families and other populations assumes that there is a fixed, unchanging population of people who are "chronically homeless," and that "freed up" shelter beds will go to serve other populations. Neither assumption is true.

—National Policy and Advocacy Coalition on Homelessness (NPACH) Questions & Answers about the "Chronic Homelessness" Initiative

The National Coalition for the Homeless recognizes the obligation placed on units of government at all levels to collect and report data pertaining to homelessness, directly and by compelling or requesting organizations to participate in homeless data collection and reporting efforts as a condition of receiving public funds. As the nation's strongest voice for the protection of the civil rights of people experiencing homelessness, the National Coalition for the Homeless urges that this obligation not overtake the fundamental right to privacy and confidentiality of the individuals from whom data is being collected.

—National Coalition for the Homeless Position Statement on Homeless Data Collection and Reporting

The reactivation of the council is a positive step, but its focus has been primarily on convincing states and cities to develop ten-year plans to end homelessness in their communities. How can cities and states end homelessness—or even develop realistic plans to do so—when federal housing and other anti-poverty funds are being cut? How can the administration state a commitment to ending even the most limited kind of homelessness while at the same time pressing for these cuts? And how can we, as advocates, respond?

—National Law Center on Homelessness and Poverty, In Just Times June 2005

Where Are the Resources to Prevent and End Homelessness?

Federal Spending on Homelessness

Federal spending for people who are homeless increased every year in the last decade, more than doubling to over $5 billion. This spending includes both targeted dollars in homeless-specific federal programs and the estimated spending for people who are homeless and using nontargeted federal programs.

By federal agency, these resources include HUD (McKinney-Vento programs, HUD-VASH housing vouchers, Family Unification Program housing vouchers); HHS (Health Care for the Homeless, PATH Block Grant, SAMHSA Mental Health Programs of Regional and National Significance, Runaway and Homeless Youth Programs, Head Start); FEMA/DHS (Emergency Food and Shelter Program); VA (Health Care for Homeless Veterans, Domiciliary Care, Compensated Work Therapy, Nontargeted Medical Care, Grant and Per Diem Program, Transitional Housing Loan Program); Education (Education for Homeless Children and Youth); DOL (Homeless Veterans Reintegration Projects); USDA (meal programs); and Social Security Administration (Homeless Outreach and Project Evaluation). The federal Interagency Council on Homelessness is also included in this budget total.

Mainstream Resources

Little had been done to tap the deeper federal mainstream resources available primarily to families and children to augment the much smaller pool of federal HUD homeless funds (HUD because other targeted funds existed in other federal agencies, whether distributed to states and providing the opportunity to work with policy makers on targeting and set-asides of funds or competitive funds not currently being sought by state, local, or nonprofit agencies). Instead, many communities had come to use HUD homeless dollars heavily for supportive services for homeless programs, leaving HUD, the federal housing agency, the funder of everything from child care to drug treatment and mental health services to veterans services.

In 1994, the Government Accountability Office (GAO), an independent, nonpartisan agency that works for Congress, published a report on the impact of the McKinney programs that noted: "The experts generally agree that mainstream assistance programs for low-income people must also be expanded and made more accessible to the homeless to significantly improve the current situation" (GAO, 1994).

A subsequent 2002 GAO report noted that "the underlying structure and operations of federal mainstream programs are often not conducive to ensuring that the special needs of homeless people are met. Federal programs do not always include service providers with expertise and experience in addressing the needs of homeless people. These providers may not be organized or equipped to serve homeless people, may not be knowledgeable about their special needs, or may not have the sensitivity or experience to treat homeless clients with respect. For example, many providers delivering Medicaid services for states are not adept at dealing with homeless patients' special needs and characteristics, such as their inability to store medicines or their lack of adequate shelter, nutrition, and hygiene" (GAO, 2002).

Observing that mainstream programs, themselves fragmented in a complex system, often lacked incentives to serve those with complex needs and experiencing transience, instability, and a lack of basic resources, GAO added, "Numerous studies have demonstrated that the multiple and complex needs of homeless people—which may include medical care, mental health care, substance abuse treatment, housing, income support, and employment services—should not be addressed in isolation but rather through programs that are integrated and coordinated" (GAO, 2002). Few initiatives to fill this gap had emerged, chief among them the "First Step" screening tool developed among federal agencies and the SSA SOAR initiative. But benefits screening and homeless-specific strategies for mainstream resources—including 10-year plans—to ensure that no resources that could assist an individual or family were left untouched were few and far between.

Mainstream resources are a wide-ranging category, and new opportunities have come into play with the economic downturn. The Recovery Act (ARRA) resources included many dollars that could assist various homeless populations in prevention, rehousing, income support, health access, homeless education, and more.

Federal health care reform legislation in 2010 included Medicaid expansion to anyone under 133 percent of poverty in 2014. According to the National Health Care for the Homeless Council, this amounts to about $14,400 annual income for a single adult, the most likely profile of those uninsured. Community health centers, already dramatically expanded over the last decade, will expand capacity again. Health Care for the Homeless programs derive their budgets from the community health centers line item. Given 2010 research published by the *American Journal of Public Health,* showing that 73 percent of homeless clients surveyed reported that they had difficulty getting medical or surgical care, prescription medications, mental health care, eyeglasses, and dental care, such expansion is warranted (Bagget et al., 2010).

Legislation was moving in 2010 to provide more than one billion dollars for the National Housing Trust Fund, which would target 75 percent of its rental allocation to people below 30 percent of AMI (NLIHC, 2010a).

In some places, state and local advocacy—based on data, outcomes, and costs—had produced gains in targeting mainstream resources to people who are homelessness, including to provide the "support" in supported housing. The reliance on HUD dollars for social services, including treatment and training instead of housing, simply represents a gap in state and local advocacy strategies to target the relatively deeper federal resources coming to state agencies and local communities. A simple example would be the state of Florida. According to HUD data, HUD's competitive homeless awards for 2009 totaled over $73 million, while the federal formula award for the state for substance abuse and mental health programs as reported in HHS data was over $130 million, with another $47 million in discretionary or competitive awards. States have broad discretion in how they target and invest formula funds (HHS, 2010b).

Mainstream resources are a path forward for moving individuals away from risk in a broader group of poverty-oriented programs that do not require homelessness as an eligibility factor. Critics question whether creating homeless-specific systems to parallel mainstream systems is a good use of scarce resources, when an alternative is creation of access points and practices that can help bridge homeless clients to mainstream resources.

The partnership of state and local jurisdictional officials provides an additional venue for educating officials and building commitments for these resources. In a provider-driven decision-making process, where maintaining funding may compete with adopting new ideas, there have been few incentives to change course.

Several examples of partnership and investment strategies by states are included in chapter 6.

Largely through business-minded leadership for 10-year plans, some cities and counties have created dedicated revenue streams for investing in their plans, following a best practice that the targeting of funds will help ensure the resource meets the deepest need and not be dissipated on higher income users. Issued by the Atlanta Development Authority in 2005, new local bonds created the Homeless Opportunity Fund representing new revenue targeted to 10-year plan goals. Public sector partners executed a multipart resource realignment, including a local car rental tax, existing bonds, and tax increment funds, a creative approach to using bonding authority and revenues to produce new targeted resources. Funds have been invested in permanent supportive rental housing, assessment centers for women and children, and other plan goals. This initiative raised $22 million in public resources in four years (USICH, 2008b).

A Homeless and Domestic Violence Tax has long been collected on all food and beverage sales in Miami/Dade County state-licensed establishments that sell alcoholic beverages for consumption on the premises, except for hotels and motels. Eighty-five percent of the tax receipts go to the Miami-Dade County Homeless Trust, and 15 percent go to domestic violence centers. The initiative generated $11.9 million in 2007 for homeless programs (Miami-Dade, n.d.).

An increase in the real estate transaction recording fee in Indianapolis was approved by the city and county and increased the city's housing trust fund for Indianapolis' efforts to reduce homelessness and build more housing that is affordable for those in need. The fee was projected to generate $1 million annually targeted to homeless and housing programs (USICH, 2008c).

Seattle supported a series of high-performing multiyear housing levies from local property taxes. The initiative includes new rental production, preservation, and emergency homelessness prevention and stabilization assistance as eligible uses. The levy fund targets its largest component to capital funds for rental development. For 2010–2011 the levy projected $8.76 million in rental resources to extremely low income households and people who are homeless or disabled (City of Seattle, 2010).

Transportation revenues were identified as an available source of investment funds for Chicago's 10-year-plan, including earmarking city parking meter revenues for homeless programs. The 2010–2011 initiative earmarked $1.4 million in city parking meter revenues for homeless programs (USICH, 2006b).

What about Prevention?

One of the debates about homelessness concerns the issue of prevention. Surely it was cheaper and less harmful to individuals and families to intervene before people became homeless or separated to avoid homelessness. A 2010 HUD study examined 9,000 individuals in six places in the nation and found that, while housing costs were usually higher than the fair market rent levels that direct federal housing assistance, transitional programs or permanent supported housing for families costs either the same or less than shelter. Further, the majority of both individuals (50–65 percent) and families (58–72 percent) used a homeless program only once in the 18 months covered by the data. Ten percent of the individuals were tallied as using over 80 percent of the costs accrued to homeless programs (HUD, 2010a).

Historically, if a family needed a back rent or utility payment, most communities received annual resources through the FEMA Emergency Management Agency (FEMA) Emergency Food and Shelter Program and the former Emergency Shelter Grant (ESG) program. These were the only prevention assistance under the HUD homeless programs until new recovery initiatives in 2009. ESG is used by a small number of localities under a 30 percent cap for prevention to provide short-term subsidies for rent and utility debt; security deposits or first month's rent to permit individuals or families at risk of homelessness to obtain permanent housing; mediation programs for landlord-tenant disputes; and other similar uses.

Local prevention resources were always distributed quickly in communities, and little was known through data about outcome indicators other than numbers served and average payments. There was no insight from investment or research into what was most effective, the profile most at risk, and the likelihood that—absent the aid—the individual or family would have fallen into homelessness.

With the 2009 passage of the American Recovery and Reinvestment Act, the Homelessness Prevention and Rapid Rehousing Program (HPRP) was created at HUD with $1.5 billion in resources to prevent and end homelessness through short-term rental subsidies. Communities reporting to HUD through HMIS will now have a vehicle to track a larger resource and examine its effectiveness.

Other resources have received increased attention for their effect in preventing and ending homelessness. HUD awards Family Unification Program rental assistance vouchers—2,500 rental assistance vouchers to more than 40 public housing authorities in 2010—to reunite more than 2,500 families where a lack of adequate housing is a primary cause of parents being separated or near separation from their children. About 20 percent of the rental vouchers provide assistance for about 750 young adults (ages 18–22) who have "aged-out" of the foster care system (HUD, 2010b).

The recent expansion of these resources in the federal budget reflects the data that show that keeping children in foster care is more expensive than housing costs. According to the National Center for Housing and Child Welfare (NCHCW), "On average, it costs more than $48,000 annually per family when children enter foster care. By contrast, housing and services to keep a family together costs approximately $15,000 annually. Supportive services for FUP families and youth are provided by agencies funded through the U.S. Department of Health and Human Services. This $20 million investment in FUP vouchers will save more than $134 million in foster care costs" (NCHCW, 2010).

Discharge into Homelessness from Other Systems

Another form of prevention need identified during the 1990s as shelter numbers surged was the direct path between publicly funded care, treatment, custody (hospitals, addiction and mental health treatment, jails and prisons, foster care, the military), and homelessness. While numbers were only being documented in a few places to show the impact of releases and discharges, the homeless shelter system was being used to rectify a lack of access and availability both for community-based residential placements and for treatment. People leaving from both long and short stays regularly appeared at shelters with a printed list of programs given to them upon exit.

Better discharge planning was needed to affect this situation at the local level, but there has rarely been effective advocacy to create change. HUD added coordination of discharge to its application process in the 1990s, and discharge strategies and partnerships were a component of the federal policy academies for states. By convening state teams of interagency personnel, the goal was to create the kind of partnerships that could begin discharge planning with mainstream resources upon an individual's entry into an institution or hospital. Federal efforts to highlight these resources were intended to avoid formalizing homeless programs as a de facto discharge site that relieves public institutions and systems of planning responsibility for the stability of their clients and the justification of the investment already made.

One place where early work was done on discharge planning that gained national attention was in Massachusetts. Interagency Council director Philip Mangano, who spent more than 20 years working in Massachusetts advocacy for families and individuals, led the Massachusetts Housing and Shelter Alliance in its pre-HMIS work to identify dynamics of adult shelter use in a state where more than $30 million was spent annually on shelter for individuals (NHCHC, 2002).

Moving the discharge issue in an overflowing emergency shelter system from anecdote to data required "front door" data about where new shelter guests were coming from as well as research into state system data on discharges. The early data showed about 1,000 entries annually from jails and prisons directly to shelter, and over 500 young adults with state system histories. Over 1,200 people were coming from a detox program into a shelter without sobriety requirements. Up to 800 were coming from hospitalization, with most coming from private hospitals.

With street death data from Dr. James O'Connell of the Boston Health Care for the Homeless program showing that more than one person who died in his study group had been discharged to the streets within a short time of death, and with over a quarter of aging-out foster care youth nationally experiencing homelessness after leaving the child welfare system, there was ample evidence to develop new approaches (NHCHC, 2002).

Federal resources that addressed diverse needs related to homelessness and its prevention were increasing during the last decade. Policy makers were quick to point out to local providers the need to identify and use these dollars for prevention. Among the new resources were the U.S. Department of Health and Human Services' (HHS) Access to Recovery Substance Abuse Treatment Vouchers, which supported client choice in seeking treatment, the U.S. Department of Labor's (DOL) Prisoner Reentry Initiative, national expansion of community health centers, which automatically expanded the Health Care for the Homeless program, and Foster Care Independent Living Vouchers.

With the economic crisis and the return of veterans from Iraq and Afghanistan, this number may continue to increase. In order to better serve this population, HUD plans to increase housing resources available to homeless veterans, to focus efforts to ensure that coordination between local VA Medical Centers and Continuums of Care are strengthened, and to utilize Recovery Act resources provided through the Homelessness Prevention and Rapid Re-Housing Program (HPRP) to assist veterans who are at risk of becoming homeless.

In 2009 HUD developed a new $10 million homelessness-prevention initiative for veterans through a demonstration program in both rural and urban areas, at the direction of Congress. Focused primarily on veterans from Iraq and Afghanistan, including the National Guard and Reserve units, HUD, VA, and DOL will coordinate housing, services, and employment (HUD, 2010c).

Not all effective initiatives require new dollars; some can be forwarded through coordination. A no-cost initiative proposed by Interagency Council director Mangano and adopted by the U.S. Department of Labor (DOL) was a new relationship between state foster care systems and the DOL Job Corps program. Job Corps provides training and residential placement for young adults, offering access to aging-out youth that addresses both the need for education and training and stable housing. DOL reported in 2008 that over 11,000 aging out youth joined Job Corps from 2001 to 2007 (USICH, 2008a).

Homelessness and Legal Issues

Civil Rights

Housing First models are deemed to be consumer responsive, providing the very housing that people living on the streets and in shelters ask for as a priority. For most, it ends their homelessness when supported by the appropriate and consumer-driven choice of supportive services. If it is a goal to end homelessness, especially for those who have been homeless the longest, is it reasonable to examine closely the investment made by national and local advocates in city after city to protect the civil rights of those living outdoors?

As noted in chapter 1, the HEARTH Act requires the federal Interagency Council on Homelessness to devise constructive alternatives to criminalization measures that can be used by cities around the country. Punitive measures, such as laws against sleeping, camping, food distribution, storing belongings, and more, had never proven successful in reducing the street presence of individuals. National organizations regularly issued reports on the nation's "meanest cities" for homeless people, including both punitive measures and attacks on people (NLCHP/NCH, 2009).

The inclusive partnerships of stakeholders to homelessness convened by results-oriented 10-year plans were seen by both the Interagency Council and local jurisdictional partners as affirmative means to steer away from a part of the issue focused on making homelessness less of an assault on those living outdoors, rather than support street homelessness. For local officials who could learn from other cities, 10-year plans presented an opportunity to close encampments and similar settings through affirmative strategies rather than punitive response.

There was no denying that physical danger was present, as attacks on those living outdoors were reported in cities of all sizes; homelessness means constant exposure to violence, leaving people on the street vulnerable (Hombs, 1994). Legal advocates had given only passing response to the potential of 10-year plans for people who are homeless and living outside. Instead they emphasize protection of the rights of individuals. Some oppose the use of "special courts" such as those targeting drug offenses, mental health issues, and veterans, creating more consumer-oriented outcomes that may remove legal barriers to housing and employment. Such courts are often a feature of the Project Homeless Connect innovation, helping clear warrants and fines so that ID, housing, and jobs move closer.

Many shared the view that it was an individual's choice to make to stay outside, that ensuring protections of person and property was vital where so-called "banishment" practices were instituted, and that addressing homelessness without addressing poverty was futile. There was little affirmation of the business or law enforcement partners key to many plans (ABA, 2010).

The American Bar Association Commission on Homelessness & Poverty (ABA) described the debate as: "Banishment stems from the faulty belief that if the experience of homelessness or extreme poverty is made painful enough, then individuals targeted will (1) choose to stop being homeless and become self-sufficient; or (2) choose to relocate to an area that is less hostile to their peace and survival." Other commentators went further, seeing punitive efforts as simply extensions of the goals of downtown business interests that wanted clean sidewalks. Banishment practices themselves were deemed to increase costs to taxpayers. The ABA presented just two constructive alternatives in its report and did not include any affirmation of proven housing innovations that remove the need for people to remain on the streets.

Panhandling had long been an issue that was perceived as hand in hand with street homelessness but also as a quality of life issue for downtown residents and businesses. With 10-year plans came the opportunity to examine the data on panhandling more effectively and forward alternatives for residents and visitors.

The International Downtown Association (IDA), a partner to federal initiatives, conducted a 2000 study of successful downtown partnerships and reported several lessons summarized here. First, IDA noted that "homelessness, poverty and mental illness are of society, not outside it." Indicating that there would be no quick or one-size-fits all answers, IDA emphasized that a partner "with an interest in the problem has a legitimate set of goals that need to be respected and reflected in the program response." Stressing that the public sector must accept its role in creating "bipartisan and community wide" goals, IDA placed front and center the importance of "leadership, mutual respect, and the agreement to cooperate" (IDA, 2000).

Denver's Road Home (DRH), the city's 10-year plan, worked with the Denver Business Improvement District to survey panhandling and its results in one downtown area. Denver prioritized public education and community engagement as essential to the successful implementation of its plan. The results were startling: 72 percent of Denver adults saw panhandling as a serious problem and a problem across the city; 42 percent of Denver adults had given money to panhandlers in the last year, and those who gave to panhandlers averaged $1.84 each time, $24.58 per year, which equated to a total of $4.5 million dollars per year.

A Denver Donation Meter Program initiated in 2007 provided an opportunity for individual citizens to participate directly and productively to provide housing, employment, behavioral health treatment, and other services to homeless and at risk individuals and families in the community. The Donation Meter Program, which grew to over 85 meters, was a response to citizen and business concerns (DRH, 2010b).

Redecorated meters—painted red with 10-year plan decals—were placed downtown where panhandling occurred as part of the Better Way to Give campaign. Passersby could put money in the meters and know that 100 percent would be directed by the

United Way partner into local initiatives that provide meals, job training, substance abuse counseling, housing, and other programs. Local businesses could support the initiative by adopting the meters for $1,000 each per year. Denver, through the very "legitimate larceny" being encouraged among cities, had adopted the meter idea to its own community, and others studied the Denver example to tailor it to their own jurisdictions. Panhandling in Denver's target area decreased more than 80 percent from 2006 to 2009.

In Calgary, a 2003 survey found that over 29 percent of people over 18 (approximately 200,000 people) had given money to people on the street in the prior year. Of that number, most gave between $1 and $3 twice per month. The survey concluded that there are approximately 60 panhandlers in the downtown core making approximately $50/day, or per year—approximately $1,000,000.00 in after-tax dollars (Cameron Strategy, 2003).

Panhandling is just one issue that is frequently entwined with other street activity where local enforcement efforts that also included street sweeps and destruction of personal property frequently resulted in community polarization and discussion of the civil rights of homeless people and their service providers. Some cities sought to regulate the distribution of food—so-called drive-by feeding—that occurs on sidewalks and in parks through the efforts of volunteers and is seen by some as providing resources that keep people living outdoors (NLCHP, 2009).

As part of Denver's 10-year plan, the city engaged feeding programs to offer indoor settings combined with service engagement. "Come On In" was the new Denver partnership of Denver's Human Services Department, other public entities, faith-based organizations, service providers, and neighborhood associations and targeted more than 20 public feeding programs in the city to create a match between resources—an indoor place to sit and eat, and restrooms—and access to other resources and services, such as health care and counseling. Feeding programs can pose a challenge for communities that also experience issues related to garbage, sanitation, and traffic (DRH, 2010a).

Violence toward homeless people was deemed to be on the rise. Legal advocates focused their efforts on securing the status of "hate crimes" for such attacks, which were then subject to greater penalties.

One national organization reported on several such measures. In 2010, Florida governor Charlie Crist signed a hate crimes bill for his state, which has experienced a disproportionate number of reported attacks on homeless people. Maryland, the first state to have such a law, and Washington, D.C., have such protections. A 2004 California law requires police training on hate crimes, especially for homeless persons with disabilities. Judges in Maine can incorporate a homeless crime victim's circumstances in their sentencing of offenders. Miami-Dade County and Los Angeles acted to increase school-based education on homelessness (NCH, 2010).

Siting Homeless Housing and the "Not in My Backyard" Problem

Opposition to the placement of housing for people who have experienced homelessness has raised issues usually associated with the "Not In My Backyard" or NIMBY response to choosing sites. Some communities have encountered this opposition as they have sought to implement 10-year plan housing goals. Even with research from coast to coast showing that existing property values are not negatively affected by such housing and that, in fact, some practitioners restore vacant or deteriorated stock to being assets in a neighborhood, opposition remains. Addressing neighborhood concerns often means time and financial resources expended to address myths and misinformation about people with mental illness or addiction, as well as reentering prisoners and others. Communities have even encountered opposition to housing homeless veterans.

In 2001, President George Bush signed an executive order creating the New Freedom Commission, which stated as its mission: "We envision a future when everyone with a mental illness will recover, a future when mental illnesses can be prevented or cured, a future when mental illnesses are detected early, and a future when everyone with a mental illness at any stage of life has access to effective treatment and supports—essentials for living, working, learning, and participating fully in the community." The president's order subsequently identified three barriers for people with mental illnesses that needed to be addressed: stigma, treatment limitations and financial requirements, and a fragmented mental health service delivery system (President's New Freedom Commission, 2003).

In its final report to the president, the commission noted the role of housing in achieving "a life in the community for everyone." According to the commission,

> The lack of decent, safe, affordable, and integrated housing is one of the most significant barriers to full participation in community life for people with serious mental illnesses. Today, millions of people with serious mental illnesses lack housing that meets their needs.
>
> The shortage of affordable housing and accompanying support services causes people with serious mental illnesses to cycle among jails, institutions, shelters, and the streets; to remain unnecessarily in institutions; or to live in seriously substandard housing. People with serious mental illnesses also represent a large percentage of those who are repeatedly homeless or who are homeless for long periods of time.
>
> In fact, people with serious mental illnesses are overrepresented among the homeless, especially among the chronically homeless. (President's New Freedom Commission, 2003)

In 2008, the Furman Center for Real Estate and Urban Policy at New York University released a study that focused on the impact of supportive housing among a range of factors that affect property values. The data included 7,500 units in 123 developments opened between 1985 and 2003. Units were either new construction or major renovation projects (Furman Center, 2008).

The center's report found that, in the five years following construction, property values increased more within two blocks of a supportive housing building than for properties not nearby. Neighborhood density was not a factor in the outcomes, and neither was building size.

The *New York Times*, editorializing on the data in *Good Neighbors* on November 7, 2008, observed, "This strategy is taking root all over the country and proving beyond a doubt that people who were once homeless can be good neighbors and good citizens. . . . Politicians and business leaders across the country should pay attention."

Fair housing and antidiscrimination measures have been used in some instances to counter NIMBY campaigns. The Americans with Disabilities Act (ADA; 42 U.S.C. §§ 12101-12213) prohibits discrimination against people with disabilities, including in employment, provision of government services, and such public accommodations as hotels and restaurants. The federal Fair Housing Act prohibits discrimination against people with disabilities, minorities, and others in selling, renting, and building housing (HUD, 2009).

References

ABA (American Bar Association Commission on Homelessness & Poverty). *No Such Place As "Away": Why Banishment Is a Wrong Turn on the Path to Better and Safer Cities*. Washington, D.C.: 2010. Available at http://new.abanet.org/homeless/PublicDocuments/ABA_CHP_%20 Banishment_White_Paper%20February%202010.pdf.

Bagget, Travis P., James J. O'Connell, Daniel E. Singer, and Nancy A. Rigotti. "The Unmet Health Care Needs of Homeless Adults: A National Study." *American Journal of Public Health*, Volume 100, Number 7 (July 2010): 1326–1333.

Cameron Strategy, Inc., 2003. Calgary Downtown Association Issue Tracking—Panhandling: 2003 City Omnibus Survey. Calgary, 2003.

Cisneros, Henry, Jack Kemp, Kent Colton, and Nicolas Retsinas. *Our Communities, Our Homes: Pathways to Housing and Homeownership in America's Cities and States*. Cambridge, MA: Joint Center for Housing Studies, Harvard University, 2007.

City of Seattle, Office of Housing. Seattle Housing Levy, 2010. Available at http://www.seattle.gov/housing/levy/default.htm.

CSH (Corporation for Supportive Housing). *Forging Ahead: The State of the Supportive Housing Industry in 2010*. New York: CSH, 2010. Available at http://documents.csh.org/documents/pubs/StateOfIndustryReport.pdf.

Culhane, Dennis P., and Stephen Metraux. "Rearranging the Deck Chairs or Reallocating the Lifeboats? Homelessness Assistance and Its Alternatives." *Journal of the American Planning Association*, Volume 74, Issue 1 (2008): 111–121.

DRH (Denver's Road Home). *Come On In: Public Feeding Campaign*. Denver, CO: Mile High United Way, 2010a. Available at http://participate.denversroadhome.org/get-involved/programs/come-on-in-public-feeding-campaign/.

DRH (Denver's Road Home). *Denver's Ten-Year Plan to End Homeless 2010 Annual Update: Year 5*. Denver, CO: DRH, 2010b. Available at http://denversroadhome.org/files/DRH_AnnualReport2011_vF_crops.pdf.

Furman Center for Real Estate and Urban Policy, New York University. *The Impact of Supportive Housing on Surrounding Neighborhoods: Evidence from New York City*. New York: Furman Center, 2008.

GAO (Government Accountability Office). *Homelessness: McKinney Act Programs Provide Assistance but Are Not Designed to Be the Solution.* Washington, D.C.: Government Accountability Office, GAO/RCED-94-37, May 1994.

GAO (Government Accountability Office). *Homelessness: Improving Program Coordination and Client Access to Programs: Statement of Stanley Czerwinski.* Washington, D.C.: Government Accountability Office, GAO-02-485T, March 6, 2002.

HHS (U.S. Department of Health and Human Services). HHS Poverty Guidelines for the Remainder of 2010 (August 2010). Washington, D.C.: U.S. Department of Health and Human Services, 2010a. Available at http://aspe.hhs.gov/poverty/.

HHS (U.S. Department of Health and Human Services). SAMHSA Grant Awards—State Summaries FY 2010/2011. Washington, D.C.: HHS, 2010b. Available at http://www.samhsa.gov/Statesummaries/index.aspx.

Hombs, Mary Ellen. "A Continuum of Violence: Rethinking Advocacy Priorities in Homelessness." *Clearinghouse Review,* Volume 28, Issue 407 (1994–1995), Chicago, IL: Sargent Shriver National Center on Poverty Law.

HUD (U.S. Department of Housing and Urban Development). *Costs Associated with First-Time Homelessness for Families and Individuals.* Washington, D.C.: HUD, 2010a. Available at http://www.huduser.org/portal/publications/povsoc/cost_homelessness.html.

HUD (U.S. Department of Housing and Urban Development). "HUD Provides Rental Assistance Vouchers to Help More Than 2,500 Families Stay Together" (press statement). Washington, D.C.: HUD, 2010b.

HUD (U.S. Department of Housing and Urban Development). Notice of FY (FY) 2009 Implementation of the Veterans Homelessness Prevention Program. Federal Register, Volume 75, Number 143 (2010c).

HUD (U.S. Department of Housing and Urban Development). *Worst Case Housing Needs 2007: A Report to Congress.* Washington, D.C.: U.S. Department of Housing and Urban Development, 2010d.

HUD (U.S. Department of Housing and Urban Development). *Fair Housing—It's Your Right.* Washington, D.C.: HUD, 2009. Available at: http://www.hud.gov/offices/fheo/FHLaws/yourrights.cfm

IDA (International Downtown Association). *Addressing Homelessness: Successful Downtown Partnerships—A Report of Strategies to Assist Homeless Persons with Serious Mental Illnesses.* Washington, D.C.: IDA, 2000.

Kowal, Jessica. "Homeless Alcoholics Receive a Permanent Place to Live, and Drink." *New York Times,* July 5, 2006.

Levin-Epstein, Jodie, and Webb Lyons. Target Practice: Lessons for Poverty Reduction. Washington, D.C.: Center on Law and Social Policy (CLASP), January 2009. Available at http://www.clasp.org/admin/site/publications/files/0453.pdf.

MHC (Millennial Housing Commission). *Meeting Our Nation's Housing Challenges: Report of the Bipartisan Millennial Housing Commission.* Washington, D.C.: U.S. Government Printing Office, 2002.

Miami-Dade County, Florida. *What You Pay: Tourist and Convention Development Tax -Homeless and Domestic Violence Tax on Sale of Food and Beverages.* (n.d.). Available at http://www.miamidade.gov/taxcollector/tourist_pay.asp.

NAEH (National Alliance to End Homelessness). Fact Sheet: Questions and Answers on Homelessness Policy and Research—the Decennial Census and Homelessness. Washington, D.C.: NAEH, April 28, 2010. http://www.endhomelessness.org/content/article/detail/2971.

NAEHCY (National Association for the Education of Homeless Children and Youth). Comments of the National Association for the Education of Homeless Children and Youth submitted to the U.S. Interagency Council on Homelessness Federal Strategic Plan Families with Children Workgroup. Washington, DC: NAEHCY, 2010 Available at http://www.naehcy.org/ich.html.

NAEHCY (National Association for the Education of Homeless Children and Youth), National Health Care for the Homeless Council, National Policy and Advocacy Council on Homelessness, and Volunteers of America. Questions and Answers about Expanding HUD's Definition of Homelessness. May 30, 2006. Available at http://www.npach.org/deffaqFINAL.pdf.

NCH (National Coalition for the Homeless). *Poverty Versus Pathology: What's "Chronic" about Homelessness.* Washington, D.C.: NCH, February 2002. Available at http://www.nationalhomeless.org/publications/chronic/full.html.

NCH (National Coalition for the Homeless). Take Action to Support Hate Crimes Protections. (2010). Available at http://www.nationalhomeless.org/hatecrimes/SenateHearingTakeAction.html.

NCH (National Coalition for the Homeless) and National Law Center on Homelessness & Poverty (NLCHP). A Place at the Table: Prohibitions on Sharing Food with People. Washington, D.C.: NCH/NLCHP, 2010. Available at http://www.nlchp.org/view_report.cfm?id=338.

NCHCW (National Center for Housing & Child Welfare). (2010). HUD's Family Unification Program. Available at http://www.nchcw.org/fup/.

NHCHC (National Health Care for the Homeless Council). *Essential Tools for Discharge Planning*. Nashville, TN: NHCHC, 2002. Available at http://www.nhchc.org/discharge.html.

NHCHC (National Health Care for the Homeless Council). Statement of Executive John N. Lozier, MSSW in Supplemental Document to the Federal Strategic Plan to Prevent and End Homelessness, June 2010, External Experts' Briefs. Available at http://www.usich.gov/PDF/OpeningDoors/ExpertsBriefs_All5Workgroups.pdf.

NLCHP (National Law Center on Homelessness & Poverty) and National Coalition for the Homeless (NCH). *Homes Not Handcuffs: The Criminalization of Homelessness in U.S. Cities*. Washington, D.C.: NLCHP/NCH, 2009. Available at http://nlchp.org/content/pubs/2009HomesNotHandcuffs1.pdf.

NLIHC (National Low Income Housing Coalition). The New National Housing Trust Fund: Frequently Asked Questions. Washington, D.C.: NLICH, 2010a. Available at http://www.nlihc.org/doc/NHTF-FAQ.pdf.

NLIHC (National Low Income Housing Coalition). *Out of Reach 2010: Renters in the Great Recession, The Crisis Continues*. Washington, D.C.: National Low Income Housing Coalition, 2010b. Available at http://www.nlihc.org/oor/oor2010/.

NPACH (National Policy and Advocacy Council on Homelessness). *Fact Check: Updating HUD's Definition of Homelessness in the Reauthorization of the HUD McKinney-Vento Act Programs*. Washington, D.C.: NPACH, November 16, 2007. Available at http://www.npach.org/HEARTH/.

NPACH (National Policy and Advocacy Council on Homelessness). *A Plan Is Still Not a Home*. Washington, DC: NPACH, February 16, 2010. Available at http://npach.org/2010/02/a_plan_is_still_not_a_home_1.html.

NPACH (National Policy and Advocacy Council on Homelessness). *Questions & Answers about the "Chronic Homelessness" Initiative*. Washington, D.C.: NPACH, n.d. Available at http://www.npach.org/chronicq.html.

President's New Freedom Commission on Mental Health. *Achieving the Promise: Transforming Mental Health Care in America*. Washington, D.C.: President's New Freedom Commission on Mental Health, 2003. Available at http://www.mentalhealthcommission.gov/reports/reports.htm.

Sherman, Arloc, Robert Greenstein, Danilo Trisi, and Paul Van De Water. "Poverty Rose, Median Income Declined, and Job-Based Health Insurance Continued to Weaken in 2008—Recession Likely to Expand Ranks of Poor and Uninsured in 2009 and 2010." Washington, D.C.: Center on Budget and Policy Priorities (CBPP), September 10, 2009.

Available at http://www.cbpp.org/research/index.cfm?fa=viewAll&id=36&type=&year=2009&numReturn=100.

U.S. Census Bureau. "Census Bureau to Develop Supplemental Poverty Measure." Washington, D.C.: U.S. Census Bureau press-release of March 2, 2010. Available at http://www.commerce.gov/news/press-releases/2010/03/02/census-bureau-develop-supplemental-poverty-measure.

USCM (U.S. Conference of Mayors). Hunger and Homelessness Survey: A Status Report on Hunger and Homelessness in America's Cities—a 27-City Survey. Washington, D.C.: U.S. Conference of Mayors, copyright December 2009. Available at http://www.usmayors.org/pressreleases/uploads/USCMHungercompleteWEB2009.pdf.

USICH (U.S. Interagency Council on Homelessness). "In Washington: Council Reviews Federal Agency Definitions of Homelessness." Washington, D.C.: USICH, 2006a. Available at http://www.usich.gov/e-newsletterarchive.html.

USICH (U.S. Interagency Council on Homelessness). "Results in the Cities: Chicago's Mayor Daley Reports 10-Year Plan Progress—5,775 Assisted Through Homeless Prevention Program." Washington, D.C.: USICH, 2006b. Available at http://www.usich.gov/e-newsletterarchive.html.

USICH (U.S. Interagency Council on Homelessness). "In Washington: U.S. Department of Labor Reports Results as 11,000 Youth Identified as Homeless, Runaway, and Aging Out Foster Care Youth Enroll in Job Corps." Washington, D.C.: USICH, 2008a. Available at http://www.usich.gov/e-newsletterarchive.html.

USICH (U.S. Interagency Council on Homelessness). "Innovation Number 4: Atlanta's Homeless Opportunity Bonds: New Resources Invested in 10 Year Plan Solutions." Washington, D.C.: USICH, 2008b. Available at http://www.usich.gov/e-newsletterarchive.html.

USICH (U.S. Interagency Council on Homelessness). "In the Cities: Indianapolis Takes New Steps to Analyze and Address Homelessness." Washington, D.C.: USICH, 2008c. Available at http://www.usich.gov/e-newsletterarchive.html.

3

Worldwide Perspective

Introduction

Fundamental change in research and policy on homelessness occurred during the last decade in the United States and yielded new results in ending homelessness. Similar change emerged in countries across both the Atlantic and Pacific oceans. In the United Kingdom (which includes England, Northern Ireland, Scotland, and Wales), Canada, Australia, and the European Union countries, new national and state/provincial government initiatives, research, partnership, and investment have emerged. Important to these developments was the partnership between peers in these governments and U.S. counterparts.

As noted in chapter 1, the worldwide economic crisis of the last few years has provided new understanding of the global economy and its impact on financial, housing, and labor markets. At the same time, the problem of homelessness has become more widely understood through recent research and data. As new strategies and solutions have emerged and became international dialogues about preventing and ending homelessness, learning across borders and sectors has taken on fresh relevance. Active partnerships among governments of the United States, the United Kingdom, Canada, and Australia—first initiated by the federal U.S. Interagency Council on Homelessness under the leadership of Philip Mangano—moved the issue and its remedy in a new direction.

The Blair government initiative on rough sleeping in England offered valuable lessons and partnership for U.S. policy makers and researchers to examine new strategies and results and commit to new goals. Themes that emerged in both the United Kingdom and the United States, despite differences in government structure and social safety net programs, had much in common. These themes included development of new policy and strategies based on data and research, the development of 10-year business plans through expansive partnership, the identification and dissemination of field-tested and evidence-based initiatives, accountability and measurement of outcomes (versus traditional reliance on numbers of beds and meals), and partnership of government with other sectors.

The specifics of how these strategies were carried out in the field included use of cost analysis, new forms of consumer engagement, multidisciplinary teams accountable for individuals deemed most vulnerable, Housing First and rapid rehousing strategies, employment initiatives, and prevention resources.

Earlier chapters looked in detail at the background of change in the United States as well as new directions in legislative and policy initiatives. This chapter focuses more closely on contemporary strategies in selected other nations that have pursued similar new paths and faced similar challenges, despite significant differences in government structure, revenues, and policy. Included are highlights of key policies and documents from the United Kingdom, Canada, Australia, and the European Union.

Ten-year plans include key strategies that make them research and data driven, consumer focused, performance based, and results oriented. Plans reflect expansive and inclusive partnership, are driven by the political will of elected officials and shaped by business principles that integrate baseline data, set benchmarks for outcomes, utilize best practices, and identify budget implications. Plans emphasize consumer preferred solutions in housing, employment, and services, as well as field-tested strategies to increase and expedite access to mainstream resources for income and social supports.

Homelessness in the United Kingdom

England's Strategy on Street Homelessness

In 1999, British prime minister Tony Blair issued an ambitious new plan for addressing the needs of the country's "rough sleepers," who are people living on the streets in England. The Labor government had created a Social Exclusion Unit (SEU) in the top level of government to set priorities on important social issues. When rough sleeping became a priority focus, the Rough Sleepers Unit was established in the SEU, with leadership by Louise Casey. Casey was appointed by Blair and brought both experience in the field on the issue and a view that change was needed and possible.

After achieving its targets, the Rough Sleepers Unit became the Homelessness Directorate in 2002, and its work was subsequently headquartered in the government's Department for Communities and Local Government (DCLG), moving from the Cabinet Office of the Deputy Prime Minister (ODPM). An interministerial work group in DCLG is discussed later.

The new government strategy focused on a goal of reducing rough sleeping by two-thirds within three years. *Coming in from the Cold: The Government's Strategy on Rough Sleeping* reflected months of dialogue with individuals and nongovernmental organizations as well as with homeless individuals. New policies demonstrated the "joined-up" approach of partnership, which, as the plan promises, offers "a better deal for rough sleepers, and better value for the taxpayer."

The Rough Sleepers Initiative achieved its targeted decrease in numbers by November 2001, reducing the rough sleepers' census reflected in government data from 1,850 to 550. An introduction and the key principles of this initiative are covered in chapter 6.

Following is a portion of Prime Minister Blair's introductory statement to the government strategy document. Blair's comments reflect the commitment to acknowledge the unacceptable situation of people sleeping outside and to move policy, investment, and practice in new directions. As was subsequently demonstrated in the United States in the commitment of the Bush administration to end chronic homelessness, the articulation of the goal by the government's highest official conveys the significance of the commitment being made. The excerpt here is from *Coming in from the Cold: The Government's Strategy on Rough Sleeping,* published in 1999 (SEU, 1999).

> On the eve of the 21st century, it is a scandal that there are still people sleeping rough on our streets. This is not a situation that we can continue to tolerate in a modern and civilised society. That is why, in a report last year by

the Social Exclusion Unit, I set the tough but achievable target of reducing rough sleeping in England by at least two thirds by 2002 . . .

Many of the proposals set out in this strategy will build on and refine the valuable work that has been going on for many years. But some will require radical change.

The Rough Sleepers Unit has taken a long hard look at everything being done to help rough sleepers. It is clear that some things work, and others do not.

In the long term, we can only make a lasting difference on the streets by stopping people from arriving there in the first place. That is why prevention is a key part of this strategy, and why more will be done to address the reasons why particular groups such as careleavers, ex-servicemen and ex-offenders are disproportionately likely to end up on the streets. The strategy also sets out support for new temporary and permanent beds, better help in finding jobs and a more focused approach to helping people off the streets. Above all, it focuses on how a real difference can be made to the lives of the most vulnerable.

Too many people are still coming onto the streets. And too many people who were sleeping rough five or ten years ago are still out there. That is why we need a new approach, with services to help people come in from the cold, and support to help them rebuild their lives.

Government will provide the tools, and the funding. But we know that this approach will only succeed as part of a genuine partnership—between central and local government, the voluntary sector, statutory bodies, businesses, community groups and rough sleepers themselves.

I believe that this strategy sets out a way forward which can deliver our vision—a vision of a society where no one needs to sleep in doorways, and where rough sleeping has become a thing of the past.

Targeting the Population and Changing Policy

The new rough sleepers' strategy identified the 30 largest known concentrations of rough sleepers in England, a key step since reliance on data and local authority were cornerstones of the Blair initiative. According to government data, the largest numbers of rough sleepers were found in Westminster (the portion of Central London where many government and historic sites are)—234; Camden—66; Oxford—52; Lambeth—46; Manchester—44; Birmingham—43; Brighton and Hove—43; City of London—36.

Costs associated with homelessness were also a factor in the new approach, though not nearly as prominent in the dialogue as they became in the United States. In the U.S. context, cost analysis became the chief tool for making the new economic argument that supplemented other existing motivations, such as moral and humanitarian reasons to address homelessness. The Social Exclusion Unit had long collected data on the costs to society of social exclusion. Homelessness was viewed as the most extreme version of this exclusion, and while cost analysis began with the rough sleepers' initiative, it continued with a broader look at family homelessness when progress on rough sleeping showed the way for new policy and investment initiatives on families. The Office for the Deputy Prime Minister sought cost studies related to family homelessness, including estimating the impact on families of time in shelter rather than simply focusing on costs to local communities.

The rough sleepers strategy summarized the government's costs since 1990 in addressing rough sleeping at more than £250 million. The strategy estimated that these resources had supported outreach and placement for approximately 1,300 hostel spaces and 3,500 permanent housing placements. Yet an estimated 635 individuals remained on the streets of London alone as a fairly steady population for whom prior initiatives had not proven effective.

Calling for a "new, braver approach," the 1999 strategy stated, "We need to do more. We need to change our approach. The balance in the system must be tipped towards the most vulnerable rather than making the streets a fast track for the most able." Maintaining that earlier efforts had, in fact, supported individuals in their life on the street rather than addressing their homelessness or trying to prevent homelessness, the strategy sought to concentrate focus and resources, end fragmentation of effort, and move to a stronger focus on the population at each step of day services, outreach, and permanent housing.

Clearly stating the point of view that "people should not in the 21st century have to sleep on the streets. . . . This strategy recognises the complexity of need that we must respond to, and aims to offer rough sleepers options which acknowledge their atypical and frequently chaotic lifestyles. Our long-term objective is to provide services which ensure that sleeping on the streets is never the preferred option."

The strategy proposed a partnership that included the interests of rough sleepers, taxpayers, government, and public agencies, local government officials, voluntary organizations, businesses, and members of the public.

New Resources for a New Direction

New resources targeted to meet the specific needs of rough sleepers were seen as key to achieving change. In addition, the new strategy called for a different and more focused type of street engagement for this population in the form of contact and assessment teams, recognizing that prior efforts had not achieved results for this group of individuals. Along with accountability for outcomes, the new plan sought vigilance against measures that supported life on the street instead of offering alternatives that ended homelessness and created stability. The Blair strategy included the following key elements for implementation.

More beds would be available for rough sleepers in London, in the form of three tiers of resources: (1) hostels and shelters, which could serve as the initial point of entry and assessment; (2) specialized hostels and supportive services aimed at deeper levels of needs or complex sets of needs; and (3) permanent housing with necessary supports to sustain housing placement and stability.

Street engagement would be more targeted and dynamic as evidence of a rethinking of the role of continuing contact with people who had experience years of outreach that provided blankets and hot food and beverages but did not seek to end their homelessness or consider their preferences for services or housing. Along with rethinking the premise of engagement, the new plan sought clear responsibility and accountability for outcomes so that the emphasis was on ending homelessness, not supporting life on the streets.

Services on the street would be structured according to the presence of rough sleepers. The population generally was on the streets from late night to early morning. This would be the key period in which to offer services and to identify the most effective means of bringing people inside.

Individuals with mental health and drug and alcohol issues were deemed most in need. Services to bring people indoors would need to account for these often intertwined issues. In fact, the new plan stated clearly, "There should be no reason for someone who is severely mentally ill to be out on the streets." Sixty new specialists would ensure support to rough sleepers as they moved off the streets and continued on a path to housing. At the start, Homeless Mentally Ill Initiative teams already in London were to be integrated with contact and assessment efforts.

Data were developing in the United States at the same time to illustrate the vulnerability of those living on the street. Through the research of Dr. Dennis Culhane of the University of Pennsylvania in 1998 and Dr. James O'Connell of Boston Health Care for the Homeless in 1999, the widespread nature of mental health and alcohol and drug issues in the street population as well as major medical conditions that resulted in extreme vulnerability and risk of death were illustrated. While it would later be a focus of U.S. advocates—when the federal goal to end chronic homelessness was announced in 2002—to question research findings and whether the long-term population with disabilities was in fact at the most risk among people who were homeless, the Blair strategy similarly asserted the level of risk for those living on the streets. The recognition that some individuals need intervention, due to their circumstances or health issues, requires that there be appropriate emergency response resources for medical needs and mental health issues. The new strategy recognized that current systems were not meeting these needs and that there was urgency in the situation.

Using Existing Resources in New Strategies

Disaster conditions, such as those that followed hurricanes Katrina and Rita in the United States, can provide the circumstances to administer wholesale reorganization to service delivery. But there are seldom real opportunities to develop new policy and practice with a clean slate. Given history, resources, and changing policy directions, the configuration of existing services at the local level—which itself includes the application of local, state, and national government resources as well as philanthropic and faith community resources—must be taken as it has developed and exists and then retargeted or realigned. This usually means that there is inherent fragmentation and overlap as well as organizational autonomy. Proposing changes generally means proposing challenges to existing ways of doing business.

Dr. O'Connell's Boston research on street deaths was expected to illustrate the anonymity and exclusion of the individuals who died, people seen as disconnected from available services and resources that could help. Instead, the research underscored the wide variety of systems and resources that touched those lives regularly, frequently, and over time. Rather than being anonymous, those homeless individuals were found to be well known to multiple public systems, including hospitals, ambulance and emergency services personnel, and police as well as outreach workers. Multiple street outreach teams were at work on downtown streets, during different hours on different days, focusing on different populations (the young, the old, individuals with specific issues), offering different resources. Yet they were seldom in coordination or communication with one another to the benefit of the individuals who were homeless. Regular meetings of all outreach teams, along with police and emergency workers, became a new standard (O'Connell et al., 2005).

The Blair strategy tackled a similar set of issues, citing the need for focus and coordination and the recalibration of street resources to establish a clear trajectory away from rough sleeping. The trajectory was expected to provide a consistent and ongoing base for supporting the individual rough sleeper who came inside, ensuring support in housing, to move practice beyond past failures of these resources to sustain individuals: "Experience shows that we have not in the past got this right." The strategy also looked to end "street lifestyle" issues, noting that some individuals who had moved to housing continued to see the street as a daytime resource (SEU, 1999).

The path from the street was intended to be a reciprocal one. New incentives would be offered to meet individual needs and ensure a focus away from street life. The government asserted an additional point clearly: Rough sleepers were expected to take the opportunity being offered. "If their needs can be provided through one or other of the accommodation, treatment or support routes that we are funding, rough sleepers themselves have a responsibility to come in. Once we are satisfied that realistic alternatives are readily available, we—and the public at large—are entitled to expect those working on the streets to seek to persuade people to take advantage of them" (SEU, 1999).

The Role of Engagement

Part of the change in the rough sleepers' census was subsequently attributed to change in engagement strategies, similar to what would be seen in U.S. results. In June 2002, *Helping Rough Sleepers off the Streets* was published by the government to evaluate the work being done. The following section identifies some of the key changes, changes that would subsequently be seen in U.S. strategy (SEU, 1999).

The role of effective engagement, as compared to the old style of outreach efforts that sustained life on the streets, was vital to achieving change. The "assertive and persistent" engagement initiatives that were a hallmark of change were understood by agency partners to be key. Among the factors contributing to greater success was a dramatic shift in the time workers actually spent on the street, thus emphasizing where their key focus was. From less than a third of their time, work shifted to up to a 75 percent presence on the streets. This level of presence coincided with persistent daily contact with their target population. Gone were the approaches that allowed individuals on the streets to decline interventions. To the forefront came measures to move individuals first and then to conduct deeper assessment (SEU, 1999).

Ensuring Stability off the Streets

Work was seen as essential for the foundation of a life away from the streets, in part because it builds self-esteem. Developing skills and creating social networks separate from the streets was seen as key to supporting individuals in moving into the mainstream. U.S. initiatives, such as Housing First, initially did not take this approach with a population deemed to require many other supports. Mainstream employment, especially for persons with disabilities and including volunteerism for those with limited work opportunity, emerged as a fundamental strategy for people achieving stability in their housing.

The Blair strategy saw "daytime occupation" as important to resettlement in housing and also as a buffer against isolation in a new life. The workplace, whether focused on education, training, production, or volunteerism, develops strengths for life and work and offers a path into social relations outside work. For people who have lived lives oriented to the streets or in an isolation brought about by individual health, addiction, mental health, or family challenges, the need is real for a new social network as part of sustaining and stabilizing the new trajectory.

Enhancing the Role of Prevention

Prevention was understood as the important task of ending rough sleeping by ensuring that individuals did not fall into the population through future systemic failures that could be curtailed. Chief among the approaches to sustain reductions would be targeting vulnerable populations, especially those termed "care-leavers." Two areas of effort would address prevention. First, government would put new measures in places, and second, "practical projects" would be undertaken for the care-leaver population.

Stated *Rough Sleeping: The Government's Strategy,* "For the long term, efforts must be targeted on those groups that we know are particularly vulnerable to homelessness and to rough sleeping: young people leaving care; people leaving prison; people who have experienced family breakdown; and people leaving the armed forces. There is a central role here for Government, both in what we can achieve directly, and what we can achieve through the work of others, especially local authorities. This is a crucial challenge for us all. We must ensure that those who have been in our care as children, as prisoners or as servicemen, are properly equipped for and supported towards independent living. Rising to this challenge must be a major component not only of our work to tackle rough sleeping, but also our efforts to deal with social exclusion more widely" (SEU, 1999).

New legislation was introduced in the form of the Government's Children (Leaving) Care Bill. Much like similar legislation targeted to foster care in the United States, the legislation sought to improve conditions for young people in care and for those "aging out," including preventing the inappropriate discharge from care of 16- and 17-year-olds. Based on the Department of Health's 1999 paper *Me, Survive, Out There?*, new funding was made available to local government to meet the needs of this population and ensure suitable housing. Local government authorities would commence supporting young adults as they made the transition from care to age 21, and to age 24 if the individual was receiving education and training (U.K. Department of Health, 1999).

As was true in U.S. research that demonstrated the role of so-called childhood antecedents in adult homelessness, a 2001 survey of rough sleepers in *Leaving Care: A Time for Change; Government Response* found that about 25 percent were formerly in care, with the results primarily among rough sleeping adults who had been in care as children (SEU, 1999).

So-called care leaving packages (usually including support funds for the individual) available to those who had been in public systems were to be reexamined in coordination with the Rough Sleepers Initiative to ensure use of best practices.

Prisoners reentering the community were another special population at risk of falling into rough sleeping. The Rough Sleepers Unit was directed to study current practice with prison and probation authorities to identify what steps were in place to reduce risk of rough sleeping. Performance measures for "resettlement" (generally called "reentry" in the United States) would be combined with a review of available benefits and resources.

A 2002 report commissioned by the government, *Blocking the Fast Track from Prison to Rough Sleeping,* used interviews with professionals and former prisoners and found several key elements that closely parallel U.S. experiences. The findings demonstrated that stable housing, legal income and available and accessible benefits, and access to treatment were essential to successful reentry. The "reception and induction" process or intake did not prepare prisoners for reentry. Discharge planning best practice for public systems was understood in the United States to start upon intake, not at the brink of discharge itself. The report found that few prisoners were properly supported in a process described as "haphazard" even where best practices were identifiable. Individuals who had been unstably housed upon entry were among the high numbers who were discharged without specific housing plans (ODPM, 2002).

The focus on prisoners has continued, as officials reported in October 2010 that one-third of London's rough sleepers reported spending time in prison. The report by Housing Minister Grant Shapps and Prisons Minister Crispin Blunt noted that some individuals described committing crimes to be rehoused. Given that 20 percent of ex-offenders have no housing upon release and that two-thirds of prisoners commit new crimes within two years, it is believed that stable housing could reduce this recidivism outcome by at least 20 percent.

Service members were also deemed at risk upon discharge. The U.K. Ministry of Defence, under its "policies for people" initiative, was already underway with efforts to reduce risk of homelessness. The Rough Sleepers Unit committed to work with the ministry to examine the role of community organizations who could assist rough sleepers who formerly served in the military to achieve successful reintegration.

Service members were prioritized by the Rough Sleepers Initiative at a time before the start of war in Iraq and Afghanistan. Yet, as has been true in the United States, the need for health and mental health services, employment, housing, and social services was identified in the resources compiled in a guide issued by the government, titled *Resources for Ex-Service Personnel in London*. The guide was produced by the Rough Sleepers Unit with the Ex-Service Action Group on Homelessness (ESAG). ESAG is a partnership of ex-service welfare organizations working to address homelessness among service members (RSU/ESAG, 2004).

Each of the three target populations for prevention resources—young adults, ex-prisoners, and service members–has also emerged in U.S. policy on homelessness. Each is a population that needs to achieve successful transition from a form of institutional living into residential stability, income, and needed services. Individuals in these specific populations frequently express mistrust of efforts not rooted in their own experience and value guidance from others who faced the same issues and succeeded, whether a military veteran, a successful young adult, or a former prisoner integrated in the community.

"Rough sleeping is at the sharp end of social exclusion," stated *Coming in from the Cold: The Government's Strategy on Rough Sleeping*. Acknowledging that the numbers of people affected by rough sleeping are small, just as they would be shown through research to be in the United States, the direction of policy and resources made clear that change would be the theme carrying efforts forward and that there was public support for this new direction.

"This will not always be easy and will require courage. But, meeting our target is not just about numbers, it is about making a difference to people's lives. The strategy outlines action that will help those currently out on the streets exposed to danger and ill-health, and it puts in place measures to stop new groups becoming tomorrow's rough sleepers. We must work together so that we can be proud of living in a country that does not have rough sleepers on the streets at night" (SEU, 1999).

In the subsequent strategy for England that looks forward from the successful reduction in rough sleeping to bringing all rough sleeping to an end in England in 2010, policy makers issued what it called "good practice" notes. The government's report identified three key areas for future strategy: prevention, diversion to shorten stays in rough sleeping, and ensuring stability once individuals were placed in housing, to prevent a return to the streets (SEU, 1999).

The good practice guide identified the chief elements of a new toolkit based on outcomes already highlighted. This approach included securing accommodations for eligible individuals, those "unintentionally" homeless, and those without priority needs.

The toolkit included a data strategy for developing information about the rough sleepers population and a checklist for local authorities to review with their partners to create their community strategy on rough sleeping. Among the checklist elements review elements were strategy and partnerships, resources for early intervention, prevention and emergency services, outreach, resources for moving from streets to stability, and specialized interventions. A scorecard for assessing outreach performance and a "reconnections protocol" for those from outside the local area were also elements of the toolkit.

By examining the paths individuals followed into rough sleeping, policy makers hoped to identify way to prevent new individuals from falling into the population. The development of PrOMPT, the Prevention Opportunities Mapping and Planning Toolkit, was central to this goal. The counterpoint, MOPP: Move On Planning Protocol, focused on housing and service needs.

With the toolkit came the announcement of the identification of 15 "champions," individuals who demonstrated best practices in prevention and intervention and the strategy at work in urban and rural areas of all sizes. Champions represented local housing government authorities, community organizations, and partnerships.

The success of the Rough Sleepers Initiative in reducing numbers led to the examination of policy and expansion of focus on family homelessness. Measurable outcomes in the rough sleeping strategy provided a record on which to forward new research and policy for families and youth.

In 2008, the Department of Communities and Local Government issued a research report on other forms of homelessness. The goal of the report was to provide data on families and 16- and 17-year-olds that could inform future policy. The government report examined the characteristics and needs of the population, causes of homelessness, and the experience and impact of temporary shelter situations (DCLG, 2008).

Ongoing oversight of homelessness initiatives is the current responsibility of the Ministerial Working Group on Preventing and Tackling Homelessness. Members of the group, which meets quarterly, and their areas of focus include the following: Department for Communities and Local Government (housing and homelessness) (chair); Ministry of Defence (welfare of veterans);

Department for Business, Innovation and Skills (adult skills); Department of Health (health and care services); Department for Work and Pensions (housing benefit); Ministry of Justice (criminal justice); Home Office (crime prevention); and Department for Education (children and youth services). Other current issues being addressed include the influx of migrants, including impoverished Eastern Europeans, who were estimated to make up more than half of London's rough sleepers at the beginning of 2010.

Other U.K. Strategies on Homelessness

A 10-Year Plan for Wales

The Welsh Assembly Government in Wales published *10-Year Plan Homelessness Plan for Wales 2009–2019* in 2009. Calling homelessness "one of the most significant social problems" in Wales, the plan sought to reduce the "distress, deprivation and disadvantage" associated with it. The plan, which its authors described as a "working document" that would be calibrated as it moved forward, included a strategy to create more detailed action plans as part of its implementation, to ensure the "widespread acceptance, ownership and engagement in delivery" that would make the document a plan for the entire country (Welsh Assembly Government Housing Directorate, 2009).

England and Wales share a definition of homelessness under the 1996 Housing Act, which finds a person to be homeless if they have no accommodation or they have accommodation but they cannot reasonably continue to occupy it.

Key elements of the plan include keeping the consumer as a central focus and developing "sustainable housing solutions for all." To accomplish these goals, the plan included addressing rough sleeping, veterans' needs, youth homelessness, criminal justice reentry, asylum seekers and refuges, rural homelessness, housing counseling, expansion of the private markets for rentals, new tenancies, employment, financial participation, foreclosure prevention, and health care. Each section of the plan expressed its specific vision and the goal to be achieved and sought to align homelessness goals with other national strategies targeting systems or populations.

The plan's strategy for veterans noted several of the same issues identified in U.S. strategies: "The pathways into homelessness experienced by veterans are varied. The four identified groups are: those who carry vulnerabilities deriving from childhood or adolescence; those who encountered difficulties within the Armed Forces, such as the onset of alcohol or mental health problems; those who had a successful career in the Armed Forces, but found the return to civilian life very difficult; and the fourth group who had a good career in the Armed Forces but who then encountered unrelated problems later in life; this last group was the most widespread experience reported by one third of ex-service personnel affected" (Welsh Assembly Government Housing Directorate, 2009).

Scotland's Legislative Strategy

Since 1977, Scotland has passed several pieces of legislation to address homelessness. The 2003 act passed by the Scottish Parliament (referred to as "Homelessness etc. [Scotland] Act 2003") set a 2012 goal to ensure "permanent accommodation" for all people who are unintentionally homelessness and no longer use "priority" need categories to provide access to housing. Some 60 percent of those reported homeless are single adults without children, of whom the largest number are in Glasgow.

Earlier 2001 legislation had required all local governments to assess homelessness and develop strategies to prevent and address the problem. Local strategies were to be submitted to the Scottish ministers or cabinet secretaries.

A task force on homelessness had been established in 1999 by the Scottish executive. The Homeless Task Force (HTF) included more than 20 individuals, academics, members of the executive and others. This body was succeeded by the Homelessness Monitoring Group (HMG). HMG includes the Scottish Council for Single Homeless (SCSH), Scottish Federation of Housing Associations (SFHA), Scottish Executive Development Department, Greater Glasgow Health Board, Convention of Scottish Local Authorities (CoSLA), Fife Council (CoSLA), and academics and voluntary sector representatives.

Prevention of homelessness was an important aspect of Scotland's initiative: "The importance of preventing homelessness is paramount—both to avoid the harmful effects of homelessness for individuals and their families and to make most effective use of limited resources." Clear data on prevention was needed, as has been shown repeatedly in the United States and elsewhere. In 2006 the Department of Communities announced eight innovation awards to demonstration projects to test approaches for specific populations. Among the £230,000 in awards were initiatives for reentering prisoners, care-leaving youth, women, and vic-tims of domestic violence, and work to examine homelessness "triggers" and create rent arrears initiatives (Scottish Government, 2005).

Homelessness in Europe

The Role of Social Exclusion

Time magazine published "Down and Out in Europe," an article surveying the growing problem of homelessness in Europe (Ghosh, 2003). The groundbreaking recognition provided by the article underscored the role of economics and regional differences, such as high unemployment in Eastern Europe. It also noted that Western European countries found their homeless populations profiling many issues that are commonly recognized in the United States: addiction, mental health issues, and trauma.

Historically, the emphasis of the European homelessness literature has been on emergency services for the range of people who are homeless and the provision of housing as the means to address the "social exclusion" seen as both cause and effect of homelessness and poverty. Social exclusion can be seen in economic, social, cultural, and political arenas. But the causal link in explaining homeless solutions in the long term is on joblessness in the European literature. Relative to U.S. discussion and due to differences in social policy and programs, there has been less emphasis on the role of chronic disability (including physical disability, mental illness, and substance abuse) and continuity in public systems of care, treatment, and custody (including child welfare, hospitals, prisons, treatment facilities).

The EU strategy on social exclusion was launched in 2001 and reviewed in 2006. The EU practice is that national reports are submitted every three years on such measures to identify the opportunities and focus for longer-term exchange on strategies and results.

In June 2010, the heads of all member-state governments in the EU, meeting as the European Council, adopted the new Europe 2020 strategy for the next decade, reported in *European Coun-*

cil Conclusions, 17 June 2010. The unprecedented poverty target of the commitment is "promoting social inclusion, in particular through the reduction of poverty, by aiming to lift at least 20 million people out of the risk of poverty and exclusion." People in poverty are defined as those who are at risk of poverty and exclusion by three indicators (at risk of poverty; material deprivation; jobless household). Each EU country will set its target using its preferred indicator (European Council, 2010).

European Year for Combating Poverty and Social Exclusion

The year 2010 was designated as the European Year for Combating Poverty and Social Exclusion for the countries of the European Union (EU). Current member-states of the European Union are Austria, Belgium, Bulgaria, Cyprus, Czech Republic, Denmark, Estonia, Finland, France, Germany, Greece, Hungary, Ireland, Italy, Latvia, Lithuania, Luxembourg, Malta, the Netherlands, Poland, Portugal, Romania, Slovakia, Slovenia, Spain, Sweden, and the United Kingdom.

Homelessness was one of the key social exclusion issues for the EU initiative. The EU provides coordination, and EU member-states have the responsibility for policy development. At the conclusion of the year, the Council of the European Union noted that "active inclusion" is key to poverty reduction, especially stressing the "three pillars" of income support, employment, and services (EU, 2010).

As previously noted, the European Parliament in 2008 adopted a Written Declaration on Ending Street Homelessness by 2015 with 438 signatures. The EU called for member-states to develop integrated strategies to combat homelessness and called for a 2010 conference on policies to address homelessness, to bring together public sector officials, EU institutions, housing providers, and people who have experienced homelessness.

FEANTSA—the European Federation of National Organisations Working with the Homeless—launched a related campaign called Ending Homelessness. The FEANTSA campaign message was that homelessness is a problem to be solved the development of "integrated strategies rather than by investing in reactive, short-term measures." FEANTSA's work as a nongovernmental organization is frequently cited in this chapter, given the role it fulfills in research, policy, and best practice networks in the EU (FEANTSA, 2010d).

In late 2010, five members of the European Parliament launched a resolution across party lines that called on the European Council to commit by the end of 2010 to ending street homelessness by 2015. Additionally, the resolution calls on the European Commission to develop an ambitious EU homelessness strategy and to support Member States in developing effective national strategies following the guidelines of the Joint Report on Social Protection and Social Inclusion adopted in March 2010 and as part of the EU 2020; calls on Eurostat to collect EU homelessness data; supports the following priorities for action: no one sleeping rough; no one living in emergency accommodation for longer than the period of an "emergency"; no one living in transitional accommodation longer than is required for a successful move-on; no one leaving an institution without housing options; no young people becoming homeless as a result of the transition to independent living; [and] instructs its President to forward this declaration, together with the names of the signatories, to the Council, the Commission and the Parliaments of the Member States (Thomsen, 2010).

FEANTSA established the European Observatory on Homelessness to conduct research as a basis for policy across Europe. The European Observatory organizes an annual European Research Conference and publishes a research journal. Recent conferences have included U.S. government and academic participation. Conferences have addressed "Understanding Homelessness and Housing Exclusion in the New European Context" (2010); "Homelessness and Poverty" (2009); "Good Governance: The Key to Effective Homelessness Policies" (2008); "Rethinking Homelessness Policies" (2007); and "Intervention Strategies to Combat Homelessness and Social Exclusion" (2006) (FEANTSA, 2010c).

FEANTSA Report on Social Exclusion

In 1998, FEANTSA published *Europe against exclusion: HOUSING FOR ALL,* which it called "a set of practical policy proposals to promote social inclusion and ensure access to decent housing for all citizens and residents of the European Union." FEANTSA's work is supported by the European Union. The report was published with the support of the European Commission, with contributions from representatives of FEANTSA member organizations, correspondents of the European Observatory on Homelessness, and selected experts. The contents of the report were unanimously endorsed by the administrative council of FEANTSA in November 1998.

Key elements of the FEANTSA report are summarized here. Stated FEANTSA: "To be 'homeless'—that is, without access to adequate accommodation—is probably the most serious manifestation of social exclusion. If you are homeless it is almost impossible to realise your potential as an active member of society, such as by getting a job or by raising children. Therefore, ensuring an adequate provision of decent housing is one of the basic foundations for building a society in which everyone can play an active part. In this sense, one can say that access to housing is the principal key to social inclusion."

The key proposals of the FEANTSA report addressed access to housing in the EU, growing homelessness and housing barriers, demographic and socioeconomic changes in the region, trends in social welfare and housing programs, and the impact for vulnerable populations (young people, people with mental health and/or addiction issues, domestic violence cases).

The Importance of Data

The data issues related to enumerating the size of homeless populations in EU countries have certain similarities to issues identified in the United States earlier. For example, improving census results raises implications for methodology and infrastructure at the local and national level in each member-state of the EU as well as for policy direction and investment based on data. Common definitional terms are needed, including the use of a typology such as was developed in the United States through research data on adult homelessness.

FEANTSA launched a 2005 initiative to develop further insights into definition and census issues and published "Typology of Homelessness and Housing Exclusion (ETHOS)" to address these challenges. The resulting report uses existing definitions in member-states and examines homelessness according to whether an individual is (1) roofless (without shelter); (2) houseless (with a temporary place to sleep); (3) insecurely housed due to an unstable tenancy, eviction, domestic violence; and (4) inadequately housed in caravans, in unfit housing, or in overcrowded conditions. FEANTSA's work in this area has tried to recognize some of the same issues raised in the United States, including the idea of episodes of homelessness over time, duration of episodes, and the prevalence of homelessness in a given period of time (FEANTSA, 2010a).

The EU adopted a regulation on census activities in 2008. Under this proviso, population and housing census counts must be undertaken in all EU member-states in 2011. Housing arrangements are one of the core data factors in the census.

Habitact is a new peer-to-peer initiative for policy exchange regarding local homeless strategies and was launched with FEANTSA's support. Habitact was a response to the need for best practice information and strategies from local authorities in Europe. A key feature of the EU's social inclusion strategy is the so-called Open Method of Coordination (OMC), which seeks to support comparisons across national boundaries.

With similarities to the U.S. idea of seeing homelessness as a national problem with local solutions, Habitact was founded by cities to improve the exchange of ideas and results in initiatives to address homelessness. Habitact founding cities were Amsterdam, the Netherlands; Athens, Greece; Dublin, Ireland; Esch-sur-Alzette, Lithuania; Ghent, Belgium; Odense, Denmark; Madrid, Spain; and Vitoria-Gasteiz, Spain.

A first-year assessment found that Habitact was underway with a European research initiative on local welfare systems and homelessness, development of a electronic policy bank on homelessness policies at the local level, and receiving what it called "moral patronage" from the EU Committee on the Regions. Priority issues for the next year were identified as migrants, prevention, and examination of Housing First strategies.

Other European Strategies

Following are excerpts and summaries of strategies from several other European countries. In addition to the highlights presented here for Ireland, Denmark, Finland, Norway, and Sweden, there are planning processes in France, Netherlands, Poland, and Portugal.

Ireland

Ireland's Department of the Environment, Heritage & Local Government in 2008 published *The Way Home: A Strategy to Address Adult Homelessness in Ireland 2008–2013*, a five-year strategy on adult homelessness. Key strategic goals of the official initiative included homelessness prevention, an end to rough sleeping, housing resources, effective services, and coordination of funding. The introductory statement to the strategy from John Gormley, Minister for the Environment, Heritage and Local Government, and T. D. Michael Finneran, Minister for Housing, Urban Renewal and Developing Areas, addresses a new sense of direction in policy and a vision with key goals of ending long-term use of shelter and the need for rough sleeping and prevention of new rough sleeping (Government of Ireland, 2008).

The government already had a financial foundation in committing to the new approach. Budgets and earlier planning documents since 2000 had provided resources for both temporary shelter and services and then for capital investment for facilities. The future challenge was to ensure that funds were well invested for the goals of the new strategy.

Homelessness prevention, for example, requires engaging a variety of systems and sectors that provide supports to those at risk, those experiencing homelessness, and those with special needs who may fall into homelessness without ongoing interventions. Among these systems are health care, mental health, drug and alcohol treatment, public welfare, child and family supports, domestic violence, education, employment, and corrections and incarceration.

As the national strategy noted, the articulated goals point to decisions that may be needed regarding service delivery in any of the above-named systems. Reorganization, setting of standards, new collaboration, and data collection and analysis may all be examined in an effort to ensure that resources are used to meet policy goals.

The Dublin, Ireland, Strategy

Dublin's strategy published in 2006 is an example of local planning in the context of an evolving national initiative. *A Key to the Door* was the Dublin Homeless Agency's third action plan, following *Shaping the Future* (2001–2003) and *Making it Home* (2004–2006). The strategy clearly states that its overarching context is to view homelessness as solvable and preventable.

Homelessness in Dublin is defined by the Housing Act 1988 as follows:

> A person shall be regarded by a housing authority as being homeless for the purposes of this Act if—

(*a*) there is no accommodation available which, in the opinion of the authority, he, together with any other person who normally resides with him or who might reasonably be expected to reside with him, can reasonably occupy or remain in occupation of, or

(*b*) he is living in a hospital, county home, night shelter or other such institution, and is so living because he has no accommodation of the kind referred to in *paragraph (a)*, and he is, in the opinion of the authority, unable to provide accommodation from his own resources.

The Dublin planning process included many stakeholders and strands, consisting of current and former consumers, a public process, and the consultation of an intergovernmental homelessness team, local authorities in Dublin, the local authority strategic policy committees, the Dublin City Development Board, social exclusion officials for the national health service, mental health officials, local homeless forums established in Dublin under the national government strategy, the Homeless Network representing the voluntary sector, and the Irish Council of Social Housing (Homeless Agency, 2007).

The important action of consultation with consumers was conducted in a dozen sites, including the streets. Consumers were asked the reasons they became homeless, what might have prevented their homelessness, and their views on existing services.

A Key to the Door identified 10 action steps to achieve an overall vision. These steps included identifying those at risk of homelessness and appropriate multidisciplinary interventions; ensuring access to health care and other services for people who are homeless or at risk; forwarding a public education campaign; implementing new needs assessment and case management approaches for homeless services providers; expanding consumer participation; increasing housing opportunities and removing barriers in the market; evaluating housing models; and resources that might be used to incorporate best practice.

Performance indicators were identified for each area of the strategy. Among these indicators were the numbers of individuals experiencing homelessness and repeat episodes of homelessness; the number of individuals experiencing long-term homelessness; the number of individuals falling into homelessness from prison, hospitalization, or during asylum requests; the duration of homelessness; the number of rough sleepers; the number of rough sleepers unable to access emergency shelter; the numbers of individuals at risk upon discharge from care or custody; the effectiveness of prevention strategies; the number of individuals barred from shelter or services; local housing need; and the number of individuals placed in housing.

The Irish Penal Reform Trust, a nongovernmental organization with a long history on prison and reentry issues, published a report in 2010 titled *It's like Stepping on a Landmine . . .": Reintegration of Prisoners in Ireland.* As in other systems, reentry and the lack of discharge planning with housing solutions is a key problem in effective prevention of homelessness and successful reintegration.

The report identified several issues that readily correlate with similar problems identified in the United States. Existing research was cited that indicated that a quarter of all prisoners had been homeless when incarcerated and over half has previously experienced homelessness. Lack of housing was the most frequently named concern of prisoners, and barriers to housing are substantial for exiting prisoners with mental health, addiction, or dual-diagnosis issues. One of the successful initiatives is a 13-week rent-payment program by the Irish Prison Service that ensures that housing is available to prevent homelessness in cases of short sentences.

In addition to the lack of clear statutory authority for release conditions and the lack of information for prisoners on resources is the structure of release in overcrowded systems. This situation can mean that prisoners are discharged with as little as a few hours' notice or at night or on weekends. Very few resources are available under these conditions to ensure stable integration.

Denmark's Goal of Ending Homelessness

Denmark's government strategy for people who are homeless relies on its larger approach for socially marginalized adults, which states that the government's goal is that individuals will "emerge from the homeless situation and live worthwhile and stable lives in their own homes." This strategy embraces consumer participation and choice, a housing focus for solutions, and a recognition that the voluntary and social service sectors need to change and that prevention of homelessness and recurring homelessness are critical efforts (Denmark Ministry, 2009).

Denmark's Council for Socially Marginalised People was established in 2002 and is responsible for the guarantee of treatment for those who use drugs and alcohol, specialized housing strategies, employment opportunities, and necessary supports for vulnerable populations.

The national strategy on homelessness seeks to reduce and end homelessness by reducing rough sleeping, creating solutions for young people, shortening the length of homeless episodes, and addressing housing as part of discharge from prisons and institutions.

The government of Denmark released a plan to address homelessness in 2009, *The Government's Homelessness Strategy—a Strategy to Reduce Homelessness in Denmark 2009–2012*. Denmark defines homelessness as "persons who do not own or rent homes or rooms, but are obliged to avail of temporary accommodation, or live temporarily, without a rental contract, with relatives, friends or acquaintances. Homeless persons also include those who do not have a place to stay for the coming night."

The eight Danish municipalities with the largest homeless populations were invited to cooperate in the implementation of the Homelessness Strategy. They were Albertslund, Esbjerg, Frederiksberg, Høje Taastrup, Copenhagen, Odense, Randers, and Århus. Copenhagen was recorded as having the largest number of people sleeping on the street.

The key role in social, housing, and employment initiatives rests with local municipalities under government reform efforts of 2007. Thus, the Denmark strategy notes, "The councils of the participating municipalities are therefore the principal players in the application of funding under the Homelessness Strategy, and it is emphasised that the initiatives for the homeless must have a political base in the municipalities."

The key strategies embraced by the plan to support housing initiatives included assertive community treatment (ACT) teams, critical time intervention (CTI), individual case management, and discharge planning.

Planning in Other Scandinavian Countries

The Scandinavian countries of Finland, Norway, and Sweden also have national strategies on homelessness that are aligned with responsibility for implementation and data. These strategies are briefly summarized here.

Finland's 2008 commitment to reduce long-term homelessness focused on 10 population centers, with a priority on Helsinki. In its *Finnish Government's Programme to Reduce Long-Term Homelessness 2008–2011*, the government forwarded its goal to reduce long-term homelessness by half by 2011 and entirely by 2015. The national plan uses a Housing First approach, stating, "Solutions to social and health problems cannot be a condition for organising accommodation: on the contrary, accommodation is a requirement which also allows other problems of people who have been homeless to be solved. Having somewhere to live makes it possible to strengthen life management skills and is conducive to purposeful activity."

In 2010 Finland convened a national seminar on Housing First led by the Finnish housing minister in which Dr. Sam Tsemberis, the U.S. innovator of the model in Pathways to Housing in the United States, described the key elements for success and the evidence for the strategy. Dr. Tsemberis identified to participants that Canada, France, and Finland, as well as 10 cities in the EU, are studying the innovation.

Norway's 2004 strategy was titled *The Pathway to a Permanent Home*. The key components of the strategy include reducing evictions, improving prisoner reentry and other discharge planning, ensuring the quality of overnight shelter, and shortening stays in temporary shelter to three months' duration (Government of Norway, 2004).

Sweden's *Homelessness, Multiple Faces, Multiple Responsibilities—a Strategy to Combat Homelessness and Exclusion from the Housing Market, 2007–2009* guarantees shelter to all, commits to improved discharge planning, seeks to increase housing opportunity, and pledges to reduce evictions, including eliminating evictions where children are involved (Government of Sweden, 2007).

Canada's National and Local Strategies

The Homelessness Partnering Strategy (HPS) is Canada's national government model that looks to local communities to identify needs and develop solutions in which national resources are allocated. HPS invests in transitional programs and supportive housing, supports community efforts to prevent and end homelessness, and seeks partnerships and collaborations between levels of government (HRSDC, 2010).

The Canadian government department Human Resources and Skills Development Canada (HRSDC), where the national homelessness initiative is based, employs a strategy of "designated" communities. "The Government of Canada identified ten most affected communities in 1999 and fifty-one additional communities were selected in 2000 in consultation with provinces and territories. These designated communities are maintained under the Homelessness Partnering Strategy (HPS). Designated Communities funding goes directly to community projects." Communities that are selected must have plans for long-term solutions to prevent and end homelessness. HPS's strategy includes pilot projects, development of an information system, and use of federal surplus property.

Designated communities include (by province) the following: (1) British Columbia/Yukon: Kelowna, Kamloops, Nanaimo, Nelson, Prince George, Vancouver, Victoria, Whitehorse; (2) Alberta/NWT/Nunavut: Calgary, Edmonton, Grande Prairie, Iqaluit, Lethbridge, Medicine Hat, Red Deer, Wood Buffalo, Yellowknife; (3) Saskatchewan: Prince Albert, Regina, Saskatoon; (4) Manitoba: Brandon, Thompson, Winnipeg; (5) Ontario: Barrie, Belleville, Brantford, Dufferin, Guelph, Halton, Hamilton, Kingston, Kitchener, London, North Bay, Ottawa, Peel Region, Peterborough, Region of Durham, Sault Ste. Marie, St. Catharines-Niagara, Sudbury, Thunder Bay, Toronto, Windsor, York Region; (6) Quebec: Drummondville, Gatineau, Montreal, Quebec City, Saguenay, Sherbrooke, Trois-Rivières; (7) New Brunswick: Bathurst, Fredericton, Moncton, Saint John; (8) Prince Edward Island: Charlottetown, Summerside; (9) Nova Scotia: Halifax, Sydney (Cape Breton); and (10) Newfoundland and Labrador: St. John's.

"Outreach Communities" are smaller jurisdictions and rural communities. They are not required to have plans in place for HPS funding but must have a wide range of partners.

The Business Model and Canadian 10-Year Plans

In September 2010, the Canadian Chamber of Commerce supported a policy resolution at its annual conference, calling for a reallocation of federal funding to support a national plan to end homelessness. The chamber represents more than 300 local board of trade organizations and local chambers of commerce, which themselves represent more than an estimated 175,000 local businesses. The resolution was brought forward by the Burnaby Board of Trade, the Greater Victoria Chamber of Commerce, the Surrey Board of Trade, and the Metro Vancouver Homelessness Secretariat (CCC, 2010).

Provincial and local government officials and business leaders in Canada undertook partnerships with U.S. federal officials, researchers, and innovators during the 2002–2009 period to learn from their peers the new expectations, strategies, and solutions that were producing results. Many major Canadian cities adopted 10-year plans, including Calgary, Vancouver, Toronto, Montreal, Ottawa, Edmonton, Victoria, and smaller communities such as Red Deer.

While the role of business in supporting 10-year plans in the United States drew some criticism that the interests of business were more specifically revenue oriented, the resolution passed by the chamber of commerce clearly stated, "Homelessness has a direct financial impact on businesses as it deters customers, damages employee recruitment and retention, harms tourism and discourages companies from setting up offices in areas with a visible homeless population." The resolution called for a nationally benchmarked plan that would set "goals, objectives, metrics and outcomes" and called for the adoption of best practices, including Housing First.

The resolution estimated that "homelessness costs Canadian taxpayers between $4.5 and $6 billion annually, inclusive of health care, criminal justice, social services and emergency shelter costs." This figure was developed by Gordon Laird and published in 2007 as *SHELTER: Homelessness in a Growth Economy; Canada's 21st Century Paradox* for Calgary's Sheldon Chumir Foundation for Ethics in Leadership. Laird also demonstrated that, from 1993 to 2004, an estimated $49.5 billion in costs could be attributed to homelessness.

In 2005 Canada held a first-ever national conference, the Canadian Conference on Homelessness: Stories, Research, Solutions, at York University, Toronto. A key result of the conference was the development of the Homeless Hub, a web-based umbrella for research and other tools useful to policy makers, providers, researchers, and other interested persons. The Homeless Hub was launched in 2007.

Finding Home is an e-book on the Hub site. Chapters are accessible to a general readership and cover many aspects of homelessness. The e-book project is funded by the Social Sciences and Humanities Research Council of Canada (SSHRC) as a partnership with the national homelessness charity, Raising the Roof, and with the newly created SSHRC-funded Canadian Homelessness Research Network (Hulchanski et al., 2009).

Australia

In 2008, the new government of Australian prime minister Kevin Rudd launched a national government initiative to develop a new strategy on homelessness. Prime Minister Rudd became foreign minister in 2010 after a change in Labor Party leadership.

The Australian housing market has been documented as dramatically more expensive than that of the United States and has an absolute shortage of units. High-density development in existing population centers is official strategy. According to research published as the *Demographia International Housing Affordability Survey*, the median home price was more than six times the gross yearly income in 2009, compared to almost three times the income level in the United States. The same research identified 6 of the top 10 cities lacking affordability as being in Australia, compared to the United States, the United Kingdom, Canada, and New Zealand. Lack of housing and affordability pose particular challenges to those starting out in the work world or starting families and to people facing special challenges in the market because of disability and/or lack of income (Demographia, 2010).

Following are excerpts from the prime minister's remarks at a national conference in Adelaide in May 2008, which convened on the release of the government's green paper on homelessness. The green paper was part of a initial consultative process that yielded a white paper of the government's plan later in 2008. Like the Blair government's earlier initiative in the United Kingdom, Prime Minister Rudd invoked "mutual partnership and mutual responsibility" to support those who choose to move out of homelessness.

Calling the goal of addressing homelessness "a great new enterprise," Rudd stressed that government would find new approaches for prevention and for breaking the cycle of homelessness, looking outside government in its search for "what works," identifying evidence-based practices to drive long-term solutions.

"As a Labor government we are committed to a principle of social solidarity that includes private philanthropy, community action, and public responsibility to protect the most vulnerable," stated the prime minister. "But let me also say this: we don't have an old-fashioned approach." The prime minister encouraged those who shared the ambitious goal to forward "undiluted, forceful, evidence based on the issues" to move solutions forward (Commonwealth of Australia, 2008).

Both the green paper and the resulting white paper are available on line at http://www.fahcsia.gov.au/sa/housing/progserv/homelessness/whitepaper/Pages/default.aspx.

International Human Rights Treaties

International human rights treaties are a tool being used to seek recognition of housing rights for people experiencing homelessness. Both European organizations and U.S. organizations focused on the law have employed various of these instruments.

Seven key international treaties address human rights: the International Convention on the Elimination of All Forms of Racial Discrimination (ICERD) (1965); the International Covenant on Civil and Political Rights (ICCPR) (1966); the International Covenant on Economic, Social and Cultural Rights (ICESCR) (1966); the Convention on the Elimination of All Forms of Discrimination against Women (CEDAW) (1979); the Convention against Torture and Other Cruel, Inhuman or Degrading Treatment or Punishment (CAT) (1984); the Convention on the Rights of the Child (CRC) (1989); and the International Convention on Protection of the Rights of All Migrant Workers and Members of Their Families (ICMRW) (1990).

Each treaty is monitored by an expert committee examining implementation by the signers to the documents. Detailed information is available at http://www.unfpa.org/rights/instruments.htm.

Universal Periodic Review (UPR) is a process undertaken by United Nations that occurs every four years. The United States took part in its first review in November 2010 in Geneva, Switzerland. The UN Human Rights Council examines how each country is meeting its obligations under the UN charter, the Universal Declaration of Human Rights (UDHR), other human rights treaties that have been ratified by that country, any relevant voluntary commitments by the government, and international law.

The UPR Working Group conducts the review. The working group is composed of 47 members of the UN Human Rights

Council. The 2010 review was the first for the United States to address housing rights.

In a statement issued by the U.S. Department of Housing and Urban Development secretary on the review, the secretary noted the federal strategy recently released by the government and stated, "Under the Obama Administration, HUD is making a concerted effort to become fully engaged in the global discussion of creating socially and environmentally sustainable urban communities, rooted in safe, decent, and affordable shelter."

"In the context of our current economic challenges, the United States is aggressively working toward a more focused, balanced, and expansive role for housing and community development programs. The UN's Universal Periodic Review process helps to inform and influence our nation's effort to dramatically increase the amount of affordable housing, especially for those struggling to find a place to call home" (HUD, 2010).

References

CCC (Canadian Chamber of Commerce). Proposed Policy Resolutions—The 81st Annual General Meeting of the Canadian Chamber of Commerce. Gatineau, QC: September 25–28, 2010. Available at http://www.chamber.ca/images/uploads/Proposed_resolutions/2010/Proposed%20English%202010.pdf.

Commonwealth of Australia. Remarks of Prime Minister Kevin Rudd at the 5th National Homelessness Conference, Adelaide, Australia, May 2008.

Council of the European Union (EU). *Council Declaration on The European Year for Combating Poverty and Social Exclusion: Working together to fight poverty in 2010 and beyond*. Brussels, Belgium, December 6, 2010. Available at http://www.consilium.europa.eu/uedocs/cms_data/docs/pressdata/en/lsa/118250.pdf.

DCLG (Government of the United Kingdom Department for Communities and Local Government). (2002) *Leaving Care: A Time for Change; Government Response*. London, Crown copyright, April 2002. Available at http://www.communities.gov.uk/archived/publications/housing/timeforchange.

DCLG (Government of the United Kingdom Department for Communities and Local Government). (2008). *Statutory Homelessness in England: The Experiences of Families and 16–17 Year Olds* (Homelessness

Research Summary Number 7, 2008). London, Crown copyright, March 2008. Available at http://www.communities.gov.uk/publications/housing/experienceoffamilies.

DCLG (Government of the United Kingdom Department for Communities and Local Government). *No One Left Out: Communities Ending Rough Sleeping; Good Practice Notes—Developing a Strategic Response to Prevent and Tackle Rough Sleeping*. London, Crown copyright, September 2009. Available at http://www.communities.gov.uk/publications/housing/developingstrategicresponse.

Demographia. *6th Annual Demographia International Housing Affordability Survey: 2010 Ratings for Metropolitan Markets*. Belleville, IL: Demographia, 2010. Available at http://www.demographia.com/dhi.pdf.

Denmark Ministry of the Interior and Social Affairs. *The Government's Homelessness Strategy—a Strategy to Reduce Homelessness in Denmark 2009–2012*. Copenhagen, 2009. Available at http://www.feantsa.org/files/freshstart/National_Strategies/Danish_strategy_Pjece%20om%20hjeml%C3%B8sestrategien_EN.pdf.

FEANTSA (European Federation of National Organizations Working with the Homeless). ETHOS: European Typology on Homelessness and Housing Exclusion. Brusells, Belgium: FEANTSA, 2010a. Available at http://www.feantsa.org/code/en/pg.asp?Page=484

FEANTSA (European Federation of National Organizations Working with the Homeless). "European Parliament Calls upon the EU for Concrete Action Towards Ending Homelessness." (2010b). Available at http://www.feantsa.org/files/freshstart/Communications/Press%20Releases/2010/101221_WD61_Adoption_PressRelease.pdf.

FEANTSA (European Federation of National Organizations Working with the Homeless). *European Research Conferences*. Brussels, Belgium: FEANTSA, 2010c. Available at http://eohw.horus.be/code/EN/pg.asp?Page=1113.

FEANTSA (European Federation of National Organizations Working with the Homeless). Strategies to Combat Homelessness, 2010d. Available at http://www.feantsa.org/code/en/pg.asp?Page=1169.

Ghosh, Aparisim. "Down and Out in Europe," *Time*, February 10, 2003. Available at http://www.time.com/time/europe/magazine/2003/0210/homeless/story.html.

Government of Ireland Department of the Environment, Heritage and Local Government. *The Way Home: A Strategy to Address Adult Homelessness in Ireland 2008–2013*. Dublin, Ireland: Department of the Environment, Heritage and Local Government, 2008. Available at http://www.environ.ie/en/Publications/DevelopmentandHousing/Housing/FileDownLoad,18192,en.pdf.

Government of Norway. *The Pathway to a Permanent Home.* Oslo, Norway, 2004. Available at http://www.feantsa.org/files/freshstart/National_Strategies/The_Pathway_to_a_permanent_home_2005_Norway.pdf.

Government of Sweden. *Homelessness, Multiple faces, Multiple Responsibilities—a Strategy to Combat Homelessness and Exclusion from the Housing Market, 2007–2009.* Stockholm, Sweden, 2007. Available at http://www.feantsa.org/files/freshstart/National_Strategies/Homelessness_multiplefaces_multipleresponsibilities2007_Sweden.pdf.

Homeless Agency. *A Key to the Door: The Homeless Agency Partnership Action Plan on Homelessness in Dublin.* Dublin, Ireland: Homeless Agency, 2007. Available at http://www.homelessagency.ie/Research-and-Policy/Publications/Action-Plans—Homeless-Agency/A-key-to-the-door—Action-Plan-on-Homelessness-in-.aspx.

HRSDC (Government of Canada Human Resources and Skills Development Canada). *The Homelessness Partnering Strategy.* (2010). Available at http://www.hrsdc.gc.ca/eng/homelessness/index.shtml.

HUD (U.S. Department of Housing and Urban Development). "U.S. Department of Housing and Urban Development Statement on the U.S. Participation in the United Nations' Universal Periodic Review" (press statement). Washington, D.C.: HUD, November 5, 2010. Available at http://portal.hud.gov/hudportal/HUD?src=/press/speeches_remarks_statements/2010/statement-110510.

Hulchanski, David J., Philippa Campsie, Shirley B.Y. Chau, Stephen W. Hwang, and Emily Paradis. *Finding Home: Policy Options for Addressing Homelessness in Canada.* (2009). Toronto: University of Toronto Cities Centre Press.

Irish Penal Reform Trust (IPRT). *"It's like Stepping on a Landmine . . .": Reintegration of Prisoners in Ireland.* Dublin, Ireland: Irish Penal Reform Trust, 2010. Available at http://www.iprt.ie/contents/1685.

Laird, Gordon. *SHELTER: Homelessness in a Growth Economy; Canada's 21st Century Paradox.* Calgary, Alberta, Canada: Sheldon Chumir Foundation for Ethics in Leadership, 2007.

O'Connell, James J., Shawn Mattison, Christine M. Judge, H. Josiyn Strupp Allen, and Howard K. Koh. "A Public Health Approach to Reducing Morbidity and Mortality among Homeless People in Boston." *Journal of Public Health Management Practice,* Volume 11, Issue 4 (2005).

ODPM (Government of the United Kingdom Office of the Deputy Prime Minister). *2002 Blocking the Fast Track from Prison to Rough Sleeping.* London, Crown copyright, March 2002. Available at http://www.communities.gov.uk/documents/housing/pdf/prisontoroughsleeping.pdf.

RSU/ESAG (Government of the United Kingdom, Rough Sleepers Unit and Ex-Service Action Group on Homelessness). *Resources for Ex-Service Personnel in London.* London, Crown copyright, January 2004. Available at http://www.communities.gov.uk/documents/housing/pdf/138010.pdf.

Scottish Government. New funding for innovative ways to prevent homelessness (press statement). 2005. Available at http://www.scotland.gov.uk/Topics/Built-Environment/Housing/access/homeless.

Scottish Parliament. Homelessness, etc. (Scotland) Act 2003 and 2001. Available at http://www.legislation.gov.uk/asp/2001/10/contents.

SEU (Government of the United Kingdom Social Exclusion Unit). *Coming in from the Cold: The Government's Strategy on Rough Sleeping.* London, Crown copyright, December 1999.

Thomsen, Britta, Elizabeth Lynne, Ilda Figueiredo, Karima Delli, and Jacek Protasiewicz, Members. Written Declaration pursuant to Rule 123 Rules of Procedure on an EU homelessness strategy (6.9.2010). Strasbourg, France; European Parliament, 2010. Available at http://www.europarl.europa.eu/sides/getDoc.do?pubRef=//EP//NONSGML+WDECL+P7-DCL-2010-0061+0+DOC+PDF+V0//EN&language=EN.

U.K. Department of Health. *Me, Survive, Out There? New Arrangements for Young People Living in and Leaving Care.* London, Crown copyright, July 1999. Available at http://www.dh.gov.uk/en/Publicationsandstatistics/Publications/PublicationsPolicyAndGuidance/DH_4010312.

Welsh Assembly Government Housing Directorate. *10-Year Plan Homelessness Plan for Wales 2009–2019.* Cardiff, Wales, Crown copyright, 2009. Available at http://www.feantsa.org/files/freshstart/National_Strategies/Wales.pdf.

4

Chronology

Key events during the last decade demonstrate the steadily accelerating momentum that resulted from new initiatives, new ideas, and new results in preventing and ending homelessness.

This chapter includes key events from the start of the last decade, as new developments in research and planning produced new focus on homelessness in public policy and investment at the federal, state, and local government level in the United States and elsewhere. In addition to highlighting new regular federal meetings of cabinet officials, new state interagency councils on homelessness to coordinate state resources and policy, and new city and county 10-year plans to create strategies, the chapter incorporates news reports, research, and other events. Included are selected examples that demonstrate diversity (states large and small taking action, cities and counties developing creative approaches to involve partners), momentum (inaugural events for policy makers, regional and intergovernmental events to develop coordination), and results (announcements of reductions in homelessness).

2001 Department of Housing and Urban Development secretary Mel Martinez tells the National Alliance to End Homelessness annual conference that "the challenge in ending homelessness is great but so is our dedication. I say it is time to dedicate ourselves to the next great new American enterprise."

February 4, 2002 The president's FY 2003 budget includes a new "top objective" to end chronic homelessness in 10 years. The proposed federal budget is for the federal fiscal year of October 1, 2002, to September 30, 2003.

March 15, 2002 U.S. Interagency Council on Homelessness executive director Philip Mangano of Massachusetts is sworn in by Department of Housing and Urban Development (HUD) secretary Mel Martinez, council chair. Mangano brings more than two decades of experience in homeless programs for individuals and families, public policy, and business to his new appointment.

July 18, 2002 Council Chair Martinez, with Department of Health and Human Services (HHS) secretary and council vice chair Tommy Thompson, convenes first full council meeting of revitalized Interagency Council in six years. Four secretaries will rotate duties as chair: HUD, HHS, Veterans Affairs, and Labor.

July 19, 2002 Council Chair Martinez gives a progress report to the National Alliance to End Homelessness annual conference, telling the audience, "President Bush has made combating homelessness a top domestic priority."

December 5, 2002 Chair Martinez and Vice Chair Thompson gather Interagency Council members at the White House for collaborative efforts to reduce street homelessness and strengthen homeless prevention. Federal agencies report on intraagency, interagency, and intergovernmental collaborations. A new $55 million joint funding effort by the departments of Housing and Urban Development (HUD), Health and Human Services (HHS), and Veterans Administration (VA) will create permanent housing and services for chronically homeless persons.

January 21, 2003 Chicago mayor Richard Daley embraces a 10-year plan to end homelessness in the third-largest city in the nation.

January 23, 2003 Addressing the plenary session of the U.S. Conference of Mayors at their winter meeting in Washington, Interagency Council director Mangano challenges 100 mayors to develop 10-year plans to end homelessness in their cities.

February 3, 2003 The president's FY 2004 budget is released and affirms "the commitment made in 2003 to end chronic homelessness within a decade" and proposes the Samaritan Initiative to provide new federal resources for chronically homeless persons.

March 2003 Mayor Shirley Franklin unveils Atlanta's Blueprint to End Homelessness. Convened by the United Way in Atlanta and chaired by Horace Sibley, a regional commission invested months to create a plan that would engage the whole Atlanta community.

March 28, 2003 HHS secretary Tommy Thompson becomes federal Interagency Council chair, marking the first time that HHS chairs the council. The council hears results in developing a federal strategy to end chronic homelessness and initiatives to engage elected officials from states, cities, and counties.

May 12, 2003 Blair government officials discuss how they were able to reduce "rough sleeping" by two-thirds. In the Indian Treaty Room at the White House, four senior Blair government officials and senior policy officials from the Interagency Council, HUD, HHS, Labor, VA, Social Security Administration, and other federal agencies meet to discuss prevention and intervention strategies to end chronic homelessness. Led by Gordon Campbell, head of the U.K. Homelessness Directorate, and Louise Casey, former head of the "Rough Sleepers Unit," the policy delegation describes their successful effort to reduce the number of homeless persons "sleeping rough" on the streets. These initial bilateral discussions form the basis for what becomes an ongoing

2003 (*cont.*)	international dialogue among governments adopting similar strategies.
June 6, 2003	The U.S. Conference of Mayors in their annual meeting in Denver adopts a resolution to encourage cities to create and implement performance-based, results-oriented strategic plans to end chronic homelessness in 10 years.
July 15, 2003	The National Association of Counties at their annual conference in Milwaukee passes a resolution supporting the Bush administration's efforts to end chronic homelessness and endorses a 10-year planning processes for counties.
July 16, 2003	Senior officials from 40 cities come to Washington for a council-sponsored focus group on developing 10-year plans to end chronic homelessness. Also discussed is the importance of using street counts to ensure performance outcomes. A toolkit for developing 10-year plans is unveiled.
July 17, 2003	Interagency Council director Mangano addresses the annual conference of the National Alliance to End Homelessness attended by more than 1,300 people. He introduces keynote speaker VA secretary and council vice chair Anthony Principi.
July 17, 2003	A new $13.5 million federal interagency funding initiative is announced to focus on employment and housing for chronically homeless people.
October 1, 2003	The U.S. Interagency Council on Homelessness, chaired by Health and Human Services secretary Tommy Thompson, announces the award of 11 grants for an unprecedented joint federal agency announcement of $55 million by the council, HUD, HHS, and VA for the Collaborative Initiative to Help End Chronic Homelessness. Departments of Labor and Housing announce demonstration grant awards to five community partnerships to end chronic homelessness and

integrate persons with disabilities into the workforce.

November 21, 2003 Mayor Michael Bloomberg announces that the City of New York, in partnership with leaders from the business and nonprofit communities, will develop a 10-year plan to end chronic homelessness.

December 13, 2003 The National League of Cities officially adopts a resolution supporting the Bush administration goal of ending chronic homelessness in the United States in 10 years and pledging to " help advance" efforts to create 10-year plans. The National League of Cities becomes the third major association of city and county government officials to support the Bush administration's call to end chronic homelessness in 10 years.

December 19, 2003 The Bush administration announces a record $1.27 billion in federal funds to be awarded to local programs to end homelessness.

January 13, 2004 Just days after being sworn in as mayor of San Francisco, Gavin Newsom pledges to end homelessness in the city within the next 10 years. He names election opponent Angela Alioto to chair the plan.

February 2, 2004 With the release of the president's FY 2005 proposed budget, the administration again affirms the federal effort to end chronic homelessness, stating, "The Administration continues the commitment made in 2002 to end chronic homelessness within a decade."

February 13, 2004 The City of Philadelphia, which won a $3.3 million grant from the federal government to end chronic homelessness, announces that, just four months later, the first participant in the "Home First" program has signed his lease.

February 25, 2004 At a press conference that includes representatives of the United Way, Deloitte, and the Metro Dallas Homeless Alliance, Dallas mayor Laura

2004 (*cont.*)	Miller unveils a new draft 10-year plan and makes Dallas the 15th community in the nation to have developed a plan. Over 70 other cities and counties are in the process of creating plans.
February 2004	The Interagency Council launches a new weekly e-newsletter to support partners from the public and private sector in preventing and ending homelessness.
March 26, 2004	At the invitation of the Interagency Council, representatives of the governments of the United States, England, and South Africa meet in Washington to discuss national government responses to homelessness. The new government-to-government colloquy is an unprecedented opportunity for exchange on topics including innovative programs, best practices, and performance results in ending homelessness.
April 1, 2004	Secretary Anthony Principi becomes the first VA secretary to chair the federal Interagency Council, underscoring the needs of the veteran population. Federal agencies announce new investment targeted to the goal of ending chronic homelessness, including an announcement by the Social Security Administration of $6.6 million in awards to 34 sites for the HOPE (Homeless Outreach and Project Evaluation) program to assist homeless individuals who apply for Social Security or SSI benefits. SSA estimates that 5,000 homeless persons will be served through the programs receiving these funds over the next three years.
	Council meeting guests Minnesota governor Tim Pawlenty and Chattanooga mayor Bob Corker describe their new initiatives to end chronic homelessness as they partner with the Interagency Council to create state interagency councils on homelessness and jurisdictional 10-year plans to end chronic homelessness.
June 16, 2004	D.C. mayor Anthony Williams unveils a 10-year plan to end homelessness for the nation's capital.

June 23, 2004 Nonprofit and public sector leaders release the New York City plan with Mayor Michael Bloomberg, who commits his administration to the goal of ending chronic homelessness.

June 30, 2004 San Francisco mayor Gavin Newsom, community leaders, members of the Ten-Year Planning Council to End Chronic Homelessness, and local citizens unveil the city's new 10-year plan. The San Francisco Plan to Abolish Chronic Homelessness calls for 3,000 new permanent supportive housing units.

July 12, 2004 The House of Representatives Financial Services Subcommittee on Housing and Community Opportunity holds a hearing on H.R. 4057, the Samaritan Initiative Act of 2004, new legislation proposed by the administration that would authorize new federal resources to promote and support community efforts to end chronic homelessness.

July Representatives of the 11 community collaborations funded under the inaugural federal collaboration to end chronic homelessness, including housing providers, substance abuse treatment and mental health counselors, outreach workers and case management staff, meet in Washington to examine progress.

September 3, 2004 Longtime civic leader and businessman Tom Dunning is named to lead Dallas's effort to prevent and end homelessness in the eighth-largest city in the nation. The announcement of Mr. Dunning's appointment as "homeless czar" for the city is made by Mayor Laura Miller. The city's recently adopted Ten Year Plan to end chronic homelessness made Dallas the first city in the state of Texas to have developed such a plan.

September 29, 2004 VA secretary Principi chairs a meeting of the U.S. Interagency Council on Homelessness, where over $160 million in new federal resources is

2004 (*cont.*) announced. Council members hear from providers of services to veterans who have benefited from expanded resources.

Horace Sibley, who led Atlanta mayor Shirley Franklin's 10-year planning effort to end chronic homelessness, and Craig Chancellor, president of Triangle United Way in North Carolina, discuss the commitment of the United Way to the goal of ending chronic homelessness and their role in helping bring resources and partnership from the business community.

October 2004 San Francisco mayor Gavin Newsom creates the first Project Homeless Connect to engage and welcome homeless people back into the community.

October 11, 2004 An inaugural meeting of "thought leaders and visionaries, civic and government leaders who have committed themselves to ending chronic homelessness in their localities, and innovators from business and non-profits" convenes in New York City under the partnership of Common Ground, the Rockefeller Foundation, and the federal Interagency Council on Homelessness. Leaders from Denver, Atlanta, San Francisco, Dallas, Indianapolis, Nashville, Minnesota, and Massachusetts hear from business thinker Malcolm Gladwell and Blair government leader Louise Casey.

January 18, 2005 Mayors sign a new agreement on ending chronic homelessness when 39 mayors representing cities from Anchorage to Key West sign a covenant of partnership with each other and with the U.S. Interagency Council on Homelessness, agreeing to collaborate in the exchange of data, share best practices, and welcome other cities to join the collaboration. The signing is at a meeting of the Hunger and Homelessness Task Force at the U.S. Conference of Mayors Winter Meeting in Washington.

February 7, 2005 In an otherwise austere federal budget in which funding for nonsecurity-related discretionary spending would be reduced by nearly 1 percent, total funding for targeted homeless assistance programs would increase by 8.5 percent.

February 17, 2005 The continuing national innovation group convenes in New York City to focus on ending street deaths. Dr. James O'Connell of Boston Health Care for the Homeless and Philadelphia director of homeless services Robert Hess review successful strategies.

March 2, 2005 At their annual winter meeting in Washington, the nation's governors adopt a new policy statement on affordable housing, homeless assistance, and community development that supports the goal of ending chronic homelessness and "the efforts of the United States Interagency Council on Homelessness to create a working partnership that includes multiple federal agencies, states and localities."

March 21, 2005 HUD releases a funding announcement for a new $10 million two-year Housing for People Who Are Homeless and Addicted to Alcohol Initiative that will develop new housing approaches.

April 28, 2005 The national innovators group convenes in New York City to continue dialogue on solutions, cost-benefit analysis, and progress in addressing street deaths. A specific focus is the integration of street-based feeding programs into larger jurisdictional strategies.

August 11, 2005 The Department of Housing and Urban Development and the federal Interagency Council announce $10 million in funding for 11 cities in the new demonstration program called Housing for People Who Are Homeless and Addicted to Alcohol. The initiative will assist 555 homeless people with chronic alcoholism who have been living on the streets for at least 365 days over the last five years.

September 15, 2005	Reno, Nevada, joined by Sparks and Washoe County, becomes the 200th jurisdiction to commit to a 10-year plan to end chronic homelessness. Reno is where Murray Barr of Malcolm Gladwell's "Million-Dollar Murray" lived on the streets.
October 26, 2005	The Center for Mental Health Services (CMHS) of the U.S. Department of Health and Human Services convenes the Third National Conference Addressing Homelessness for People with Mental Illnesses and/or Substance Use Disorders in Washington, D.C.
December 8, 2005	Thirty cities across the country partner with the U.S. Interagency Council on Homelessness for the first National Project Homeless Connect Day, bringing volunteers from nonprofits, corporations, federal, state, and local government agencies, faith-based organizations, and homeless service programs to one-stop events for persons experiencing homelessness with services and housing to end their homelessness.
December 20, 2005	A record number of nearly 5,000 local programs that house and assist persons experiencing homelessness are awarded a record $1.33 billion in funding in an announcement made by the U.S. Department of Housing and Urban Development secretary.
February 6, 2006	Stating that the "2007 Budget continues the Administration's commitment to end chronic homelessness," the Bush administration announces an unprecedented sixth consecutive year of increased funding for targeted federal programs serving persons who are homeless, proposing over $4 billion in assistance. The president continues the federal commitment to the Samaritan Initiative for housing people who are chronically homeless.
February 13, 2006	Author Malcolm Gladwell, in the *New Yorker*, examines the economics of homelessness.

Gladwell's article, "Million-Dollar Murray," whose title reflects the example of one chronically homeless man in Reno, Nevada, examines cost-benefit analyses across the nation that are revealing the public cost of homelessness.

February 15, 2006 During a street outreach and services event to engage people who are homeless, the City of San Juan, Puerto Rico, unveils its new 10-year plan to end chronic homelessness at a ceremony hosted by San Juan mayor Jorge Santini. The Iniciativa Hacia La Esperanza ("Initiative for Hope") is a mobile one-stop event providing intensive services, treatment, and detoxification in areas of the city frequented by people experiencing homelessness.

February 18, 2006 Writer Malcolm Gladwell is interviewed on National Public Radio's *Weekend Edition* with Scott Simon, where he discusses the Bush administration's partnership with cities focusing on chronic homelessness and showing results, noting, "The thing that's driving this strategy towards homelessness is the notion that we have a very limited amount of money, a very limited amount of political will. And what are we going to do with that? Well, we're going to concentrate it on the worst part of the problem in the place where we can save the most money in the short term."

March 2, 2006 Mayors and 10-year plan leaders from 18 cities gather in San Diego for the first mayors' summit: Preventing and Ending Homelessness Among Veterans, convened by the federal Interagency Council on Homelessness with Common Ground and the Rockefeller Foundation.

April 4, 2006 The federal Interagency Council on Homelessness holds it second meeting following the Gulf Coast hurricanes. HHS estimates that 500,000 people may be in need of counseling services in

2006 (*cont.*) the region. The Department of Education reports on school rebuilding efforts and assistance for students at every level.

May 10, 2006 With reports of decreases in chronic homelessness being documented across the country, the U.S. Interagency Council on Homelessness holds a national summit for jurisdictional leaders: "Moving From Good to Better to Great in Sustaining Ten-Year Plans to End Chronic Homelessness" in Denver, Colorado. The summit brings together jurisdictional leaders developing 10-year plans, innovators, and practitioners to focus on results.

June 20, 2006 The first-ever Oregon Leadership Summit on Ending Chronic Homelessness convenes in the capital city of Salem with over 100 participants including mayors of Portland, Salem, Eugene, Corvallis, and Hillsboro, city councilors, county commissioners, federal, state and local government agency officials, 10-year plan leaders, representatives of several United Way chapters, and innovative service providers.

July 10, 2006 The federal Interagency Council on Homelessness convenes. The Department of Health and Human Services reports that the Administration for Children and Families is finalizing a study of "promising strategies to end youth homelessness," which was drafted in consultation with the Interagency Council at the request of Congress.

Denver releases a Year One report card to the community on progress in implementing Denver's Road Home. The city reports that it met or exceeded all eight of its first-year goals. The report card notes that progress was built on the spirit of Mayor John Hickenlooper's promise that the strategy would allow local government to say, "Here's your investment; here's what we delivered" and would "end much of the frustration of just throwing money at the problem without having any results."

October 24, 2006	Sixty new 10-year plans are unveiled at a statewide event in Michigan, marking the first time all geography—83 counties in Michigan—in a state is covered by a plan. A two-day Michigan Homeless Summit held in Lansing attended by more than 650 people marks the official launch of Michigan's Campaign to End Homelessness.
December 4, 2006	The federal Interagency Council's Annual Project Homeless Connect event expands to a National Project Homeless Connect Week, with 40 cities partnering with over 9,500 volunteers who welcome almost 22,000 homeless persons. Some of the participating cities host "opinion leader" screenings offered by SONY/Columbia Pictures for the feature film *The Pursuit of Happyness.* Starring Will Smith as Chris Gardner, the film depicts the true story of a homeless single father who becomes a successful broker.
January 2007	Springfield, Massachusetts, mayor Charles V. Ryan describes his city's new 10-year plan, Homes Within Reach, as a demonstration of a new outlook and commitment to "not housing after shelter, not housing never, but housing first."
February 5, 2007	The president's proposed 2008 budget "continues the administration's commitment to end chronic homelessness by creating new supportive housing options for these individuals." The Bush administration proposes an unprecedented seventh consecutive year of increased funding for targeted federal programs serving persons who are homeless.
March 1, 2007	The departments of Health and Human Services and Housing and Urban Development and the Interagency Council on Homelessness convene the National Symposium on Homelessness Research in Washington, the first such conference in a decade. Research papers presented include topics of cost studies, historic perspectives,

2007 (*cont.*) consumer involvement, homeless families and children, youth, chronic homelessness, rural homelessness, housing, employment, incarceration, and mainstream services.

March 5, 2007 The U.S. Interagency Council on Homelessness convenes its 10th meeting, now under the leadership of Department of Health and Human Services secretary Michael Leavitt as chair. Director Philip Mangano notes that the meeting coincides with the 20th anniversary of the passage of the McKinney Act, which established the federal intervention in homelessness and the Interagency Council, and marks five years since revitalization of the council by President Bush in March 2002 after a six-year dormancy.

The Department of Housing and Urban Development reports that the HUD/HHS/VA Collaborative Initiative to Help End Chronic Homelessness created over 600 permanent supportive housing tenancies with only 4 percent of homeless clients returning to the streets; all participants in the HUD/DOL Ending Chronic Homelessness Through Housing and Employment Initiative have retained their housing.

March 7, 2007 The federal Interagency Council on Homelessness's third national summit for jurisdictional leaders welcomes over 200 state and local jurisdictional leaders for "The Pursuit of Solutions: Second Annual National Summit on Innovation for Jurisdictional Leaders." The program includes remarks by Louise Casey, government architect of England's successful "rough sleepers" initiative, which successfully reduced street homelessness by 75 percent, and Chris Gardner, depicted in the feature film, *The Pursuit of Happyness,* with Will Smith.

March 15, 2007 Miami mayor Manny Diaz announces a 50 percent reduction in the number of homeless people between July 2006 and January 2007. Included in the reduction is a 27 percent decrease in the number of persons experiencing chronic homelessness.

March 29, 2007 Fort Myers and Lee County, Florida, become the 300th jurisdictional commitment to a 10-year plan, in the same week that Duluth and St. Louis County, Minnesota, adopt a plan and San Francisco announces a 38 percent reduction in homelessness since 2004.

April 2007 Dallas, in its third year of plan implementation in the nation's ninth largest city, reports further reductions in chronic homelessness. A new 23 percent reduction in chronic homelessness and a 9 percent overall reduction in homelessness are reported, bringing the reported decrease in chronic homelessness over two years to 43 percent.

April 19, 2007 Fort Worth, Texas, convenes its first Project Homeless Connect event and reports a 42 percent decrease in its unsheltered population.

May 25, 2007 University of Pennsylvania researcher Dr. Dennis Culhane releases new research results on family homelessness, showing how the needs of families and their social service histories relate to the level of service and length of stay they experience in homeless programs. Data show that most families (75 percent) leave quickly and don't return to shelter but that a small number (5–8 percent) return repeatedly.

May 31, 2007 Mayors and city councilors and other elected officials from more than 1,200 Canadian cities meet in Calgary for the Big City Mayors Caucus and the Federation of Canadian Municipalities' (FCM) 70th Annual Conference. A key conference focus is the U.S. partnership to end homelessness.

June 11, 2007 The new members of the Central Florida Regional Commission on Homelessness, established by elected officials from the City of

2007 (*cont.*)	Orlando and Orange, Osceola, and Seminole counties, meet to focus on their 10-year plan, Ten2End. The commission includes executives from Disney World and the Orlando Magic.
November 16, 2007	Mayors and county officials from across the nation sign a 12-point statement of principles and actions to end chronic homelessness at a summit convened by Denver mayor John Hickenlooper, Interagency Council on Homelessness executive director Philip Mangano, and Melville Charitable Trust president Robert Hohler and sponsored by Fannie Mae.
December 3, 2007	The Third Annual National Project Homeless Connect sponsored by the federal Interagency Council on Homelessness commences with events in 25 cities including Bridgeport, Connecticut, San Francisco (its 19th event), Miami, Nashua, New Hampshire, Oakland, California, Orlando, New York City, San Jose, California, and Detroit. More than 10,000 people who are homeless are welcomed at events.
January 2008	With the New Year comes a new 2008 federal budget, delayed but in place with new resources. Budget language emphasizes the importance of coordinating and integrating federal Department of Housing homeless resources with mainstream entitlement, benefit, and service resources. Rapid rehousing strategies are the focus of new investment, with $25 million for a demonstration program for rapid rehousing of homeless families.
January 2008	Massachusetts' Joint Legislative-Executive State Commission to End Homelessness releases its five-year plan to end homelessness, identifying as a defining principle "targeting the right resources to the right people at the right time" to reduce reliance on shelters and increase housing opportunity. State Representative Byron Rushing

cochaired the commission with Tina Brooks, undersecretary of the Commonwealth's Department of Housing and Community Development.

March 2008 The Department of Health and Human Services names Pathways to Housing, the innovative Housing First technology pioneered by Dr. Sam Tsemberis, as an evidence-based practice. Housing First, which has achieved housing stability and recovery for persons experiencing chronic homelessness, showed that about 80 percent of Housing First participants were stably housed after two years.

March 4, 2008 Ten-year plan community champions from New England gather in Boston for a first-ever summit convened by the federal Interagency Council to measure progress in 10-year plans and in the development of local community champions. Champions are one of the key innovations associated with plans, engaging business and civic leaders.

March 6, 2008 Department of Veterans Affairs secretary James Peake becomes chair of the U.S. Interagency Council on Homelessness at its eleventh meeting, with Secretary Peake committing to continue the council's leadership commitment on the issue of homelessness and a focus on "goals and measured results." HHS releases a new inventory of federal programs to serve families, showing key information on 73 programs across 11 federal agencies.

The Social Security Administration, whose three-year Homeless Outreach Projects and Evaluation (HOPE) initiative operates at 41 sites, reports that more than 9,000 individuals have enrolled under the initiative.

Norfolk mayor Paul Fraim reports to the council that his city's Blueprint to End Chronic Homelessness, now in its second year of implementation, focuses on regional solutions and includes the innovations of rapid rehousing, Housing First, and Project Homeless Connect, and permanent housing for ex-offenders. Norfolk has achieved results of a 25 percent reduction in overall homelessness and a 40 percent reduction in street homelessness as well as projecting to double local permanent supportive housing capacity this year.

March 9, 2008 New York City announces a third year of decreasing street homelessness in the city, with a 12 percent reduction since 2007 and an overall 25 percent decline in street homelessness since 2005.

March 11, 2008 Officials from city, county, and state government in California, Arizona, Utah, and Hawaii meet in Phoenix under the leadership of the federal Interagency Council on Homelessness for a peer-to-peer summit on innovation and results in preventing homelessness.

March 31, 2008 Australian First Lady Therese Rein and federal Interagency Council on Homelessness executive director Philip Mangano meet to discuss strategic partnerships, innovation, outcome measures, and results in ending homelessness during a visit of Prime Minster Kevin Rudd to Washington. Ms. Rein, a business leader, has specialized in employment services for persons with special needs.

April 9, 2008 President Bush signs the Second Chance Act, new bipartisan legislation that addresses successful prisoner reentry with support from state and local government, law enforcement, corrections, and the courts. Ensuring successful reentry will reduce and prevent homelessness and recidivism to jails and prisons. The new initiative provides grants to government agencies and nonprofit organizations for employment assistance, substance abuse treatment, housing, family programming, mentoring, victims support, and other services.

April 9, 2008 "America's Road Home: Future Directions for Policy and Investment in Abolishing Homelessness—Partnering for Results in Ten-Year Plans" welcomes over 250 state and local government partners, community champions, and business and community leaders to the Third Annual National Summit Homelessness in Washington. The National Press Club is the site of the event convened by the U.S. Interagency Council on Homelessness, which includes a special "Innovators Symposium" of experts from across the nation.

April 11, 2008 British Columbia's Leadership Prayer Breakfast in Vancouver focuses on homelessness as more than 1,200 government, business, political, political, labor, education, religious, and civic leaders assemble to welcome U.S. Interagency Council on Homelessness executive director Philip Mangano, invited to keynote the annual event.

April 23, 2008 "A Partnership to House Every North Dakotan" is convened by the federal Interagency Council on Homelessness and the North Dakota Governor's Interagency Council on Homelessness created by Governor James Hoeven. The event includes the 10-year-plan cities of Bismarck, Dickinson, Mandan, Fargo, Jamestown, and Minot, Williston. The first Native American tribal authority to create a plan, the Turtle Mountain Band of Chippewa, takes part; the three affiliated tribes are developing a plan.

May 22, 2008 Prime Minister Kevin Rudd announces a new Australian strategy, with the release of a green paper for discussion at a national homelessness conference in Adelaide.

June 3, 2008 Canada's capital city of Ottawa, Ontario, brings together a broad partnership to announce a new

2008 (*cont.*) 10-year plan, under the leadership of Mayor Larry O'Brien and the Leadership Table on Homelessness. The group hears an address by U.S. Interagency Council on Homelessness executive director Philip Mangano and brings together business leaders, government officials, representatives of community agencies, and the faith community to address the issue of chronic homelessness in Ottawa.

The European Parliament, the sole elected body of the European Union, adopts a resolution to end street homelessness by 2015. Signed by 438 of 785 members, the resolution calls for a universal definition of homelessness across the EU, the collection and reporting of standard data, use of winter emergency plans as part of larger strategies, and creation of annual progress reports on results.

June 2008 The Fort Worth City Council, with the support of the Fort Worth Chamber of Commerce, Downtown Fort Worth, Inc., and others in the business community, votes unanimously to adopt Directions Home, a new city-county 10-year plan.

June 12, 2008 *Street Sense,* D.C.'s street newspaper, inaugurates annual journalism awards at the National Press Club. Interagency Council on Homelessness executive director Philip Mangano and *Washington Post* columnist Courtland Milloy deliver remarks.

June 19, 2008 A total of 120 state and local elected officials, provider agencies, and homeless advocates representing the 12 10-year plans in Oregon gather in the state's capital city of Salem. The Oregon Ending Homelessness Advisory Council releases the state's plan called "A Home for Hope."

June 23, 2008 The nation's mayors, in their annual meeting, unanimously affirm the goal of ending homelessness and expanded their bipartisan partnership with the U.S. Interagency Council on Homelessness to end homelessness in the nation.

July 2008 A new $25 million, three-year Rapid Re-Housing for Families Demonstration Program is announced by the Department of Housing. The demonstration program will help HUD learn more about how to best serve families who are homeless and also contribute to research on families.

July 15, 2008 County officials from across the nation gather in Kansas City at their annual conference and support resolutions on innovations that are reducing and ending chronic homelessness in communities across the nation. The National Association of Counties (NACo) endorses innovative initiatives in 10-year plans, including rapid rehousing and Housing First strategies, and focuses on homeless veterans, cost-benefit analysis, and Project Homeless Connect. The national jurisdictional partnership to end homelessness, America's Road Home, is affirmed by resolution and supported by new signatories; mayor and county official signatories number more than 335 jurisdictional leaders.

July 29, 2008 Federal officials announce a second year of reduction in chronic homelessness, averaging a 15 percent decline annually from 2005 to 2007. The Annual Homeless Assessment Report (AHAR) is based on reports from a single Point in Time count from 3,800 cities and counties. AHAR for the first time reports on the scope of homelessness over a full-year period, finding that nearly 1.6 million persons experienced homelessness and found shelter between October 1, 2006, and September 30, 2007.

September 2008 Atlanta mayor Shirley Franklin launches a new "donation parking meter" initiative called "Give Change That Makes Sense," as a way for community residents and tourists to support the

2008 (*cont.*) city's goals to end homelessness. The meters on downtown streets accept donations as an alternative to giving money to people on the street.

Toronto pilots a new initiative that creates partnerships with shelters for rapid and successful housing placements, creating a "Shelter to Home" trajectory for single adults and youth who are frequent users of shelter. The new initiative shows an 88 percent housing stability rate one year after its launch.

October 3, 2008 The Paul Wellstone-Pete Domenici Mental Health Parity and Addiction Equity Act of 2008 (H.R. 6983) becomes law when signed by President Bush. The new bipartisan mental health measure will provide expanded insurance coverage for mental health treatment and addiction.

October 6, 2008 The Department of Housing and Urban Development releases $3.92 billion in funds under the new Housing and Economic Recovery Act's Neighborhood Stabilization Program (NSP). NSP resources can be used to purchase foreclosed homes and rehabilitate or redevelop them. The resources represent an opportunity for 10-year-plan communities to apply the new resources to produce housing outcomes that prevent and end homelessness.

October 15, 2008 Housing and employment are the focus of "Housing Works" for Utah under its 10-year business plan to end chronic homelessness adopted in 2005. At an annual homeless summit of over 300 state and local leaders, service providers, and other private sector and philanthropic leaders, Utah leaders reported over 2,100 housing units created as well as results of a cost study with Salt Lake City police.

October 20, 2008 The federal Interagency Council on Homelessness convenes its 12th and final meeting of the Bush administration. Meeting at the White

House, Department of Veterans Affairs secretary and council chair Dr. James Peake leads federal agencies in summarizing results and the investment of record federal resources for people who are homeless. Secretary Peake reports a 40 percent decrease in the number of homeless veterans.

December 1, 2008 The Interagency Council launches its Fourth Annual National Project Homeless Connect Week, as communities across the country welcome homeless people to one-day, one-stop events to create access to needed resources. Project Homeless Connect, promoted as a field-tested innovation by the council, has been adopted by over 200 communities in the United States, Canada, and Australia.

January 13, 2009 Jurisdictional 10-year-plan leaders from 18 cities and counties across Northern California—part of California KEYS—meet at the newest site of San Francisco's Direct Access to Housing initiative. KEYS works to strengthen partnership and share innovations with 10-year plan leaders from across California.

January 17, 2009 More than 250 of the nation's mayors hold their 77th annual winter meeting in the capital, under the leadership of the United States Conference of Mayors (USCM) president and Miami mayor Manny Diaz. The Mayors' Task Force on Hunger and Homelessness, chaired by San Francisco mayor Gavin Newsom, meets to affirm the national partnership.

February 12, 2009 In Springfield, Massachusetts, mayor Domenic Sarno announces the second straight year of a decrease in homelessness, with a 35 percent drop in street homelessness and a 9 percent overall decrease in the number of individuals.

February 17, 2009 President Obama signs the American Recovery and Reinvestment Act (ARRA) with new resources to prevent and end homelessness.

2009 (*cont.*) Resources in targeted homeless programs include the Emergency Shelter Grants program ($1.5 billion), FEMA's Emergency Food and Shelter Program ($100 million), Education of Homeless Children and Youth program ($70 million), and Violence against Women transitional residential program ($50 million) and total $1.72 billion.

February 18, 2009 The Obama administration announces $1.6 billion in record targeted homeless assistance grant funding from the U.S. Department of Housing and Urban Development to more than 6,300 local programs to provide housing, shelter, and supportive services to individuals and families. Twenty-three new sites for a national Rapid Re-Housing for Families Demonstration Program are also announced.

February 25, 2009 The New York City Department of Homeless Services (DHS) announces that street homelessness in New York City is down 30 percent since last year and 47 percent since 2005, the first year the city conducted the Homeless Outreach Population Estimate (HOPE) count citywide.

March 19, 2009 The Bill and Melinda Gates Foundation and the Washington State partners of the Washington Families Fund announce a commitment to reduce family homelessness in the state by 50 percent in the next decade though coordination with 10-year plans and use of promising practices in prevention, rapid rehousing, and service coordination.

April 1, 2009 Seattle reports a 50 percent reduction in costs and $4 million in savings from its Housing First initiative at 1811 Eastlake. Findings are published in the *Journal of the American Medical Association*. The housing success for 95 chronic inebriates shows that the residents previously cost local taxpayers $8.2 million in hospitalizations, emergency services, jail time, detox, and sobering center visits.

April 24, 2009 The U.S. Interagency Council on Homelessness partners with Paramount and Participant Media to offer "opinion leader" screenings of the new Jamie Foxx and Robert Downey Jr. movie, *The Soloist,* in 58 cities engaged in 10-year plans. The film depicts homeless musician Nathaniel Ayres and his life on Skid Row and *Los Angeles Times* columnist Steve Lopez.

May 20, 2009 President Barack Obama signs new federal legislation that reauthorizes the McKinney-Vento Homeless Assistance programs for the first time in almost two decades. The Homeless Emergency Assistance and Rapid Transition to Housing (HEARTH) Act now has an authorization level of $2.2 billion. More than a decade of work went into the new law, which emerged this year with the leadership of Senators Jack Reed and Christopher Bond and Representatives Barney Frank and Maxine Waters.

June 18, 2009 The U.S. Interagency Council on Homelessness (USICH) convenes its first meeting in the Obama administration, with Department of Veterans Affairs secretary Eric Shinseki as chair. Housing and Urban Development secretary Shaun Donovan is elected chairperson for the coming year, and labor secretary Hilda Solis is elected vice chairperson.

July 9, 2009 The U.S. Department of Housing and Urban Development issues the 2008 Annual Homeless Assessment report to Congress. HUD concludes that overall homelessness remained almost unchanged from 2007 to 2008, but the number of homeless families, particularly those living in suburban and rural areas, increased.

The U.S. Department of Labor Veterans' Employment and Training Service (DOL-VETS) announces FY 2009 and FY 2010 funds to support

2009 (*cont.*)	local stand-down events for homeless veterans. Stand-downs are community-based events targeted to homeless veterans. They offer a welcoming and safe environment and access to a broad range of services. Stand-downs are derived from the military practice of "standing down" from customary activity or the front line.
December 8, 2009	The U.S. Conference of Mayors Task Force on Hunger and Homelessness releases its annual report on more than 20 cities, finding that there is increased need for food assistance, increased family homelessness, and decreased or steady numbers of homeless individuals. According to the mayors, "Most of the cities that experienced drops in individual homelessness attribute the decline to a policy strategy by federal, state and local governments of instituting 10-year plans to end chronic homelessness among single adults."
March 25, 2010	The Department of Housing and Urban Development releases new studies on the costs of "first-time" homelessness; life after transitional housing for homeless families; and strategies for improving access to mainstream benefits programs.
June 16, 2010	The Department of Housing and Urban Development releases its fifth Annual Homeless Assessment Report (AHAR) for Congress. The new report includes data from 2009 counts across the nation and demonstrates that from 2005 to 2009, there was a 36 percent decrease in chronic homelessness. Reflecting overall economic conditions, family homelessness increased.
June 22, 2010	The federal Interagency Council on Homelessness and the departments of Housing and Urban Development (HUD), Labor (DOL), Health and Human Services (HHS), and Veterans Affairs (VA) release the new federal strategy, *Opening Doors: Federal Strategic Plan to Prevent and End Homelessness.*

July 22, 2010 The federal departments of Housing and Urban Development and Veterans Affairs announce a new $15 million demonstration program called Veterans Homelessness Prevention Demonstration Program (VHPD) to prevent homelessness for veterans. Investments in five communities near military bases will target those returning from the wars in Afghanistan and Iraq, to provide housing assistance and supportive services to veterans who might otherwise be living in homeless shelters or on the streets.

September 2010 The eighth annual Homeless World Cup of soccer concludes with host team Brazil winning both the men's and women's titles. Sixty-four countries field teams.

September 22, 2010 National and local leaders join former president Bill Clinton on stage for the first homelessness-related commitment of the Clinton Global Initiative. Deb De Santis, CEO of the Corporation for Supportive Housing, Tod Lipka of Step Up in Los Angeles, Philip Mangano of the American Round Table to Abolish Homelessness, and real estate developer Steve Bing represent the Step Up partnership, which will develop green units of permanent supportive housing.

5

Biographical Sketches

A number of individuals have had significant influence on the direction of homelessness research, policy, partnership, and investment over the last several decades. Some are in the public arena in positions as government policy makers and appointed and elected officials in the United States and elsewhere. Others are in academia or research; their work sometimes attracts media or government attention. Some individuals have been associated with local initiatives or studies of importance. Some figures are in the public eye because of their advocacy efforts in organizing or litigation.

Included in this chapter are biographical sketches of some of the key contemporary figures as well as select biographies of individuals who helped establish the importance of the issue of homelessness historically. Perhaps the most recognized name of a person who was homeless during this time is that of Murray Barr, the "Million-Dollar Murray" whose life and death on the streets of Reno, Nevada, became shorthand for the new field of cost analysis and the chronically homeless population. The details of his story identify the individual human circumstances at the heart of the issue of homelessness.

Angela Alioto

Alioto belongs to one of San Francisco's most prominent political families and is the community champion of the city's Ten-Year Plan to End Chronic Homelessness. She chairs the city's Ten-Year Plan Council formed by Mayor Gavin Newsom.

Angela Alioto was born in San Francisco; her father Joseph was mayor from 1968 to 1976. She received a law degree from the University of San Francisco in 1983. She was elected to the board of supervisors and served from 1988 to 1997, and she was board president from 1993 to 1995. While on the board, Alioto led anti-tobacco, AIDS, homelessness, and health initiatives. She ran for mayor in 1991, 1995, and 2003. She previously was vice chair of the California Democratic Party. She serves as chair of the board of directors for the National Shrine of St. Francis of Assisi.

Alioto maintains a law practice in the firm that bears her father's name, the Law Offices of Mayor Joseph L. Alioto and Angela Alioto. Her firm is known for its expertise in civil rights and employment law, representing individuals in cases regarding workplace discrimination due to race, age, disability, gender, religion, and sexual orientation.

In the 2003 mayoral election, Alioto came in third in a race where Supervisor Gavin Newsom, who had been active in issues regarding homelessness, won. Mayor Newsom turned to his election opponent to lead his new homelessness initiative. One month into his term, he appointed Alioto to lead the effort. The partnership demonstrated by such an appointment elevates the issue in visibility and underscores the importance of the planning partnership.

More than 35 partners from the public and private sector worked collaboratively to develop the plan. Mayor Newsom announced in 2010 that San Francisco's Housing First focused plan, called "Changing Directions" and released in 2004, had resulted in 12,000 people leaving homelessness. Alioto co-chairs the "California KEYS" network of leaders of 10-year-plan cities in the state, providing a model of intergovernmental collaboration and peer-to-peer partnership.

Murray Barr

Murray Barr lived and died on the streets of Reno, Nevada. His story was reported in the Malcolm Gladwell article for the February 13, 2006, *New Yorker,* "Million-Dollar Murray," which looked at the economics of homelessness and new solutions.

Gladwell reported both on Barr's alcoholism and frequent use of services as well as the compassionate relationship of two street patrol officers, Patrick O'Bryan and Steve Johns, who knew

Barr well. "I've been a police officer for 15 years," O'Bryan's partner, Steve Johns, said in the article. "I picked up Murray my whole career. Literally." Officer Johns's wife, Marla Johns, was a hospital emergency room social worker who frequently saw Barr being brought in when he was so inebriated that he needed medical care.

After years of encountering Barr and soon after the city began enforcing a new antipanhandling ordinance, the officers contacted ambulance services and local hospitals. They identified three people who were all chronic inebriates and frequently arrested. Using records from just one hospital, the officers noted that in just six months since being released from jail one individual (Murray Barr) had accumulated $100,000 in hospital bills. Adding in the officers' knowledge of use of the second city hospital and addiction treatment and other costs, they determined that Murray Barr "ran up a medical bill as large as anyone in the state of Nevada." As stated by Officer O'Bryan, "It cost us one million dollars not to do something about Murray."

Murray Barr died on the streets in 2005. His story as reported by Malcolm Gladwell became a tool passed hand to hand by policy makers and 10-year-plan partners making the new economic argument common to every city.

Ellen Bassuk, MD

Bassuk is managing director of the Center for Social Innovation (previous founder and president of the National Center on Family Homelessness) and associate professor of psychiatry at Harvard Medical School. The center operates the Department of Health and Human Services Homelessness Resource Center, an online resource for training and technical assistance.

A board-certified psychiatrist, she has published many articles, monographs, and books on the issue that report her work on some of the key research about homeless families and children. Her research and writing examines risks of family homelessness and the impact of homelessness on the mental and physical health of women and their children. She has focused on the relationship among mental illness, substance abuse, family violence, and social support in poor families. She has received many research grants and has served on national and regional health policy committees.

Bassuk received her BA from Brandeis University and her MD from Tufts Medical School and completed a residency in psychiatry at Beth Israel Hospital, where she was director of the Continuing Care Clinic and Psychiatric Emergency Services. Bassuk was a fellow at the Bunting Institute, Radcliffe College. She served as editor for the *American Journal of Orthopsychiatry* and has received numerous awards and recognitions for her work.

Ellen Baxter

Baxter is founder and executive director of Broadway Housing Communities and is nationally known for her vision, innovation, and dedication to creating comprehensive, replicable model programs to address the problem of homelessness and disadvantage. She founded Broadway Housing Communities in 1983 with the renovation of an abandoned building in the Washington Heights area of Manhattan. Broadway Housing now operates seven developments, which adhere to its model of integrated housing, where residents with different specific challenges and histories live in the same building.

In 1981, Baxter and coauthor Kim Hopper released a report titled *Private Lives, Public Spaces: Homeless Adults on the Streets of New York City,* which generated significant public attention to the issue of homelessness and the experiences of people living on the streets. The report was based on their firsthand work visiting and talking with men and women who were homeless.

Baxter serves on the boards of the New York Coalition for the Homeless and the Corporation for Supportive Housing as well as St. Francis Friends of the Poor and Common Ground. She has a BA from Bowdoin College, an MA from Columbia University, School of Public Health, and honorary doctorates of humane letters from Mount Holyoke College and Bowdoin College.

Martha M. Burt, PhD

Burt is an affiliated scholar at the Urban Institute's Center on Labor, Human Services, and Population. She retired as director of the Social Services Research Program at the Urban Institute in Washington, D.C.

In 1983, she began research on homelessness with a study of the Federal Emergency Management Agency's work. In 1987 she directed the first national survey of homeless individuals. The survey focused on meal programs and shelters in cities with populations of over 100,000, and the results were published in 1989 as *America's Homeless: Numbers, Characteristics, and the Programs That Serve Them*. In 1992 Burt wrote *Over the Edge: The Growth of Homelessness in the 1980s*, and she is the author of *Practical Methods for Counting Homeless People: A Manual for State and Local Jurisdictions*. She helped plan and conduct the National Survey of Homeless Assistance Providers and Clients, published in 1999. Her book, *Helping America's Homeless: Emergency Shelter or Affordable Housing?* (2001), was based on the National Survey of Homeless Assistance Providers and Clients.

Burt earned her PhD in sociology in 1972 from the University of Wisconsin–Madison.

Louise Casey

Under British prime minister Tony Blair, who appointed her in 1999, Louise Casey led the successful initiative to reduce the number of "rough sleepers" and led the Homelessness Directorate in the Office of the Deputy Prime Minister. The work of the Blair government to reduce "rough sleeping" by two-thirds in five years and its success in reaching that goal ahead of schedule provided a model for U.S. efforts which followed.

Casey is the victims' commissioner for the Ministry of Justice, a position to which she was named by the prime minister in 2010. Under Prime Minister Gordon Brown she headed a cabinet office review of the criminal justice system, proposing tougher penalties. Casey served beginning in 2002 as the director of the Anti-Social Behavior Unit, the government's strategy to address antisocial behavior and the issuance of "Asbos," or anti-social behavior orders. She was previously the government's coordinator for respect, a cross-government task force based in the Home Office and focused on problem families.

Casey began her professional career with the former Department of Health and Social Security, which oversees benefit payments to homeless people. She was later coordinator of the St. Mungo Association, managing the provision of services to homeless adult men. She ran the Homeless Network in London and in 1992 became deputy director of Shelter, a national homeless organization established in 1966.

In 1997, she was appointed to head the rough sleepers unit and was outspoken on the role of charitable organizations in maintaining a status quo approach to homelessness. With her government partners, she traveled to Washington, D.C., to address the newly revitalized federal Interagency Council on Homelessness in 2002, regularly participated in multilateral dialogues established by the council with the United States and Canada, and was recognized with the council's "Inspiration" award at its national summit in 2007. In accepting the award, she observed, "We were a collection of voices who said we were doing the right thing, that we had to hold our nerve. We had to be focused and clear, unnerving and unswerving in our utter and complete determination to make sure we reduced the number of people who were sleeping rough on our streets. To be unrelenting in our determination to get that number down when people wavered toward the path of the popular. . . . So as I stand before you, the number of human beings that face early death, sickness, loneliness, and a poverty of spirit, let alone a financial and social poverty as rough sleepers, are less than 700 across the whole of the United Kingdom."

Henry Cisneros

Cisneros was secretary of the U.S. Department of Housing and Urban Development in the first term of the Clinton administration. He was appointed by President Bill Clinton in January 1993 and served until 1997. As HUD secretary, Cisneros, who had walked the streets of downtown Washington, D.C., and talked with homeless people, announced that homelessness would be the agency's top priority. He proposed increased spending and realignment of the agency's programs for homeless people. In May 1993, President Clinton signed an executive order on homelessness to create a "single coordinated Federal plan for breaking the cycle of existing homelessness and preventing future homelessness." This report was issued in March 1994 and is called *Priority Home! The Federal Plan to Break the Cycle of Homelessness.*

In 1981, Cisneros was the first Hispanic mayor of a major U.S. city when he became mayor of San Antonio, Texas, the nation's 10th-largest city. As a four-term mayor, serving from 1981 to 1989, he rebuilt the city's economic base. He served as president of the National League of Cities, chairman of the National Civic League, deputy chair of the Federal Reserve Bank of Dallas, and as a board member of the Rockefeller Foundation.

Cisneros left government to become president of Univision Communications, a Spanish language television network. He remained in that position until August 2000, when he resigned to form American CityVista, a joint venture with one of the largest homebuilders in the United States. Now called CityView, the venture concentrates on investment to develop housing affordable to average families. He is the only former HUD secretary to be involved in the issue of housing.

Cisneros graduated from Texas A&M with a BA and an MA in urban and regional planning. He earned a second graduate degree in public administration from the Kennedy School of Government at Harvard University. He received a PhD in public administration from George Washington University.

Jim Collins

Collins is a business thinker and writer whose book, *Good to Great: Why Some Companies Make the Leap . . . and Others Don't*, provided a model for understanding the challenges of implementing 10-year plans over time. Collins spent five years studying companies that moved from good to great and those that didn't. He consulted with jurisdictional leaders at the first national summit convened by the federal Interagency Council on Homelessness to focus on his insights about "disciplined people, disciplined thought, disciplined action" and the importance of "the right people on the bus" for success. These principles were applied in a council toolkit on 10- year plans, "Good . . . to Better . . . to Great: Innovations in 10-Year Plans to End Chronic Homelessness in Your Community."

Dennis P. Culhane, PhD

Culhane is professor of social policy in the University of Pennsylvania School of Social Policy and Practice and director of Research, National Center on Homelessness among Veterans of the U.S. Department of Veterans Affairs.

His primary area of research is homelessness, and he has been responsible for some of the most influential data in the last decade regarding including shelter use, population typologies, and costs for both individuals and families. Culhane's research indentifying the chronic, transitional, and episodic populations of individuals reshaped thinking about the needs and costs associated with homelessness as well as solutions.

Culhane has also studied geographic and housing market factors associated with housing instability and the design and evaluation of homeless prevention programs. He has studied the mental health and substance abuse service histories of homeless adults in Philadelphia. His work includes studies of the impact of homelessness on utilization of Medicaid services, public hospitals, state psychiatric hospitals, jails, prisons, and behavioral health treatment in New York City and studies of the dynamics of public shelter use in New York and Philadelphia.

Culhane helped develop a management information system for tracking utilization of homeless services for the federal government. He completed studies of housing and neighborhood factors related to the distribution of homeless persons' prior addresses in New York, Philadelphia, and Washington, D.C. He became involved in homelessness and housing issues as a shelter worker in Philadelphia in 1982. He was an organizer for the Union of the Homeless in 1986–1988 and served as director of technical assistance and organizing for the National Union of the Homeless in 1987–1988.

Culhane earned a PhD in social psychology from Boston College and a BA from St. Bonaventure University. He was recognized with the 2009 Michael B. Katz Award for Excellence in Teaching from the University of Pennsylvania, with the 2006 National Partner Award by the United States Interagency Council on Homelessness, and the 2003 John W. Macy Award for Individual Leadership awarded by the National Alliance to End Homelessness.

Andrew M. Cuomo

Cuomo became secretary of the U.S. Department of Housing and Urban Development in 1997, after serving as assistant secretary for Housing and Community Development from 1993 to 1996 under Secretary Henry Cisneros. Cuomo served until 2001, subsequently becoming New York State attorney general in 2007. He was elected governor in November 2010.

Cuomo went to HUD from New York City, where he headed the New York City Commission on the Homeless in 1991. The

New York commission's report first defined the "continuum of care" concept later adopted by HUD for federal homeless programs. He built and operated housing for homeless people and was seen as the first HUD secretary to have experience in producing housing, as founder of Housing Enterprise for the Less Privileged (HELP) in 1986 and the Genesis Project.

He served as special assistant to his father, Governor Mario M. Cuomo (D-N.Y.), who advanced state initiatives to address homelessness in the 1980s. Cuomo graduated from Fordham University in 1979 and received a law degree from Albany Law School in 1982.

Deborah De Santis

De Santis is president and CEO of the Corporation for Supportive Housing (CSH), a position she has held since 2007. CSH is a national organization that partners with communities in creating permanent supportive housing.

Deborah De Santis came to her national role after leading the New Jersey CSH program for several years. In her state position, she increased CHS's lending, supported the creation of the state's $200 million Special Needs Housing Trust Fund, and took part in the development of Homes for New Jersey, an organization supporting development of 100,000 affordable units, including 10,000 units of supportive housing.

De Santis was previously COO and executive director of the New Jersey Housing and Mortgage Finance Agency, where she partnered in investment with state agencies including the Health Care Facilities Finance Agency and the Department of Human Services.

De Santis served as deputy chief of staff to New Jersey governor Christine Todd Whitman from 1996 to 1998 and also as deputy commissioner of the New Jersey Department of Community Affairs. Education Ms. De Santis received a BS in business administration from Babson College.

Manual Diaz

As Miami mayor from 2001 to 2009, Manual Diaz declared homelessness "an issue of critical importance to our city" during his 2004 State of the City Address. Shortly after, he released *Helping Hands, Mending Lives,* the city's 10-year plan to end chronic homelessness. The plan called for a public/private partnership and interagency collaboration. Steadily implementing its action items, Mayor Diaz announced a 50 percent reduction in the number of homeless people between July 2006 and January 2007, including a 27 percent decrease in the number of persons experiencing chronic homelessness. By the time he left office, the city had achieved over an 80 percent reduction.

Mayor Diaz's commitment made him a leader among mayors, ensuring continuing focus and partnership on the issue of homelessness at the U.S. Conference of Mayors, of which he was president in 2008. When the city adopted the innovation of Project Homeless Connect in "Miami Cares" events, Mayor Diaz personally welcomed homeless neighbors at the door. The city's Homeless Assistance Program aims to identify and engage homeless individuals and to secure housing, employment, and stability for individuals.

Many local services are supported by the innovative dedicated revenue of the Miami-Dade County 1 percent food and beverage tax in 1993 to establish a dedicated revenue source for homeless initiatives. Almost $12 million was collected in 2007 for the Miami-Dade Homeless Trust.

A native of Cuba, Diaz received his BA in political science in 1977 from Florida International University. In 1980, he earned his JD degree from the University of Miami School of Law.

Maria Foscarinis

Foscarinis is founder and executive director of the National Law Center on Homelessness and Poverty (NLCHP) in Washington. She has been involved in legal and legislative issues affecting homeless people since the mid-1980s, when she left the Wall Street firm of Sullivan and Cromwell to litigate full-time on behalf of homeless people. Using rights-based strategies that focus on common experiences of people living on the streets, Foscarinis addresses meal programs, punitive laws, and access rights.

Foscarinis worked with the National Coalition for the Homeless before starting the law center in 1989. At NLCHP she has been a public voice on issues affecting homeless children's education and the criminalization of homeless people in public places. Her efforts have increased access to educational development programs for homeless children; forced compliance with McKinney

Act provisions by state administrators and federal agencies; and increased the conversion of closed military bases into shelters, job training, child care, and food program sites. Foscarinis graduated from Barnard College and Columbia University Law School.

Mayor Paul Fraim

Paul Fraim was first elected mayor of Norfolk, Virginia, in 1994. As mayor, Fraim appointed a commission to develop the city's 10-year plan released in 2005. A new Office to End Homelessness was created by the mayor and partners proceeded with the implementation and adoption of field-tested innovations to prevent and end homelessness. Among Norfolk's strategies were Project Homeless Connect, Rapid Re-Housing and Central Intake for families, Housing First, regional partnerships, and reentry initiatives. Norfolk's commitment resulted in a more than 40 percent reduction in its homeless census.

Mayor Fraim was recognized with the federal Interagency Council on Homelessness Mayor's Award. He is a member of the board of directors of the Hampton Roads Partnership and the Hampton Roads Economic Development Alliance. He has recently been chair of Hampton Roads Mayors and Chairs Caucus. He is a past member of the board of directors of the Hampton Roads Chamber of Commerce, the Kiwanis Club of Ocean View, the Norfolk Sports Club, and the Navy League. He has been a member of the Hampton Roads Planning District Commission since 1990, and he is a member of the board of directors of the Greater Norfolk Corporation.

Mayor Fraim is a Norfolk native. He received a BA from Virginia Military Institute, his MEd from the University of Virginia, and his JD from the University of Richmond.

Shirley Franklin

Shirley Franklin was elected mayor of Atlanta in 2001 as a first-time candidate for public office. She launched a 10-year plan initiative cochaired by local business and civic leader Horace Sibley, whom Mayor Franklin appointed as community champion, and the United Way.

The key initiative of the plan, which was supported by Atlanta and the counties of Clayton, Cobb, DeKalb, Douglas Fulton, Gwinnett, and Rockdale, was the 24/7 Gateway Center, which opened in 2005 to serve as a central point of services and reaches 500 people a day in collaboration with dozens of community partners. Over $22 million in new private funds were raised for plan goals. A model reunification initiative assisted 6,000 people in the first five years to return to family and friends, leaving homelessness and Atlanta.

Atlanta's creative strategy for financing new housing relied on the issue of a tranche of Homeless Opportunity Bonds issued by the Atlanta Development Authority. In total $22 million in Homeless Opportunity Bonds are invested in 17 capital housing projects resulting in over 485 permanent supportive housing units. Involved in the creation of the new revenue stream were a wide range of players, including the Atlanta Development Authority, a Phillips Arena parking garage, existing bonds, and a tax increment.

Mayor Franklin is the William and Camille Cosby Professor at Spelman College. She was a cochair of the 2008 National Democratic Convention. She has held leadership roles in the U.S. Conference of Mayors, including as the chair of the Women's Caucus.

Mayor Franklin earned her BA degree in sociology from Howard University and was awarded her MA degree in sociology from the University of Pennsylvania. She has received honorary degrees from Howard University, the Atlanta College of Art, Cambridge College, Spelman College, Morehouse College, Clark Atlanta University, Tuskegee University, Oglethorpe University, and the University of Pennsylvania.

Malcolm Gladwell

Malcolm Gladwell is a staff writer with the *New Yorker* magazine, a position he has held since 1996. His writing often focuses on unusual ideas or counterintuitive findings, and two of his works have particularly influenced strategies on homelessness.

Gladwell is the author of *The Tipping Point: How Little Things Make a Big Difference,* released in 2000. For many working on the issue of homelessness, the idea of reaching a "tipping point" that could produce new results was captured in Gladwell's work.

Gladwell particularly made the point that modest new resources had to be concentrated on the most visible part of a social problem to achieve the visible result that could lead to greater investment.

Gladwell's writing and his exposure to homelessness in New York City led him to address a 2004 launch meeting of public and private partners focused on innovation and economics and convened by New York's Common Ground, the Rockefeller Foundation, and the federal Interagency Council on Homelessness. From his exposure to the local specifics of these leaders came his 2006 *New Yorker* article, "Million-Dollar Murray," which used the story of Murray Barr, who lived and died on the streets of Reno, Nevada, as an illustration of, as the article's subtitle stated, "Why problems like homelessness may be easier to solve than to manage." Gladwell reported on several of the local examples where Housing First was resulting in better outcomes for individuals and better stewardship of public resources. "Million-Dollar Murray" became required reading and was shorthand for the reality of frequent users of public and private services in the community by people experiencing homelessness.

In 2009, Gladwell published *What the Dog Saw* as a compilation of his personally selected writings from the *New Yorker.* He included "Million-Dollar Murray" in the book, noting that it was one of his favorite pieces and in keeping with his belief that a writer's role is to start conversations.

In 2005 Gladwell was named one of *Time* magazine's 100 Most Influential People. He had previously worked from 1987 to 1996 as a reporter with the *Washington Post.* He reported on business and science and served as the New York City bureau chief. He graduated from the University of Toronto, Trinity College, with a degree in history. Gladwell grew up in rural Ontario.

Rosanne Haggerty

Haggerty is the president and founder of Common Ground, a New York City nonprofit housing development and management organization that creates supportive housing for homeless and low-income individuals. Common Ground has over 3,000 units of permanent and transitional housing in New York City, Connecticut, and upstate New York. Its Street to Home initiative to engage people living in Times Square reduced homelessness by 87 percent in a 20-block area.

Common Ground's efforts are focused on those who are chronically homeless; intensive transitional housing programs designed to move chronic homeless adults into permanent housing within a six-month period; scattered site housing programs targeted to the chronic homeless; and homelessness-prevention programs focused on high-risk families, recent veterans, and young people leaving foster care.

Haggerty founded Common Ground in 1990 to rehabilitate the Times Square Hotel, a single-room occupancy site. Common Ground has since developed numerous other transitional and permanent housing sites. Common Ground partnered in a successful outreach and housing initiative for the chronic homeless population living on the streets surrounding Times Square. A key component of Common Ground's innovative approach to homelessness is the establishment of ancillary services at its facilities including job training and placement programs, health care, computer centers, and other services. Haggerty's work to spread Common Ground's success has led to partnerships with other cities through the 100,000 Homes campaign to house the nation's most vulnerable individuals by 2013.

Haggerty is a recipient of the MacArthur Foundation Fellowship for her work on the problem of homelessness in the United States and an Ashoka Fellow for social entrepreneurship. She won the 1998 Peter F. Drucker Award for Nonprofit Innovation. Prior to founding Common Ground, Haggerty held the position of coordinator of housing development at Brooklyn Catholic Charities, operating in Brooklyn and Queens. She is a graduate of Amherst College and studied for a graduate degree in real estate and development at Columbia University Graduate School of Architecture, Planning and Historic Preservation.

Robert M. Hayes

Hayes filed the landmark New York City right-to-shelter case *Callahan v. Carey* in 1979 while an attorney at the Wall Street firm of Sullivan and Cromwell, where he concentrated on banking, securities, and antitrust litigation. He subsequently left the firm in 1982 and founded both the Coalition for the Homeless, oriented to New York City issues, and the National Coalition for the Homeless, a legal and policy advocacy organization with offices in Washington, D.C., and New York City. Hayes directed major class-action lawsuits, organized advocacy groups across the country, and led legislative campaigns before Congress and state legislatures.

He is a graduate of Georgetown University and New York University School of Law. He received a MacArthur Foundation Fellowship in 1985 and numerous awards from state and national bar associations. He was named one of the nation's 10 most influential lawyers for the 1980s by the *American Lawyer* magazine, and the *National Law Journal* named him among the nation's 50 leading attorneys of his generation.

Robert Hess

Hess served as New York City's Commissioner of Homeless Services from 2006 to 2010. During his tenure, the number of people living on the streets in New York City declined by 49 percent and over 100,000 people moved from shelters to permanent housing in a period of four years. He oversaw a federal-city partnership to decrease homelessness among veterans as well as managing new initiatives to reduce family homelessness, support employment and education, and prevent homelessness. He joined the Doe Fund as vice president in 2010.

Prior to working in New York, Hess was deputy managing director for special needs housing for the City of Philadelphia, where his leadership on reducing homelessness in Center City led to greater visibility for jurisdictional officials. Hess developed the mayor's 10-Year Plan to End Homelessness, reduced the number of individuals living on the streets by over 60 percent, and created the first Housing First programs for chronically homeless individuals. Hess's approaches to the Center City street population relied on data collection and new engagement strategies. During his tenure Philadelphia won one of 11 federal awards under the HUD-HHS-VA Collaborative Initiative to Help End Chronic Homelessness, putting the Housing First approach to work in the City. Hess instituted "code" protocols to reduce deaths during hot, cold, and wet weather for people living on the streets.

Hess previously served as the president and CEO of the Center for Poverty Solutions in Baltimore, Maryland, and the president and CEO of the Maryland Food Committee. He earned a BS from the University of Maryland and served in the U.S. Army.

John W. Hickenlooper

John Hickenlooper was elected mayor of Denver in 2003 and reelected in 2007. A local businessman and former geologist, he was a first-time candidate for public office. Mayor Hickenlooper launched a 10-year plan initiative by appointing the Denver Commission to End Homelessness in 2003. He was elected governor in November 2010.

Denver's Road Home, the city's plan, adopted innovations ranging from Housing First to Project Homeless Connect, recruiting private sector partners including professional sports teams, academia, and business. Mayor Hickenlooper established a replicable faith partnership that brings teams from local congregations into ongoing support roles for families leaving homelessness.

In making a 2009 progress report on the plan, Mayor Hickenlooper stated, "The most important thing we've learned, is A: It's possible to succeed at this; and B: To do so makes economic sense." In 2008 he announced that, having documented savings in public systems, the city would reinvest $20 million in additional housing.

In November 2005, Mayor Hickenlooper was named by *Governing* magazine as one of the top public officials of the year. In April 2005 *Time* magazine named him one of the top five "big-city" mayors in America. Mayor Hickenlooper graduated from Wesleyan University, where he received a BA degree in English in 1974 and a MA in geology in 1980.

William Hobson

Hobson is executive director of Seattle's Downtown Emergency Service Center (DESC). The Center's 1811 Eastlake project, a controversial Housing First initiative begun in 2005 for 75 homeless men and women with chronic alcohol addiction, has demonstrated $4 million in cost savings for taxpayers, according to research published in the *Journal of the American Medical Association*.

Under Hobson's leadership, DESC received a Best Practice Award from the U.S. Department of Housing and Urban Development, an Exemplary Program Award from the U.S. Department of Health and Human Services, and two MetLife Awards for Excellence in Affordable Housing. The program was also recognized with an Innovator's Award by the federal Interagency Council on Homelessness. The 1811 Eastlake program was selected by the Fannie Mae Foundation and Partnership to End Long Term Homelessness for the 2007 "Maxwell Award of Excellence."

Nearly half of the residents of the 1811 site have a co-occurring mental illness, and almost all have other chronic and disabling health conditions. While addiction treatment and mental health services are provided on site, residents are encouraged, but not required, to participate in treatment. The housing approach was characterized by one local talk show host as "bunks for drunks," drawing enormous media focus to the initiative.

Hobson began his work at DESC as a shelter counselor in 1984 and became executive director in 1988. He is an adjunct professor at Seattle University, teaching on homelessness. He received a BA in history and philosophy (Phi Beta Kappa) and an MA in political science from Baylor University.

Kim Hopper, PhD

Hopper is professor of clinical sociomedical sciences at Columbia University's Mailman School of Public Health. He has been active in local and national initiatives to address homelessness since 1980. Hopper is a medical anthropologist and a research scientist at the Nathan S. Kline Institute for Psychiatric Research. There he codirects the Center for the Study of Issues in Public Mental Health. Hopper is the author of *Reckoning with Homelessness*, a retrospective on 20 years of research and advocacy.

Hopper served as president of the National Coalition for the Homeless from 1991 to 1993. He earned his PhD from Columbia University. He received the Anthony Leeds Awards in Urban Anthropology in 2003 and was a finalist for the C. Wright Mills Award in 2003.

Jack Kemp

Kemp was a Republican political figure, former professional athlete, and former secretary of the U.S. Department of Housing and Urban Development and the U.S. Interagency Council on Homelessness chair in the George H.W. Bush administration.

Kemp became HUD secretary and council chair in February 1989, serving until 1993. The McKinney Act had been passed less than two years before, creating a federal response to homelessness and establishing the Interagency Council. Once confirmed as secretary, Kemp undertook a tour of East Coast cities organized by Robert Hayes of the National Coalition for the Homeless to see and hear the experiences of people who were homeless.

Secretary Kemp committed to interagency collaboration and with former Department of Veterans Affairs secretary Ed Derwinski moved forward the HUD-VASH permanent housing initiative in 1990. In March 1992, Secretary Kemp and Council vice chair and U.S. Department of Health and Human Services secretary Louis Sullivan released *Outcasts on Main Street*, a report outlining a national strategy to eradicate homelessness among people with severe mental illness. The report presented more than 50 steps federal agencies would take to improve substantially the system of care and housing options for the nation's homeless mentally ill individuals. The report proposed two major federal initiatives: Safe Havens and the Access to Community Care and Effective Services and Supports (ACCESS) program.

Philip F. Mangano

Mangano is president and CEO of the American Round Table to Abolish Homelessness, a national nonprofit organization whose mission is to be a strategic partner with every level of government and every element of the private and faith-based sectors to prevent and end homelessness. Internationally recognized for his bold leadership on an issue seen as intractable, Mangano's blend of business experience, public service, and personal commitment energized partners to focus on solutions. The round table is committed to strategies that are research and data driven, performance based, consumer centric, and results oriented and to rapid dissemination of innovation, information, and inspiration to its partners.

From 2002 to 2009, under both the Bush and Obama administrations, Mangano led the national strategy to prevent and end homelessness in his position as the executive director of the United States Interagency Council on Homelessness. Mangano was appointed as the council's executive director in 2002, when the newly independent agency was charged to forward the administration's goal of ending chronic homelessness. Mangano's successful results-oriented strategies and innovative initiatives focused the council's mission to coordinate the federal response to homelessness and to create partnerships throughout government and the private sector to end homelessness.

Mangano's new strategies resulted in an unprecedented national partnership of 20 federal agencies, 53 governors, and over 1,000 mayors and county executives partnered in over 350 local jurisdictional 10-year plans. With his leadership, new interagency and community collaborations were established across the country. The prioritization of prevention of homelessness and rapid rehousing of homeless people focused federal policy and encouraged local plans and investments from the public and private sectors.

Mangano led the application of cost-benefit analysis and business planning to the issue of homelessness. His work at the council gained the attention of mainstream media and some of the foremost business thinkers in the nation. Mangano has spoken across the country on the abolition of homelessness and in Canada, England, Scotland, Australia, New Zealand, Germany, and Denmark, at United Nations and European Union sponsored events, and at national meetings in a number of countries. In 2004 he initiated international dialogue on homelessness, which included peers from the Blair government's successful Rough Sleepers Initiative, on which the United States modeled its strategy, and Canadian and Australian counterparts.

Mangano's work has been nationally honored by a public and private sector, media, academic, business, and community partners. He was honored in May 2009 with a doctor of humane letters degree (honoris causa) by the University of Puget Sound. He was nominated as one of *Time* magazine's 100 Most Influential People in 2007. He was recognized by the International Downtown Association (IDA) in 2008 with a Lifetime Achievement Award, IDA's most prestigious award, for "leadership, dedication, and generosity." He was named in 2006 by *Governing* magazine as the first and only federal official ever to be honored with its Public Official of the Year Award. His work was named by Harvard University's John F. Kennedy School of Government one of the 2009 "Top 50 Government Innovations" in the nation, recognition also awarded in 2007. He was presented with the National Alliance to End Homelessness Private Sector Award in 2001. Mangano is a member of the board of directors of the Dalai Lama Center for Ethics and Transformative Values at MIT. He is a Knight of La Nuova Porziuncola of St. Francis of Assisi in San Francisco.

Mangano was founding executive director of the Massachusetts Housing and Shelter Alliance, a position he held with the statewide advocacy organization from 1990 to 2002. He began his work in homelessness in the 1980s, after leaving behind a successful business career in the music industry, starting as a full-time volunteer on a Boston breadline. Mangano holds an MA from Gordon-Conwell Theological Seminary in Massachusetts, a BS from Boston University, and certificates in business law and entertainment law from UCLA.

Mel Martinez

Martinez became the first secretary of Housing and Urban Development in the Bush administration in January 2001 and chair of the newly revitalized Interagency Council on Homelessness. He served as secretary until 2003 when he resigned to run for the U.S. Senate.

Under Martinez's leadership, the new Bush administration goal to end chronic homelessness in 10 years resulted in new interagency initiatives to test new strategies including Housing First. A $55 million initiative of the council, HUD, HHS, and VA was awarded to 11 cities to address chronic homelessness and an employment and housing initiative in five cities. More than 40 cities were awarded Social Security Administration funds to increase access to benefits for chronically homeless individuals.

Martinez had previously served as the chairman of Orange County, Florida, the elected chief executive of the regional government. He was first elected to a four-year term in 1998, and he began a series of initiatives emphasizing public safety, growth management, the needs of children and families, clean neighborhoods, improved transportation, and streamlining government. In 1962, at age 15, he left his birthplace of Cuba and went to Florida as part of an organized evacuation of young people. He was reunited with his family in Orlando in 1966. He graduated from Florida State University College of Law in 1973. He practiced law in Orlando for 25 years. Martinez is chairman of JP Morgan Chase operations in Florida, Mexico, Central America, and the Caribbean.

George T. McDonald

McDonald is founder and president of the Doe Fund in New York City, an employment and housing innovation to break the cycle of homelessness, addiction, and incarceration. McDonald's model is notable for his emphasis on work, or, as his program motto states, "Work works," to achieve self-sufficiency and stability.

Over 3,000 formerly homeless individuals and ex-offenders have graduated from the Doe Fund's Ready, Willing & Able (RWA) program, where the "men in blue" are seen on the more than 150 miles of New York streets which they clean daily. Trainees have access to programs in culinary arts, security services, business services, pest control, resource recovery, building maintenance, animal care, and computer education. The Doe Fund also operates a targeted program for veterans.

RWA has been recognized by the federal Department of Housing and Urban Development, receiving the Community Service Excellence Award, the Outstanding Partnership Award, and the first ever Best Practices Award. McDonald received the New York Post Liberty Medal; the 2008 William E. Simon Lifetime Achievement Award, given annually by the Manhattan Institute's Social Entrepreneurship Initiative; St. John's University's 2008 Spirit of Service award; the 2008 Honor of Hope award from the White House Faith-Based and Community Initiatives; and the 2008 Innovator of Special Merit award from the U.S. Interagency Council on Homelessness.

McDonald was appointed in 1991 to Mayor David Dinkins' Commission on Homelessness, headed by Andrew Cuomo. The commission created *The Way Home,* a model for addressing homelessness that has influenced homeless policy locally and nationally. He is chair of the New York State Independent Committee on Reentry and Employment, cochair of the Employment Committee of the Discharge Planning Collaboration developed by the New York City Departments of Correction and Homeless Services, and a member of the New York City Workforce Investment Board's Prisoner Reentry Steering Committee.

Representative Stewart B. McKinney

McKinney, for whom the McKinney Homeless Assistance Act was named, was a Republican member of the House of Representatives at the time of his death from AIDS in 1987. McKinney represented Connecticut's 4th District for over 16 years. From 1983 until his death, he was the ranking Republican member of the Banking Subcommittee on Housing and Community Development, where he fought to preserve domestic programs in the 1980s. It is believed that he contracted fatal AIDS-related pneumonia from being outdoors in the cold during the demonstrations for the homeless that occurred at the U.S. Capitol during the winter of 1987, when the bill first introduced as "The Urgent Relief for the Homeless Act" was being considered.

Gavin Newsom

Mayor Gavin Newsom took office in 2004 as San Francisco's youngest mayor in 100 years. He immediately launched a 10-year plan initiative, naming his election opponent Angela Alito to head a new plan for one of the city's most vexing issues.

More than 35 partners from the public and private sector worked collaboratively to develop the plan, which was unveiled in 2004. Mayor Newsom announced in 2010 that San Francisco's Housing First focused plan, called Changing Directions, had resulted in 12,000 people leaving homelessness, including those reunited with friends and family elsewhere.

The one-day, one-stop innovation called Project Homeless Connect was developed in San Francisco to support the plan's focus on consumers and the goal of engagement, which was part of every action step in the 10-year plan. San Francisco developed an effective and replicable model of mobilizing civic will through volunteerism, to involve thousands of community residents who embraced the opportunity to welcome homeless neighbors in a dignified and accessible setting that offers many needed resources.

Project Connect, which has occurred 35 times from 2004 to 2010, is a field-tested model of effective engagement and delivery of services and benefits for people who are homeless. The federal Interagency Council on Homelessness recognized Project Homeless Connect as national innovation. Project Connect has been visited by planners from across the country and adopted in more than 250 cities in the United States, Canada, and Australia.

In 2005, Mayor Newsom earned an honorable mention as one of *Time* magazine's Best Big City mayors. He was a successful businessman before taking office. He was elected lieutenant governor in November 2010. Mayor Newsom was a member of the San Francisco Board of Supervisors, 1996–2004. He received a BA from Santa Clara University in 1989 in political science.

James O'Connell, MD

O'Connell is president of Boston Health Care of the Homeless, where he serves as a physician, and medical director of the Andrew House Dual Diagnosis Detoxification Unit as well as medical director of Bay Cove Substance Abuse Center.

O'Connell graduated from Harvard Medical School in 1982 and completed his residency in internal medicine at Massachusetts General Hospital in 1985. In 1985, he began working full-time with people experiencing homelessness at the Boston Health Care for the Homeless Program. The program now serves over 11,000 homeless persons each year in three hospital-based clinics and over 80 shelters and other outreach sites in Boston. O'Connell holds positions as clinical assistant professor of Medicine at Boston University, clinical instructor in medicine at Harvard Medical School, assistant in medicine at Massachusetts General Hospital, and attending physician at Boston Medical Center.

In 1999, O'Connell undertook research on the deaths of more than a dozen people who were chronically homeless in downtown Boston and died within a few months. He identified a common profile that included specific factors for risk, with multiple major medical problems key among them. This groundbreaking work to identify vulnerability has been translated to a "vulnerability index" now used in many communities to identify and list those most at risk on the streets in order to prioritize individuals to move to Housing First locations. O'Connell is nationally recognized for the leadership and results of his work to develop and train practitioners and clinicians on successful strategies to secure Social Security benefits for homeless people.

In 1993, O'Connell founded the Barbara McInnis House, a medical respite program that has grown to over 100 beds and provides acute, rehabilitative, recuperative, and palliative care for homeless men and women. Working with the Massachusetts General Hospital Laboratory of Computer Science, O'Connell designed the first computerized medical records for a homeless program in 1995.

O'Connell was the national program director of the Robert Wood Johnson Homeless Foundation Families Program from 1989 to 1996. He sits on the boards of directors of the Massachusetts Shelter Alliance, the Albert Schweitzer Fellowship and the Urban Health Project at Harvard Medical School. In addition to his Harvard Medical School training, O'Connell received a MA in theology from Cambridge University and a BA as salutatorian of his class at Notre Dame. He has written extensively on medical issues for people who are homeless. Boston Health Care for the Homeless has undertaken research on the chronic population, medical respite care, utilization of hospital care, health outcomes for people housed after chronic homelessness, and integrated care.

M. Dene Oliver

Oliver is the chair of the Leadership Committee for the Plan to End Chronic Homelessness in the City of San Diego and community champion of the plan. San Diego's plan was chaired with the support of San Diego County and the United Way and a leadership council of business and civic partners. Oliver has helped define the role of champion, including as co-convener of the California KEYS network of 10-year plan leaders. Under his leadership, San Diego developed a plan that emphasizes regionalism, data and evaluation, Housing First, and prevention strategies.

A native of San Diego, Oliver is the CEO of Oliver McMillan, an award-winning commercial development firm he established in 1978 with a lifelong friend. He is a graduate of the University of California at Berkeley where he received a BS in real estate and urban land economics from the School of Business Administration. He graduated from the University of Southern California School of Law and attended the University of Southern California Graduate School of Business Administration.

Barton "Bart" R. Peterson

Peterson was mayor of Indianapolis, Indiana, from 1999 to 2007. He was the earliest mayor in the nation to support a jurisdictional plan. Indianapolis's Blueprint to End Homelessness was a Housing First and prevention-oriented plan that called for new strategies. "Can the Indianapolis community really end homelessness? Those who have worked on the Blueprint are absolutely convinced that homelessness can, in fact be ended. . . . Setting our sights any lower—concluding, in essence, that some level of homelessness is acceptable or inevitable—is unworthy of the caring community known as Indianapolis."

A native of Indianapolis, Peterson attended Purdue University and the University of Michigan law school.

Michael S. Rawlings

Since 2005, Rawlings has been the community champion of the Dallas Ten-Year Plan, bringing a lengthy business history to the leadership and results of the initiative, which was announced in 2003. Dallas's plan has resulted in decreased homelessness, a new service center and housing placement initiative, and reductions in community costs. Downtown crime rates, hospital use, and arrests and jail stays were reduced, with a reported $2.7 million savings to Dallas County. Rawlings has been active in national initiatives to share results among community champions and innovators.

Rawlings is managing partner of CIC Partners LP in Dallas, a large private equity fund. He previously served as president and chief concept officer for Pizza Hut, Inc., the world's largest pizza chain, from 1997 until 2003, creating dramatic increases in sales and profits. He also leads Dallas's Parks and Recreation Board. Rawlings graduated magna cum laude from Boston College with a degree in philosophy and communications.

Priscilla Ridgway, PhD

Ridgway is credited as the innovator of the idea of permanent supported housing. Her emphasis on consumer choice, the concept of recovery, and the importance of "home" in ending homelessness underscores the priority she assigns to identifying the aspirations of those in recovery from mental illness and the critical role of services.

Dr. Ridgway is assistant professor, Department of Psychiatry Program for Recovery & Community Health, at Yale University School of Medicine, where her work includes developing and evaluating consumer recovery education in Connecticut. She has done innovative work on consumer preference, created supported housing models, and conducted housing research including on evidence-based practices.

Dr. Ridgway has worked in the field of mental health for more than 30 years, in roles ranging from psychiatric aide, case manager, advocate for psychiatric inpatients, and program director in a psychosocial rehabilitation agency to coordinator of research and planning for a state mental health department. For the last 20 years her work has focused on building knowledge about recovery, including at the Center for Psychiatric Rehabilitation at Boston University, the University of Kansas Office of Mental Health Research and Training, and Advocates for Human Potential, Inc.

She earned a BA from the University of Southern Maine, an MSW degree from the University of Connecticut, and a PhD in social welfare from the University of Kansas. She identifies herself as a consumer, having had the personal experience of recovery from brain trauma and post-traumatic stress disorder. She is the co-author of *Pathways to Recovery: A Strengths Self-Help Workbook* for personal recovery. She has worked with a team primarily of consumer researchers on the project What Helps and What Hinders Recovery? Her work includes recovery and resilience, hope, and spirituality; defining recovery; and development of recovery performance indicators.

Debra J. Rog, PhD

Rog is vice president of the Rockville Institute, a position she assumed in 2007 at the research and evaluation organization. She is an associate director with Westat, a statistical services research corporation. She is known both as a researcher on homelessness and as a leading expert on program evaluation. Dr. Rog was 2009 president of the American Evaluation Association (AEA). She has expertise in family and individual homelessness, mental health, and cost issues as well as experience in evaluating collaborative initiatives.

In 1990 she became director of the Washington Office of the Center for Mental Health Policy of the Vanderbilt Institute for Public Policy Studies, a position she held for 17 years. Dr. Rog has published and presented widely and edited books, series, and journals. She has been project manager for research initiatives supported by the Robert Wood Johnson Foundation, the Department of Health and Human Services' Center for Mental Health Services and Substance Abuse and Mental Health Services Administration, the National Institute of Mental Health, the National Mental Health Association, and the Bill and Melinda Gates Foundation.

Dr. Rog received a BS in psychology from American International College, an MA in social psychology from Kent State University, and a PhD in social psychology from Vanderbilt University.

Nan Roman

Roman is president of the National Alliance to End Homelessness (NAEH). She was previously vice president for policy and programs with the alliance, where she has worked since 1987. She has helped build the organization into a leading voice on homelessness in Washington, D.C., with more than 2,000 nonprofit members. She oversees all program and policy activities, including congressional and federal agency advocacy, training, technical assistance, and research.

Roman was part of the U.S. delegation to Habitat II in Istanbul. She received the Miss America Woman of Achievement Award, which is awarded annually to a woman who has demonstrated zeal, devotion, and contribution to an issue of benefit to American society. In 2000 she unveiled a 10-year alliance plan to end homelessness around which NAEH hoped to organize support for new programs. She has been active in antipoverty and community organizing activity at the local and national levels for over 20 years. Roman received her BA and MA from the University of Illinois.

Sister Mary Scullion

Scullion of Philadelphia belongs to the Sisters of Mercy religious order. She is cofounder and executive director of Project HOME and has more than 35 years of experience working with people who are homeless, especially people with mental illness. Sister Mary has been active in advocacy for people who are homeless and mentally ill, and she cochaired the Philadelphia 10-year plan steering committee.

In 1985 she cofounded Woman of Hope, a program of permanent housing and services for women. She helped establish the Outreach Coordination Center in 1988 to improve coordination of public and private organizations doing outreach to people who are chronically homeless.

Sister Mary was named as one of *Time* magazine's most influential people in 2009 and has been recognized by the Philadelphia Bar Association, presented with the Prudential National Nonprofit Leadership Award and the 1992 Philadelphia Award. In 2002, she was a national awardee of the Ford Foundation "Leadership for a Changing World" award. She earned a BA from St. Joseph's University in psychology and an MSW from Temple University.

Marybeth Shinn, PhD

Shinn is professor of human and organizational development at Vanderbilt University. Her research focuses on poverty, homelessness, and mental illness. She has been involved in research to identify effective prevention strategies, successful housing models for homeless families, and homelessness among older adults. She is currently involved in an evaluation of the federal multisite initiative to develop rapid rehousing models for homeless families.

Prior to her Vanderbilt position, Shinn held positions at New York University's Steinhardt School of Culture, Education, and Human Development, as professor of applied psychology and public policy, at the Robert F. Wagner School of Public Service, as professor of psychology and public policy, on the Faculty of Arts and Science as chair, Department of Psychology.

Shinn focuses on the use of research to guide public policy. She has done collaborative studies with New York City's Department of Homeless Services, Human Resources Administration, and Department of Health. She has participated in state policy academies run by the federal Interagency Council on Homelessness and served on research advisory panels for the New York City Department of Homeless Services and the National Low Income Housing Coalition, among others.

Shinn earned her PhD from the University of Michigan in community and social psychology, an MA in social psychology from Michigan, and a BA in social relations from Radcliffe College, Harvard University.

Horace Sibley

Sibley retired in 2009 as chair of the Atlanta Regional Commission on Homelessness, the implementing body of the Blueprint to End Homelessness in Atlanta in Ten Years. Having recently retired as a partner at Atlanta's King & Spalding law firm, Sibley helped develop the regional plan as community champion appointed by former mayor Shirley Franklin in 2002. Sibley's leadership and partnership with other cities helped define the potential of community champions and the importance of their private sector partnerships in ending homelessness.

The commission worked for 90 days to develop the plan adopted in early 2003. Over $30 million in private investments has been leveraged into the plan to date. Outstanding accomplishments of the partners include creation of the Gateway Center as a focus of services, new housing developed with a bond issue, development of housing secured from Fort McPherson when it closed, and a model reunification initiative that helps people return to their community of origin.

Mr. Sibley, a native of Philadelphia, has numerous civic and charitable involvements. He was one of the original group of Atlanta citizens who organized to bring the 1996 Summer Olympics to Atlanta. He was on the executive committee of the Atlanta Organizing Committee and chairman of the International Affairs Committee, serving as general counsel to and as a member of the board of directors of the Atlanta Committee. He has served on the Carter Center board of advisors and serves on the board of the Calloway Gardens Foundation.

Sibley received a BA from Vanderbilt University; an LLB from the University of Georgia; and an MBA from Georgia State University. He served as a captain in the U.S. Army Third Infantry Division in Germany.

Mitch Snyder

Snyder was a member and highly visible spokesperson for the Community for Creative Non-Violence (CCNV) in Washington, D.C., which he joined in 1973 to open a small residence for homeless people who would otherwise be held in jail because they lacked a fixed address.

He had recently been released from federal prison, where he had met antiwar activists who influenced his thinking about social justice. Snyder was born in Brooklyn, New York, and quit school as a teenager. He committed numerous acts of nonviolent civil disobedience, fasted publicly, and lived on the streets for extended periods of time to draw attention to the needs of homeless people.

He engaged the interest and participation of many policy makers and celebrities who joined and supported some of the more visible protests against homelessness, including the landmark HOUSING NOW! March in Washington, D.C., in 1989. He led the campaign for Initiative 17, a D.C. ballot measure that was passed with a 72 percent vote in support of providing shelter for all in need in 1984. He led the 1986–1987 campaign to develop and pass comprehensive federal legislation to help homeless people. As part of this effort, he slept outside the U.S. Capitol from the time the bill was introduced until its ultimate passage as the Stewart B. McKinney Homeless Assistance Act. Advocates, providers, and homeless people joined the effort by traveling to Washington and sleeping outside the Capitol at night and visiting members of Congress during the day.

He co-authored *Homelessness in America: A Forced March to Nowhere* with Mary Ellen Hombs. He was well-known as an organizer and activist as well as a speaker on poverty and homelessness. He committed suicide in 1990.

Sam J. Tsemberis, PhD

Tsemberis is founder and CEO of the innovative Pathways to Housing program created in 1992. Pathways has since defined the widely adopted Housing First strategy for people experiencing chronic homelessness. Pathways to Housing provides immediate access to independent permanent apartments to individuals who are homeless and who have psychiatric disabilities and substance use disorders. More than 85 percent of individuals have succeeded in their housing. The strategy was named an evidence-based practice by the federal Department of Health and Human Services in 2007. Tsemberis authored *Housing First: The Pathways Model to End Homelessness for People with Mental Illness and Addiction* published in 2010 as a guide to creating Housing First.

Pathways has been replicated in Philadelphia and Washington, D.C., and is under development in numerous other cities worldwide. Pathways to Housing has been widely profiled by national media, including NPR, PBS, the *New York Times,* the *Washington Post,* and the *Christian Science Monitor.*

Tsemberis, who had worked as part of a New York psychiatric street outreach team prior to establishing Pathways, has served as principal investigator for several federally funded studies of homelessness, mental illness, and substance abuse. He has published numerous articles and book chapters on the topics of effective housing and treatment interventions for individuals who are homeless and have psychiatric disabilities and consumer choice.

His work has been widely recognized, including by the federal Interagency Council on Homelessness, New School for Social Research, National Alliance for the Mentally Ill, American Psychiatric Association, and National Alliance to End Homelessness. Tsemberis earned a BA in psychology and English from Sir George Williams University, an MA in psychology from the New School for Social Research, and a PhD in psychology from New York University. He completed internships in psychology at Bellevue Hospital, NYU Medical Center.

Representative Bruce Vento

Vento was a 12-term Democratic member of the U.S. House of Representatives from St. Paul, Minnesota. He served on the Housing and Community Opportunity Subcommittee, where he helped lead congressional efforts to assist homeless people by establishing the Emergency Shelter Grants program and sponsoring legislation on homeless programs throughout the 19080s and 1990s.

Vento was elected to the House of Representatives in 1976. He was born in St. Paul and attended the University of Minnesota and Wisconsin State University. He was a science and social studies teacher before being elected to a seat in the state legislature in 1970.

Vento died in October 2000 of a rare type of cancer caused by inhaling asbestos fibers. Upon his death, the McKinney Act, named for his late colleague Stewart McKinney, was renamed the McKinney-Vento Act.

6

Data and Documents

Introduction

This chapter provides a documentary overview of modern homelessness that highlights key data, speeches, testimony, and government reports and plans from the past decade. Key policy, research, and legislative documents that demonstrate some of the primary facets of homelessness and the response to it in the United States are included here. The focus of this chapter is primarily on the United States, though the initiatives of the European Union, Canada, the United Kingdom, and Australia are introduced here. Further coverage of strategies outside the United States is provided in chapter 3.

Collecting Data on Homelessness Nationally

The federal initiatives to develop and aggregate local data that could be reported nationally began to shows results during the first decade of the 21st century. HUD's Homeless Management Information System (HMIS), which collects data from local users, is based on two categories of information: universal data collected by service agencies from all clients and program-specific data, which programs that receive certain types of funding must collect.

Universal data elements include name, date of birth, race, ethnicity, gender, veteran's status, Social Security number, prior residence, and disabling conditions. Program-specific data elements are amount and sources of income, receipt of noncash benefits, physical and developmental disabilities, HIV status, mental illness, substance abuse status, and domestic violence status. Special provisions apply to data collected from domestic violence programs.

Congress directed that data be reported from HUD annually, and in 2007, HUD released the first analysis of data from a sample of communities participating in HMIS in a report called the Annual Homeless Assessment Report (AHAR).

Since communities needed several years to implement their HMIS systems, locating financial, staff, and computer resources to produce the required data, HUD also established a nationally representative sample of communities that could move ahead with reporting to produce unduplicated estimates of users of emergency shelter and transitional programs. (An unduplicated figure means that each person is counted once during a given time period, even if the person is served multiple times or seen at multiple programs.)

AHAR uses two data sources described here in the 2008 HUD report. Continuum of care applications are submitted to HUD annually as part of the competitive funding process and provide one-night, Point-in-Time (PIT) counts of both sheltered and unsheltered homeless populations. The PIT counts are based on the number of homeless persons on a single night during the last week in January, and the most recent PIT counts for which data are available nationally were conducted in January 2008.

Homeless Management Information System (HMIS) are electronic administrative databases that are designed to record and store client-level information on the characteristics and service needs of homeless persons. HMIS data is used to produce counts of the sheltered homeless population over a full year—that is, people who used emergency shelter or transitional housing programs at some time during the course of a year.

According the first AHAR, "Since 2005, communities have been submitting unduplicated counts of shelter users as well as other information about their demographic characteristics and patterns of service use for analysis and reporting in the AHAR. HUD has supported local efforts to submit data to the AHAR by providing technical assistance on how to increase participation in HMIS among homeless service providers and on improving the accuracy and reliability of the data."

To date, five AHAR reports have been submitted to Congress. The 2005 AHAR covered a three-month period in 2005 and used HMIS data reported by 63 communities. The 2006 AHAR covered six months, January through June 2006, and included information from 74 communities.

The 2007 AHAR was the first report to cover an entire year, October 2006–September 2007, and serves as the baseline for analyzing trends over time. The number of communities providing useable data had increased to 98. The 2008 AHAR used HMIS data provided by 222 communities nationwide, covering about 40 percent of the total U.S. population, to produce nationwide estimates of sheltered homelessness. The report covers the period from October 2007 through September 2008.

The 2009 AHAR, which covers the period from October 2008 to September 2009, reports an increase of 66 percent in the number of participating communities when compared to 2008. A total of 2,988 counties and 1,056 cities contributed data.

Finally, as part of the American Recovery and Reinvestment Act of 2009, Congress allocated $1.5 billion for a Homelessness Prevention Fund, which supports HPRP. The purpose of HPRP is to provide homelessness prevention assistance to households who would otherwise become homeless—many due to the economic crisis—and to provide assistance to rapidly rehouse persons who are homeless. HPRP data are included in HUD's Pulse Report.

What the AHAR Data Reveal

Here are key findings from the 2009 AHAR, reporting data through September 30, 2008.

Data from Point-in-Time Estimates of Homeless Persons in 2008 On a single night in January 2009 when counts were conducted across the nation, there were an estimated 643,067 people experiencing homelessness (including both sheltered and unsheltered people). More than 60 percent were in shelter or transitional programs, and 37 percent were living on the streets or in places unfit for human habitation according to the homeless definition. Just 31.8 percent were from rural or suburban areas.

Individuals accounted for 63 percent of the population, and 37 percent of those counted were in a family. Just 21 percent of family members were without shelter, compared to almost half of all homeless individuals. The estimate of people experiencing chronic homelessness was 110,917, demonstrating over a 10 percent decrease from the 2008 count of 124,135 chronically homeless people, and a total 36 percent drop in chronic homelessness since 2005. All of the 2009 decrease was among unsheltered chronically homeless people.

Per the findings of research, a chronically homeless person is defined as an unaccompanied homeless individual with a disabling condition who has either been continuously homeless for a year or more or has had at least four episodes of homelessness in the past three years. To be considered chronically homeless, a person must have been on the streets or in emergency shelter (e.g., not in transitional or permanent housing) during these stays.

The reported data for 2009 were collected in the context of the effects of the economic downturn, which was expected to show more widespread effects for families.

AHAR estimates the number of people who experience homelessness in the course of a year. The 2009 AHAR reported that almost 1.56 million people used either emergency shelter or a transitional program during the year. Two-thirds of those counted were individuals, and one-third were members of families. Thirteen of sheltered homeless people were veterans.

As was true in 2008, the number of homeless families in shelter increased, and the number of homeless individuals in shelter dropped. In 2009, approximately 1,035,000 individuals used sheltered or transitional programs at some time during the year. About 535,000 people who were part of a family used these programs. (A family is a household that includes an adult 18 years of age or older and at least one child. All other sheltered homeless people are counted as individuals.)

The profile of homeless individuals is also revealed by the data: "A typical sheltered homeless person in 2009 was an adult male, a member of a minority group, middle-aged, and alone. Men are overrepresented in the sheltered homeless population—63.7 percent of homeless adults are men, compared to 40.5 percent of adults in poverty. African Americans make up 38.7 percent of the sheltered homeless population, about 1.5 times their share of the poverty population. Only 2.8 percent of the sheltered homeless population is 62 years old or older. Homeless people have higher rates of disability than either the poverty population or the total U.S. population; slightly over two-thirds of sheltered homeless adults have a disability, according to HMIS data."

Adults in sheltered homeless families have a very different profile. Most families are headed by women under age 31. Very few of these women are either veterans or have a disability. Some

60 percent of family members are children, with the majority under age 6.

Most people who were counted stayed fairly briefly in shelter. For individuals, the median length of stay was 17 days, and for families it was 36 days.

Homeless individuals and families are also identified by geography, and analysis shows that they offer a very different picture from both the general population and the poverty population. Homeless people in shelter in cities are nearly twice the number of people in poverty, 68.2 percent versus 35.6 percent. Over 70 percent of homeless individuals are in cities, versus just over 60 percent of homeless families.

Besides demographics and the location of people who were counted, there is also data on where people came from to the location where they were counted. Almost 40 percent of those in shelter or transitional programs came from other homeless situations. Another 40 percent came to shelter for housing of their own or shared housing, and the balance of those counted were either in institutions or settings such as motels. Families were more likely to have been in housing before coming to shelter. Of more than 60 percent who were in housing, 20 percent were in their own housing, 29 percent were with family, and 14 percent were with friends.

HUD found that more homeless individuals came to shelter from places not meant for human habitation than in 2008. According to HUD, "This may suggest that communities are having some success in getting people off the 'street' and into shelter or other forms of housing, especially since the overall number of unsheltered homeless individuals reported by communities in the PIT count did not go up."

HUD analyzed some of the trends as follows:

> The overall number of sheltered homeless people increased slightly between 2007 and 2008 before dropping slightly—by about 2 percent or 35,000 people—between 2008 and 2009. The continued rise in family homelessness across the three years, from 131,000 families in 2007 to 170,000 families in 2009, is almost certainly related to the recession. However, the increase was more pronounced between 2007 and 2008, even through unemployment rates remained high during the 2009 reporting period (October 2008 through September 2009). It may

> be that many families already at risk of becoming homeless lacked sufficient support networks and became homeless almost immediately after the economy turned down. A much larger group turned to family and friends and may be doubled up and still at great risk of becoming homeless. The percentage of adults in families who reported that they had been staying with families before entering shelter increased steadily over the three-year period, from 24.2 percent in 2007 to 29.4 percent in 2009, as did the total percentage reporting that they had been in some sort of 'housed' situation before becoming homeless, reaching 62.5 percent in 2009.

HUD counted and analyzed the resources to shelter people. In 2009, data showed a total of 643,423 "beds" nationwide in 20,065 shelter, transitional programs, permanent supportive housing, and safe haven programs. HUD uses the term "beds" to apply to all these settings. HUD noted that 2009 data show the first increase in permanent housing (versus shelter) in the count. According to data, permanent supportive housing—key to reducing chronic homelessness—increased by almost 60,000 beds in the period 2006–2009.

Various geographic patterns are identified in the data. AHAR found that the largest numbers of people who are homeless are counted in specific coastal states: California, New York, and Florida account for 39 percent of those enumerated in the one-night count in 2009. HUD analyzed the regional percentage of the total homeless population counted and found the following distributions. The Northeast counted 18 percent of the total homeless population, the same percentage of the total U.S. population that it represents. The Midwest had 12 percent of the homeless population and 22 percent of the U.S. population. The South reported 32 percent of the homeless population and 37 percent of the general population. Finally, the West showed 37 percent of the homeless population and just 23 percent of the U.S. population.

Homelessness in the States

The 2009 AHAR provides insights into the number of people who are homeless on a state-by-state basis and compares the data to the entire homeless population and establishes a rate of homelessness in the state. The five states with the largest homeless population are listed in Table 6.1.

TABLE 6.1
The five states with the largest homeless population

California	133,129
New York	61,067
Florida	55,599
Texas	36,761
Washington	22,782

Measuring homelessness as a percentage of total state population, the five states with the highest percentage are listed in Table 6.2.

When comparing the number of people counted as homeless, HUD also examined the ratio of available shelter and other beds by state by population. Washington, D.C., while not a state, has the highest ratio, at 17.1 beds per 1,000 people. New York reports 4.8 beds per 1,000 and reports the largest inventory (94,500) in the nation, in part because of the requirement that many people be sheltered. California follows with 88,688, and then the numbers drop dramatically to 32,000. California and New York together have 29 percent of the nation's capacity. Wyoming has the smallest number of beds (835), and Mississippi the fewest per capita (0.6 per 1,000).

The Homelessness Pulse Project

HUD began a new limited data project with quarterly reports to look at possible trends in more current time than the annual collection reported in AHRA. Called the Homelessness Pulse Project, the data for May 2010 showed the following.

TABLE 6.2
Measuring homelessness as a percentage of total state population, the five states with the highest percentage

Nevada	0.55 percent
Hawaii	0.45 percent
Oregon	0.45 percent
California	0.36 percent
Washington	0.34 percent

Pulse reports the number of people homeless, the number of newly homeless people served during the quarter, and certain socioeconomic data. Nine sites were involved in the 2009 launch of the project: Bridgeport, Connecticut; Cleveland, Ohio, Kentucky; New York; Phoenix; Polk County, Florida; Richmond, Virginia; Shreveport, Louisiana; and Washington, D.C.

Data are reported for shelters and transitional programs, along with existing point-in-time count data. For new clients, data includes household type, disability, veteran status, living arrangements before coming to shelter, and length of stay in prior living situation.

All sites experienced increased unemployment in 2009. However, six of the nine sites reported improvements in late 2009, with having reporting declining unemployment and one reporting stable numbers. Shreveport, Louisiana, reported the largest decline. Other sites reported increased unemployment.

Other findings include the following. The December 2009 point-in-time count found a slight decrease in the total sheltered homeless population from the previous quarterly count. For seven sites that reported data for four quarters, the total number of persons in families decreased by 1.6 percent in the last quarter. The total number of individuals decreased by 1.3 percent. Five of the eight sites reported more new homeless individuals than new family members among newly sheltered homeless persons. Thirty-two percent of new clients were children (1 percent were unaccompanied youth).

All Homelessness Pulse Reports are available at http://www.hudhre.info/documents/HomelessnessPulseProjectMay10.pdf.

The 2010 AHAR Report

According to HUD, "The 2010 AHAR will continue to provide Congress and the nation with updated counts of homelessness nationwide, including counts of individuals, persons in families, and special population groups such as chronically homeless people and persons with disabilities. These topics will be explored using data from an ever-expanding group of communities that participate in the AHAR, which now includes the majority of continuums of care nationwide. The 2010 AHAR also will add another full-year of HMIS data to further highlight trends in homelessness and identify any long-term impacts of the economic recession."

The 2010 AHAR will be released in 2011 and will include new data on people served in permanent supportive housing programs in addition to the existing data from emergency shelter and transitional programs. The 2010 AHAR will examine homelessness among veterans, comparing the 2009 supplemental report on homeless veterans with the 2010 supplemental report.

All AHAR reports are available at http://www.hudhre.info.

Recent Issues in Federal, State, and Local Government Programs

Passage and Implementation of the Federal HEARTH Act

Reauthorization of the McKinney-Vento program and fundamental change to their structure and approach occurred with passage of the Homeless Emergency Assistance and Rapid Transition to Housing (HEARTH) Act of 2009. The legislation was incorporated in the Helping Families Save Their Homes Act, signed into law by President Barack Obama on May 20, 2009. This section provides highlights of the program changes.

The HEARTH Act consolidates the existing McKinney-Vento homeless assistance programs; codifies HUD's continuum of care process in use since the 1990s as the local provider process for developing projects and preparing funding applications; and establishes a goal that families who become homeless return to permanent housing within 30 days. Applications will be more focused on performance, including reducing lengths of homeless episodes, reducing returns to homelessness, reducing the number of people who become homeless, and emphasizing prevention, rapid rehousing, chronic homelessness, a focus on outcomes, and rural flexibility. The legislation continues the requirement that people who are homeless participate in decision-making bodies about these resources.

Defining Homelessness

One key change to federal programs was the expansion of the definition of homelessness and the addition of several other definitions, including one to determine eligibility for prevention resources.

Under the HEARTH Act, being implemented for the 2011 federal funding competition, the term "homeless," "homeless individual," and "homeless person" means—

(1) an individual or family who lacks a fixed, regular, and adequate nighttime residence;
(2) an individual or family with a primary nighttime residence that is a public or private place not designed for or ordinarily used as a regular sleeping accommodation for human beings, including a car, park, abandoned building, bus or train station, airport, or camping ground;
(3) an individual or family living in a supervised publicly or privately operated shelter designated to provide temporary living arrangements (including hotels and motels paid for by Federal, State, or local government programs for low-income individuals or by charitable organizations, congregate shelters, and transitional housing);
(4) an individual who resided in a shelter or place not meant for human habitation and who is exiting an institution where he or she temporarily resided;
(5) an individual or family who—

    (A) will imminently lose their housing, including housing they own, rent, or live in without paying rent, are sharing with others, and rooms in hotels or motels not paid for by Federal, State, or local government programs for low-income individuals or by charitable organizations, as evidenced by—(i) a court order resulting from an eviction action that notifies the individual or family that they must leave within 14 days; (ii) the individual or family having a primary nighttime residence that is a room in a hotel or motel and where they lack the resources necessary to reside there for more than 14 days; or (iii) credible evidence indicating that the owner or renter of the housing will not allow the individual or family to stay for more than 14 days, and any oral statement from an individual or family seeking homeless assistance that is found to be credible shall be considered credible evidence for purposes of this clause;

(B) has no subsequent residence identified; and
(C) lacks the resources or support networks needed to obtain other permanent housing; and

(6) unaccompanied youth and homeless families with children and youth defined as homeless under other Federal statutes who—

(A) have experienced a long term period without living independently in permanent housing,
(B) have experienced persistent instability as measured by frequent moves over such period, and
(C) can be expected to continue in such status for an extended period of time because of chronic disabilities, chronic physical health or mental health conditions, substance addiction, histories of domestic violence or childhood abuse, the presence of a child or youth with a disability, or multiple barriers to employment.

Defining at Risk

"At risk of homelessness" is also defined, and this is especially important in a new national dialogue about homelessness prevention, what works to prevent homelessness, and the use of federal recovery resources for prevention. The HEARTH Act defined "at risk of homelessness" as a family or individual with income below 30 percent of median income for the geographic area (referred to as "extremely low income" in housing programs); with insufficient resources immediately available to attain housing stability and having moved frequently because of economic reasons; living in the home of another because of economic hardship; already notified that their right to occupy their current housing or living situation will be terminated; living in a hotel or motel or severely overcrowded housing; exiting an institution; or otherwise lives in housing that has characteristics associated with instability and an increased risk of homelessness.

Defining Chronic Homelessness

The HEARTH Act put into law a definition of "chronic homelessness," which expanded the definition that had been in use under targeted federal initiatives since 2003 and that had been used to identify those individuals whose long-term homelessness—often on the streets—was accompanied by disability (defined as a physical, mental, or emotional impairment, including an impairment caused by alcohol or drug abuse, post-traumatic stress disorder or brain injury, a developmental disability, or AIDS). Families were added to the definition.

The new definition is summarized as: "The term 'chronically homeless' means, with respect to an individual or family, that the individual or family (i) is homeless and lives or resides in a place not meant for human habitation, a safe haven, or in an emergency shelter; (ii) has been homeless and living or residing in a place not meant for human habitation, a safe haven, or in an emergency shelter continuously for at least 1 year or on at least 4 separate occasions in the last 3 years; and (iii) has an adult head of household (or a minor head of household if no adult is present in the household) with a diagnosable substance use disorder, serious mental illness, developmental, post-traumatic stress disorder, cognitive impairments resulting from a brain injury, or chronic physical illness or disability, including the co-occurrence of 2 or more of those conditions."

The new law noted, "A person who currently lives or resides in an institutional care facility, including a jail, substance abuse or mental health treatment facility, hospital or other similar facility, and has resided there for fewer than 90 days shall be considered chronically homeless."

Eligible Activities for New Funding

Eligible activities for funding under HEARTH include construction of new housing for transitional or permanent housing; acquisition or rehabilitation to provide supportive services or transitional or permanent housing; leasing property for supportive services or transitional or permanent housing; rental assistance to provide transitional or permanent housing, including project-based, tenant-based, and sponsor-based assistance; and operating costs for transitional or permanent housing.

Supportive services for individuals or families who are homeless, who were homeless up to six months ago, or who are in permanent supportive housing are also eligible. Supportive services are defined as child care services program for homeless families; employment assistance, including providing job training; outpatient health services, food, and case management; assistance in obtaining permanent housing, employment counseling, and nutritional counseling; outreach services, advocacy, life skills training, and housing search and counseling services; mental health services, trauma counseling, and victim services; assistance in obtaining other federal, state, and local assistance available for residents of supportive housing (including mental health benefits, employment counseling, and medical assistance, but not including major medical equipment); legal services for purposes including requesting reconsiderations and appeals of veterans and public benefit claim denials and resolving outstanding warrants that interfere with an individual's ability to obtain and retain housing; transportation services that facilitate an individual's ability to obtain and maintain employment; and health care; and other supportive services necessary to obtain and maintain housing, including housing search, mediation or outreach to property owners, credit repair, providing security or utility deposits, rental assistance for a final month at a location, assistance with moving costs, or other activities that help homeless people move immediately into housing or would benefit people who have moved into permanent housing in the last six months.

Emergency Solutions Program (ESG) The HEARTH Act made major changes to the prior ESG program, renaming it the Emergency Solutions Grants Program. Allocations will be made to local government.

Programmatically, the HEARTH Act also made the following changes summarized here.

The act authorized eligible homeless assistance activities: shelter and street outreach, short-term rental assistance, medium-term rental assistance, security deposits, utility deposits and payments, and moving costs. It identified housing relocation and stabilization services as a focus for both homeless assistance and homeless prevention, including outreach, housing search, legal services, and credit repair. It also established rapid rehousing as a major focus for homeless assistance. Rapid rehousing helps people experiencing homelessness return to permanent housing as soon as possible.

Improving Discharge Planning

The HEARTH Act directs that the HUD secretary may not provide a grant for any governmental entity unless there is developed and implemented to the maximum extent practicable and where appropriate policies and protocols for the discharge of persons from publicly funded institutions or systems of care (such as health care facilities, foster care or other youth facilities, or correction programs and institutions) in order to prevent such discharge from immediately resulting in homelessness for such persons.

Incentives for High-Performing Communities

HEARTH created a funding category for communities that score well and will be eligible for a bonus for proven strategies, including for permanent supportive housing for individuals or families with children experiencing chronic homelessness, rapid rehousing that serves homeless families, and other activities that HUD determines are effective at reducing homelessness.

The HUD secretary will annually identify 10 high-performing communities as measured by reliable data for five requirements: mean length of episodes of homelessness for that geographic area is less than 20 days; or for individuals and families in similar circumstances in the preceding year was at least 10 percent less than in the year before. Of individuals and families who leave homelessness, fewer than 5 percent of such individuals and families become homeless again at any time within the next two years; or in similar circumstances who leave homelessness, the percentage of such individuals and families who become homeless again within the next two years has decreased by at least 20 percent from the preceding year.

The communities that compose the geographic area have actively encouraged homeless individuals and families to participate in homeless assistance services available in that geographic area, and included each homeless individual or family who sought homeless assistance services in the data system used by that community. If recipients in the geographic area have used funding in previous years, the activities were effective at reducing the number of individuals and families who became homeless in that community.

New Rural Program

The HUD secretary will establish a new rural housing stability grant program for rehousing or improving the housing situations of individuals and families who are homeless or in the worst housing situations in the geographic area; stabilizing the housing of individuals and families who are in imminent danger of losing housing; and improving the ability of the lowest-income residents of the community to afford stable housing. Half of the funds will go to communities under 10,000 in population with priority to communities with fewer than 5,000 people and communities receiving little federal aid.

Rural funds may be used to provide rent, mortgage, or utility assistance after two months of nonpayment in order to prevent eviction, foreclosure, or loss of utility service; security deposits, rent for the first month of residence at a new location, and relocation assistance; short-term emergency lodging in motels or shelters, construction of new housing units to provide transitional or permanent housing, acquisition or rehabilitation of a structure to provide supportive services or to provide transitional or permanent housing, other than emergency shelter, leasing of property for use in providing transitional or permanent housing or providing supportive services; provision of rental assistance to provide transitional or permanent housing, payment of operating costs for housing; development of comprehensive and coordinated support services that use and supplement, as needed, community networks of services, including outreach services to reach eligible recipients; case management; housing counseling; budgeting; job training and placement; primary health care; mental health services; substance abuse treatment; child care; transportation; emergency food and clothing; family violence services; education services; moving services; entitlement assistance; and referrals to veterans services and legal services; and costs associated with making use of federal inventory property programs to house homeless families, including the program established under title V of the Stewart B. McKinney Homeless Assistance Act and the Single Family Property Disposition Program.

Federal Strategic Plan

The HEARTH Act directed the U.S. Interagency Council on Homelessness to develop a federal strategy on homelessness and update it annually. The strategy was released in June 2010. As stated in President Obama's introductory letter:

> Since the founding of our country, "home" has been the center of the American dream. Stable housing is the foundation upon which everything else in a family's or individual's life is built—without a safe, affordable place to live, it is much tougher to maintain good health, get a good education or reach your full potential.

When I took office in January 2009, too many of our fellow citizens were experiencing homelessness. We took decisive action through the American Recovery and Reinvestment Act by investing $1.5 billion in the new Homelessness Prevention and Rapid Re-Housing Program. We have made record Federal investments in targeted homeless assistance in the FY2010 budget and FY2011 budget request. And the recently passed Affordable Care Act will provide new and more effective methods for targeting uninsured, chronically ill individuals as well as children, youth, and adults experiencing homelessness. In addition, through the leadership of the United States Interagency Council on Homelessness, we are coordinating and targeting existing homelessness resources, as well as mainstream programs that can help prevent homelessness in the first place.

But there is still much more work to do. Veterans should never find themselves on the streets, living without care and without hope. It is simply unacceptable for a child in this country to be without a home. The previous Administration began the work to end chronic homelessness. Now is the time to challenge our Nation to aspire to end homelessness across *all* populations—including families, youth, children, and veterans.

This will take a continued bipartisan effort, as Republicans and Democrats in Congress have collaborated for years to make progress on fighting homelessness.

And preventing and ending homelessness is not just a Federal issue or responsibility. It also will require the skill and talents of people outside of Washington—where the best ideas are most often found. Tremendous work is going on at the State and local level—where States, local governments, nonprofits, faith-based and community organizations, and the private and philanthropic sectors are responsible for some of the best thinking, innovation, and evidence-based approaches to ending homelessness. These State and local stakeholders must be active partners with the Federal Government, and their work will inform and guide our efforts at the national level.

As we undertake this effort, investing in the status quo is no longer acceptable. Given the fiscal realities that families, businesses, State governments, and the Federal Government face, our response has to be guided by what works. Investments can only be made in the most promising strategies. Now more than ever, we have a responsibility to tackle national challenges like homelessness in the most cost-effective ways possible. Instead of simply responding once a family or a person becomes homeless, prevention and innovation must be at the forefront of our efforts.

I was excited to receive *Opening Doors: Federal Strategic Plan to Prevent and End Homelessness.* The goals and timeframes set forth in the Plan reflect the fact that ending homelessness in America must be a *national* priority. Together—working with the Congress, the United States

Interagency Council on Homelessness, mayors, governors, legislatures, nonprofits, faith-based and community organizations, and business and philanthropic leaders across our country—we will make progress on ensuring that every American has an affordable, stable place to call home.

Vision, Goals, and Themes Following are the vision, goals, and themes from the federal strategy, *Opening Doors.*

Vision: No one should experience homelessness—no one should be without a safe, stable place to call home.

Goals: Finish the job of ending chronic homelessness in 5 years

Prevent and end homelessness among Veterans in 5 years

Prevent and end homelessness for families, youth, and children in 10 years

Set a path to ending all types of homelessness

Themes: Increase Leadership, Collaboration, and Civic Engagement

Objective 1: Provide and promote collaborative leadership at all levels of government and across all sectors to inspire and energize Americans to commit to preventing and ending homelessness

Objective 2: Strengthen the capacity of public and private organizations by increasing knowledge about collaboration, homelessness, and successful interventions to prevent and end homelessness

Increase Access to Stable and Affordable Housing

Objective 3: Provide affordable housing to people experiencing or most at risk of homelessness

Objective 4: Provide permanent supportive housing to prevent and end chronic homelessness

Increase Economic Security

Objective 5: Increase meaningful and sustainable employment for people experiencing or most at risk of homelessness

Objective 6: Improve access to mainstream programs and services to reduce people's financial vulnerability to homelessness

Improve Health and Stability

Objective 7: Integrate primary and behavioral health care services with homeless assistance programs and housing to reduce people's vulnerability to and the impacts of homelessness

Objective 8: Advance health and housing stability for youth aging out of systems such as foster care and juvenile justice

Objective 9: Advance health and housing stability for people experiencing homelessness who have frequent contact with hospitals and criminal justice

Retool the Homeless Crisis Response System

Objective 10: Transform homeless services to crisis response systems that prevent homelessness and rapidly return people who experience homelessness to stable housing

The federal Interagency Council, which developed the strategy, identified six core values:

1. Homelessness is unacceptable.
2. There are no "homeless people," but rather people who have lost their homes who deserve to be treated with dignity and respect.
3. Homelessness is expensive; it is better to invest in solutions.
4. Homelessness is solvable; we have learned a lot about what works.
5. Homelessness can be prevented.
6. There is strength in collaboration and USICH can make a difference.

The council decided that the development of the strategy should be guided by several key principles. It should be collaborative, solutions driven and evidence based, cost effective, implementable and user friendly, lasting and scalable; and measurable, with clear outcomes and accountability.

The implications for existing systems were identified based on analysis of the populations experiencing homelessness. According to the strategy,

- We need coordinated leadership at the federal, state, and local levels.
- There must be more program coordination and simplification. Mainstream programs, those not targeted to homeless populations, need to be a part of the solution rather than a set of uncoordinated targeted programs as has been the approach historically.
- Programs must adapt to meet the unique needs of people who have experienced homelessness. Systems must be organized to meet the needs of people with histories of trauma and violence and must be responsive to the special needs of other populations.
- Interventions—mainstream and targeted—must focus on prevention and achieving the outcome of housing stability.
- People must have better access to affordable housing, health, and behavioral health care as well as income and work supports.

The strategy does not include more than general timelines for ending homelessness among several populations, does not incorporate percentage reductions as benchmarks of progress, and does not reflect individual federal agency commitments of resources to be invested in the goals. Each strategic goal is explained, and federal agencies are identified for key responsibilities.

The entire strategy is available at http://www.usich.gov/.

The Federal Role and Results

U.S. Department of Housing and Urban Development secretary Shaun Donovan was the first chair of the U.S. Interagency Council on Homeless in the Obama administration. Following are excerpts from remarks he made to a national homeless conference in 2009, in which he draws on the "Million-Dollar Murray" article of writer Malcolm Gladwell.

> By developing the "technology" of combining housing and supportive services—delivering permanent supportive housing via a targeted pipeline of resources—we've "moved the needle" on chronic homelessness, reducing the number of chronically ill, long-term homeless by nearly a third in the three years since *Million Dollar Murray* was published.
>
> The fact is, we have now proven that we can house anyone.
>
> Our job now is to house everyone—to prevent and end homelessness.
>
> *All* homelessness.
>
> . . . And here's why. For the general public, Murray Barr's story captured something this audience is all too familiar with:
>
> The cost of homelessness—not only in the dollars we spend as taxpayers, but also in the terrible price individuals and families experiencing homelessness pay when we spend those dollars in a disjointed, fragmented way.
>
> It wasn't that the system wasn't spending enough money on Murray. As the title of the article suggests, the bill paid by the local, state, and Federal government reached seven figures.
>
> Nor was it that no one cared about Murray. In fact, when he died, police officers in Reno gave him a moment of silence.
>
> Think about that for a moment—city police officers, bowing their heads in silence in honor of a homeless man.
>
> From cops and social workers to doctors and nurses, a lot of people cared about Murray Barr.
>
> What was missing wasn't money.
>
> It wasn't compassion.
>
> What was missing was leadership—leadership that recognized when we harness public resources and the enormous wellspring of

human capital in this country we can provide everyone-from the most capable to the most vulnerable-the opportunity to reach their full potential (HUD, 2009).

Lessons Learned from the National Partnership

Former U.S. Interagency Council on Homelessness executive director Philip Mangano, who went on to establish the American Round Table to Abolish Homelessness, has continued to take the lessons of the national partnership constellated by the council from 2002 to 2009 to local jurisdictions that are developing and implementing plans. Following are excerpts from 2009 remarks he made to the Vancouver Board of Trade on what's working and what doesn't work.

Whether for moral and spiritual reasons, or quality of life, or social and humanitarian, or just to rid our community of the nuisance, or for obvious economic reasons, we are united in our appetite to end homelessness, beginning with those who are on our streets and long term in shelters.

The research tells us that the majority of those who experience homelessness do so only once or twice, move beyond fairly quickly, and once out into the stability of housing, never return again.

Our focus is then on those who are long term or chronically homeless, who without an intervention would live on our streets or languish in our shelters.

So what has worked over the past seven years to achieve the reductions we all seek?

Nothing has created more public interest or generated more political will than understanding the economics of homelessness, especially for those experiencing chronic homelessness. People with one or more disabilities and living on the streets or in shelters … to know that it costs $35,000 to $150,000 to maintain people in ad hoc crisis interventions, versus $13,000 to $25,000 to solve homelessness through housing with support services, is the compelling argument.

In the work we've done in the States to change the national mind set on homelessness, to fashion strategic plans shaped around business principles and practices, and to create reductions in street homelessness in cities coast to coast, border to border, we learned what the key elements were that correlated with solution oriented reductions …

The single most important factor in reducing street homelessness in those cities was the determined and unflinching political will of the jurisdictional CEO. When mayors in major metropolitan centers partnered with us in the creation of strategic plans informed by business and economic principles and practices and extended their political will to reduce and end street homelessness, results were achieved …

Second was a reframing of the issue from the social service frame of the previous two decades to the business and economic frame of the past seven years.

For two decades we have looked through the lens of a social service frame, seeing homeless people and wondering how to service them, the approach when government ceded the issue to well intentioned provider agencies.

For the last half decade we added a business frame and when we look through the lens of that frame and see homelessness, we wonder, how can we solve that problem.

It is that evolution from servicing to solving that has captured the imagination of the public and private sector across the United States and now cities here in Canada …

Now, having worked with hundreds of mayors and communities across America, when that will is extended and the rhetoric emboldened, there is an expectation of change. Rapid change. As if daring to utter the bold goal was in itself the solution. It's not.

But it is a most important first step without which results will not follow.

So the expectation that some may have that visible and real change can come in a month or six months or even a year fails to understand that this is a problem that's been incubating in most places for two decades. And that policy failings of the past and institutionalized policy and program missteps have only contributed to a status quo of managing, maintenancing, and accommodating.

That turnaround from servicing to solving takes times. We wish it could happen quickly, of course. But what we have seen in the States is that the kind of tangible, quantifiable outcomes of street reductions on a community-wide basis took between a year and a half and 2½ years to begin.

But once the change began to happen, the results continued to mount. Whether in New York which has experienced four consecutive years of reductions representing a 46 percent decrease or Denver's three years and 36 percent reduction or Oakland's recent 18 percent reduction, St. Louis and other cities are seeing that multi-year reduction even in the face of the downturn in the economy.

What are the other factors that have created and sustained the increases? What works? And, as importantly, what doesn't?

Here is some of what we've learned has not worked to reduce street homelessness on a community-wide basis:

1. Ad hoc, uncoordinated crisis interventions only correlate with increased homelessness and economic irresponsibility. Without a plan, things only get worse. Worse on our streets, in our

emergency rooms, for police, firefighters, judges, and jailers. That shuffling of homeless people through crisis intervention after crisis intervention is ineffective and inefficient.
The research now tells us that it is morally wrong, morale deflating, and economically irresponsible.

2. We've learned that good intentions don't get the job done. If good intentions, well meaning programs, and humanitarian gestures could end homelessness, it would have been history decades ago. They don't and it isn't.
Now the moral and spiritual and humanitarian are most important to the vast majority of those of us concerned with this issue. But if they don't correlate with the strategies that remedy and cure and end the human tragedy and long misery, we need a new strategy.
3. Just increasing resources doesn't create the reduction. We've increased resources targeted to homelessness between 1987 and 2002 by 500% and the numbers of homeless people increased dramatically. Outside of a strategic plan, increased resources do not correlate with a community-wide decrease.
4. Implementing innovative program ideas has not correlated with community-wide decreases.
Only in the past five years have we seen these initiatives, contextualized in a strategic plan and part of the reduction strategy, have their intended impact of reducing numbers.
5. A refined intervention strategy without a priority on prevention doesn't work to reduce the numbers. We simply bail the leaking boat of homelessness. Some move beyond, others fall in.
6. Provider driven responses and programs do not correlate with community-wide reductions. Only when contextualized in larger, jurisdictionally led, business informed plans.
Well, what does work? What has demonstrated in the real world, on city streets results? What is beyond conjecture and anecdote and has demonstrated visible and quantifiable reductions?

I've already identified the two most important factors:

1. The leadership and political will of the jurisdictional CEO. Without which we are left with ad hoc crisis interventions or plans that migrate to a shelf and are subject to a future public policy archeological dig.
2. And a strategic, time limited plan informed by business principles and practices and shaped by economic analysis.
Additionally what works for a community includes:
3. Identification and investment only in field-tested, evidence-based initiatives. Innovations that can be visited and supported

by the research. The assurance that when you invest, there will be a return.

4. Business community involvement to foster a business mind set. To move the response from servicing to solving, from managing to ending. And from inputs to outcomes; from process to performance; from anecdote to data; from conjecture to research.
5. Read and disseminate cost studies and cost benefit analysis and engage to do a local one. We had long hoped that moral, spiritual, and humanitarian arguments would drive political will to remedy the problem.

Not in one place has that happened. The economic data has stimulated unprecedented political will to solve the problem as a cost effective strategy (Mangano, 2009).

The Role of the States

With the commitment of the Bush administration in the FY 03 budget of a new "top objective" to end chronic homelessness in 10 years and the revitalization of the U.S. Interagency Council on Homelessness in 2002, a new emphasis was placed on the role of each level of government—federal, state, and local.

To demonstrate their support for these new initiatives, the National Governors Association in 2003 passed the following resolution:

> The Governors support the goal of ending chronic homelessness and recognize the shared responsibility that state and local governments and the federal government have in combating this social problem. This recognition of shared responsibility has been made tangible by the establishment of State Interagency Councils on Homelessness in 50 states and territories to date. These State Interagency Councils establish a framework at the highest level for coordinating and focusing state resources on performance-based and results-oriented policies to prevent and combat homelessness and for ensuring that the state is coordinating its efforts effectively with the federal government and with local efforts including ten-year planning efforts to end chronic homelessness. The Governors support the efforts of the United States Interagency Council on Homelessness to create a working partnership that includes multiple federal agencies,

states, and localities. Programs that help states and localities invest in supportive housing for homeless persons with special needs must be adequately funded. The Governors recognize that ending homelessness contributes to economic development and improves the quality of life for everyone in the community.

State Government Initiatives

Both state interagency councils on homelessness and state governments have contributed new initiatives in partnership with federal efforts and local jurisdictions. Here are summaries of a few examples.

Alabama—State Leadership for Partnership and Planning
In 2005, Governor Bob Riley signed an executive order creating the Governor's Statewide Interagency Council on Homelessness to develop and implement a plan to prevent and end homelessness in Alabama and to serve as a statewide planning and policy development resource. The council was established within the Governor's Office of Faith-Based and Community Initiatives and maintains standing agenda item to identify and address barriers to preventing and ending homelessness, resulting in initiatives such as the resolution of access issues to identification for reentering prisoners.

In 2006, the council released its "Blueprint Toward a Ten Year Plan to End Homelessness" citing fiscal optimization, increasing access to permanent housing/Housing First, and developing comprehensive and accessible statewide data on homelessness as key. In 2008, policy makers identified a "pressing need" for accurate statewide baseline data about homelessness, resulting in a new statewide data report. In 2006 the state's leadership prompted convening an alliance of more than 40 Alabama counties with largely rural populations to pursue the plan.

California—State Social Services Undertakes Intergovernmental and Interagency Initiatives Replicable Nationally In 2007, state agencies undertook an intergovernmental initiative with federal and state partners to create SSI access for aging out foster care youth with disabilities. Youth cannot apply for SSI while in foster care, so they often face instability upon discharge and a long wait for a successful SSI application. In 2008, federal and state partners identified a solution allowing application and determination for target youth to ensure receipt of SSI upon age-out. The policy was adopted in 2010 as a national SSA policy. Federal, state, and county partners also announced statewide implementation of pilot project to ensure improved access to SSI and medical exams for chronically homeless persons by providing real-time exams and needed supports such as transportation at time of application.

Colorado—Emphasizing Partnership and Vulnerable Populations In 2007, Governor Bill Ritter signed a new executive order to expand the state interagency council to make "cross-agency and community cooperation the norm" and create and implement evidence-based plans to address homelessness. The council was to facilitate "tighter partnerships and linkages" among service providers.

Governor Ritter expanded Medicaid coverage to aging-out foster care youth and signed as his first bill called "Bridging the Gap"—a consumer-driven foster care family preservation measure designed, written, and advocated for by foster care youth.

Kentucky—Action Based on Research In 2006 the Kentucky governor unveiled a 10-year business plan calling for Kentucky Housing Corporation to develop 2,400 permanent supportive housing units. Based on research showing treatment as the greatest unmet need, the governor called for establishing 10 housing recovery centers throughout Kentucky for homeless and reentry populations with 1,000 new transitional residential placements. In 2007, the state opened the first Recovery Kentucky site on donated land in a joint effort by the Governor's Office of Local Development, the Department of Corrections, the Office of Drug Control Policy, and the Kentucky Housing Corporation.

Massachusetts—the Right Resources at the Right Time In 2007 a new joint executive-legislative commission was charged to create five-year state plan. Its report calls for a new approach: "The right resources to the right people at the right time." The commonwealth committed to invest $10 million to establish a pool of flexible resources to develop and test new strategies. In 2009, new regional networks are identified for investment of state resources.

Michigan—Starting a Statewide Campaign of Planning In 2006, the Michigan governor's leadership drove the creation of 60 10-year plans for all 83 Michigan counties; plans were unveiled at a statewide summit. State housing funds were tied to the

10-year plans by the Michigan State Housing Development Authority, with new planning grants for innovations, including Project Homeless Connect.

Minnesota—Business Plan Calibrated for Results In 2004, the governor unveiled a 10-year business plan partnering the departments of Human Services and Corrections and the Minnesota Housing Finance Agency with $10 million investment in supportive housing services for 1,500 Minnesotans in 37 counties and six tribal reservations for two years. The 2006–2007 budget supported $23.3 million for Homeless Prevention and Supportive Housing activities, including a new emergency response system that shifted the focus to prevention of homelessness and a rapid move to housing and a record $17.5 million bond for permanent supportive housing, transitional programs, and new supportive housing for veterans. In 2007, the state issued a progress report and recalibration showing that results exceed goals in years one through three. The Heading Home Minnesota private-public partnership was formed to support the plans.

New Jersey—Partnership and Innovation for Housing In November 2008, the governor signed an executive order creating the New Jersey Interagency Council on Preventing and Reducing Homelessness. New Jersey's Special Needs Housing Trust Fund targets housing opportunity to extremely low income people through $200 million bonds underwritten by fines and tickets collected by the courts from convictions for unsafe driving violations. Seventy-five percent of the resources are targeted to develop special needs housing and residential opportunities as alternatives to institutionalization or homelessness for people below 30 percent AMI.

North Carolina—State Leadership for Local Planning In 2003, North Carolina became the first state to designate a state "point person" for homeless policy and coordination of the state's interagency council. The state's 2006 "Housing 400" Initiative created 400 units of independent and supportive housing for very low income persons with disabilities, affordable for persons at SSI income levels. A state council leadership summit for all 10-year plan leaders includes new resources to strengthen local 10-year plan efforts, such as specialized technical assistance, support to adopt Project Homeless Connect, and a $2.1 million to fund three pilot sites to create housing support teams to work with people who have a history of homelessness and cycling through publicly funded systems.

North Dakota—State Leadership Spurs Plans In 2004, the governor revitalized the state interagency council and directed it to create North Dakota's 10-Year Plan to End Long Term Homelessness by encouraging and working with local communities and reservations to develop local plans that would be "collectively rolled up" into a statewide plan. Fargo became the first North Dakota city to develop a 10-year plan. The Housing Finance Agency offered technical assistance to encourage and assist other communities and reservations to develop 10-year plans in areas with the largest concentrations of homelessness in the state. By 2008, 10 new plans were created.

Utah—Regional Approaches Supported by State In 2003, Utah state government unveiled its business plan to end homelessness. Officials set a goal to develop 12 local homeless coordinating committees chaired by mayors or county officials. The state launched initiatives to develop chronic homelessness pilot programs, with the first pilot in Salt Lake City placing 17 chronically homeless individuals in existing housing inventory using the Housing First model with supportive services. By 2007, the state reported that eight pilots were underway and 500 units identified. In 2010 Utah reported further reductions in chronic homelessness.

Washington—Statewide Initiative to Support 10-Year Plans The 2005 Homeless Housing and Assistance Act set a goal of reducing homelessness in the state by 50 percent by July 2015. The act directed resources to projects consistent with the state and local 10-year plans that will reduce homelessness; demonstrate cost savings; employ evidence-based approaches; are replicable; and include strong performance measurements. In 2007, the state announced nearly $11 million in state Homeless Grant Assistance Program (HGAP) awards to help fund three-year model projects and programs in nine counties implementing 10-year plans. The state ICH undertook new initiatives to facilitate successful offender reentry and prevent youth exiting the foster care system from becoming homeless.

Local Jurisdictional Leaders Support 10-Year Plans

Mayors and officials were encouraged by the U.S. Interagency Council on Homelessness to address homelessness at the local level with new strategies including 10-year plans to end homelessness. The national organization of mayors—the U.S Conference of Mayors—passed a 2003 resolution endorsing the goal of ending chronic homelessness and endorsing 10-year plans.

U.S. Conference of Mayors
June 2003
Endorsing 10 Year Planning Process to End Homelessness

1. WHEREAS, the Bush Administration has called for a 10 Year Initiative to End Chronic Homelessness; and
2. WHEREAS, chronically homeless individuals and families, those with the most persistent forms of homelessness, are afflicted not only by poverty but also by chronic conditions such as mental illness and substance abuse; and
3. WHEREAS, many of these individuals and families cycle repeatedly through our local shelters, hospital emergency rooms, psychiatric wards, detox programs, and even criminal justice system; and
4. WHEREAS, there exists new research findings, housing programs and discharge planning models that demonstrate that ending chronic homelessness is within the nation's grasp; and
5. WHEREAS, mayors and cities are on the front lines of response to homelessness; and
6. WHEREAS, the abolition of chronic homelessness requires collaboration and coordination of resources at all levels of government, together with community institutions, businesses, and faith-based organizations, to best determine how to implement prevention and intervention strategies; and
7. WHEREAS, the federal government is coordinating policies and resources to assist the efforts to end chronic homelessness through the Interagency Council on Homelessness; and
8. WHEREAS, a number of major cities across the country, including Chicago, Atlanta, Indianapolis and Phoenix, have already created and committed to 10 year plans to end chronic homelessness,
9. NOW, THEREFORE, BE IT RESOLVED that the U.S. Conference of Mayors will, in partnership with the Federal government, work to meet the challenge of the Bush Administration's goal of having 100 ten-year city plans to end chronic homelessness in place by January 2004; and
10. NOW, THEREFORE, BE IT FURTHER RESOLVED that the U.S. Conference of Mayors will work with the Interagency Council

on Homelessness to ensure policies and resources support the elimination of chronic homelessness; and

11. BE IT FURTHER RESOLVED that the U.S. Conference of Mayors supports the 10-year planning process and strongly encourages cities to create and implement performance based, results oriented strategic plans to end chronic homelessness in 10 years (USCM, 2003).

The above is reprinted courtesy of the United States Conference of Mayors (usmayors.org).

America's Road Home In a 2007 summit of mayors and county officials convened in Denver, local jurisdictional officials—who by 2009 numbered over 1,000—signed a new statement of commitment that demonstrated the evolution of key principles and innovations through planning and partnership. The key principles follow. Titled "America's Road Home," the statement was signed by more than 300 officials by 2009 (USICH, 2009).

America's Road Home Statement of Principles and Action

Whereas: More than 2 million Americans across our country each year experience homelessness in our local communities, compromising the quality of life of the person, and the community; and

Whereas: As elected Mayors and County officials, we are on the frontlines of homelessness and accountable to our communities for the well-being of all citizens; and

Whereas: We recognize that no one level of government can remedy homelessness alone; and

Whereas: We affirm that we will work together with our partners in state and federal government as well as in the foundation community and private sector to maintain and enhance the sustainable investment of resources needed to respond; and

Whereas: We have taken action to create jurisdictionally-led, community-based 10 Year Plans to end chronic homelessness in our communities in partnership with the United States Interagency Council on Homelessness (USICH), the U.S. Conference of Mayors (USCM), and the National Association of Counties (NACo) to end the disgrace;

Now, therefore, we resolve to work together in a national partnership of every level of government and the private sector, with our fellow cities and counties and the United States Interagency Council on Homelessness to identify, adopt, and create innovative initiatives to advance the following principles and actions:

1. End the homelessness of our most vulnerable and disabled citizens who reside on our streets and in our shelters, those

experiencing chronic homelessness, especially including homeless veterans.

2. With the support of our partners work to shorten the time any person is homeless.
3. Accept jurisdictional responsibility for accountability and results in the broader partnership that includes other levels of government and the private sector for an issue that is visible, expensive, and unacceptable in our communities.
4. Affirm our jurisdictionally-led, community-based 10 Year Plans as the community's primary planning strategy to effect accountability and results in ending and preventing homelessness.
5. Develop these plans to ensure that the measurable outcomes are sustainable and render lasting solutions to homelessness
6. Endorse housing solutions as our primary investment to end homelessness, recognizing that shelter and punitive responses are often expensive and ineffective in reducing numbers and restoring lives and affirm that permanent supportive housing and rapid rehousing models offer our most disabled citizens the housing and services they need in a cost effective response.
7. Affirm the work of faith and community based agencies for the work they have done on the frontlines for decades and partner with them to fashion innovative responses that are results-oriented.
8. Invite the business and philanthropic communities to be a partner in our efforts, especially local business associations, foundations, Business Improvement Districts, the United Way, and Chambers of Commerce.
9. Work with the United States Interagency Council on Homelessness, the United States Conference of Mayors Task Force on Hunger and Homelessness, the National Association of Counties (NACo), and the Partnership to End Long Term Homelessness to assure rapid dissemination of innovations that ensure that every community will have equal access to the best ideas that create results in ending homelessness.
10. Create Project Homeless Connect events, the one-day, one-stop, targeted to homeless people in offering an array of housing, employment, and treatment services along with quality of life resources, as a component of our 10 Year Plan response.
11. Support all local, state, and federal legislation and resources that will offer new capabilities for investment in results.
12. Invite other communities to join us in this national effort.

We, the undersigned Mayors and County officials, do hereby commit to this Statement of Principles and Actions, embrace its goals, and announce our intention to work in partnership in bringing the homelessness of our most vulnerable and disabled neighbors to an end in the United States.

Previous Federal Initiatives

In May 1993, President Bill Clinton signed an executive order on homelessness to create a "single coordinated Federal plan for breaking the cycle of existing homelessness and preventing future homelessness." This plan was issued in March 1994 and is called *Priority Home! The Federal Plan to Break the Cycle of Homelessness.* This document dates from the period before the new business-oriented sense of planning had emerged and reflects an even earlier period of addressing homelessness without the new data, innovations, investments, and partnerships that later created national results in ending homelessness. Excerpts from the federal plan follow; citations have been edited for brevity.

Priority Home! The Federal Plan to Break The Cycle of Homelessness

The Face of Homelessness: No Longer a Poor Apart

It profits us nothing as a nation to wall off homelessness as a novel social problem made up of a distinctly "different" population. Nor is it something that requires separate and distinctive mechanisms of redress, isolated from mainstream programs. In fact, the more we understand about the root causes of homelessness, the greater our sense of having been here before.

To put it plainly, homelessness in the 1990s reveals as much about the unsolved social and economic problems of the 1970s as it does about more recent developments. This Plan reveals and documents that the crisis of homelessness is greater than commonly known or previously acknowledged. Researchers have found that as many as 600,000 people are homeless on any given night. Recent research reveals the startling finding that about seven million Americans experienced being homeless at least once in the latter half of the 1980s. Hence, its resolution will require tackling the enduring roots of poverty, as well as complications introduced by psychiatric disability, substance abuse, and infectious disease. That task is rendered more difficult by today's economic realities and severe budget constraints.

By the middle of the 1980s, the number of homeless people had surpassed anything seen since the Great Depression. Disability, disease, and even death were becoming regular features of life on the streets and in shelters. For the first time, women and children were occupying quarters formerly "reserved" for skid-row men. Psychiatric hospitals continued to discharge people with little hope of finding, let alone managing, housing of their own. Crack cocaine emerged as a drug of choice for those on the margins of society. A new scourge—HIV/AIDS-joined an old one-tuberculosis—to become a major affliction of the homeless poor.

Yet for all that, there remained something disconcertingly familiar about this new homelessness. What America glimpsed on the streets and in the shelters in the 1980s was the usually hidden face of poverty, dislodged from its customary habitat.

Homelessness can be understood as including two broad, sometimes overlapping, categories of problems. The first category is experienced by people living in crisis poverty. Their homelessness tends to be a transient or episodic disruption in lives that are routinely marked by hardship. For such people, recourse to shelters or other makeshift accommodations is simply another way of bridging a temporary gap in resources. Their housing troubles may be coupled with other problems as well—dismal employment prospects because of poor schooling and obsolete job skills, domestic violence, or poor parenting or household management skills—all of which require attention if rehousing efforts are to be successful. But their persistent poverty is the decisive factor that turns unforeseen crises, or even minor setbacks, into bouts of homelessness.

For those individuals who fall in the second category—homeless men and women with chronic disabilities—homelessness can appear to be a way of life. Although a minority of those who become homeless over the course of a year, it is this group that is most visible and tends to dominate the public's image of homelessness. Alcohol and other drug abuse, severe mental illness, chronic health problems or long-standing family difficulties may compound whatever employment and housing problems they have. Lacking financial resources and having exhausted whatever family support they may have had, they resort to the street. Their homelessness is more likely to persist. Disability coupled with the toll of street-living make their situation more complex than that of those who are homeless because of crisis poverty. Those with chronic disabilities require not only economic assistance, but rehabilitation and ongoing support as well.

For the most part, homelessness relief efforts remain locked in an "emergency" register. Many existing outreach, drop-in, and shelter programs address the symptoms of homelessness and little else. Although of proven promise in dealing with the disabled homeless poor, supportive housing options remain in scarce supply. Increasingly, it has become clear that efforts to remedy homelessness cannot be fully effective if they are isolated from a broader community-based strategy designed to address the problems of extreme poverty and the inadequate supply of housing affordable by the very poor. Lasting solutions to homelessness will be found only if the issue is productively addressed in ongoing debates concerning welfare reform, health-care reform, housing, community and economic development, education, and employment policy.

The previous section provided the context of the federal report, and the following section examines causes of homelessness.

Causes of Homelessness

A decade of research and practical experience has confirmed that there are many varieties of contemporary homelessness. Manifold in its causes, duration, consequences, and coexisting disabilities, its steady growth in the early 1980s reflected the confluence of a number of factors.

In accounting for homelessness, it is useful to distinguish among a number of levels of causation. Understanding the structural causes of homelessness is especially important when considering preventive strategies. When fashioning measures to reach those who are currently on the street, personal problems that contribute to the prolongation of homelessness must be addressed.

If stable residence is the goal of policy, appreciating the role of risk factors is essential. Psychiatric disability, substance abuse, domestic violence and chronic illness not only add to the likelihood that someone will become homeless, but complicate the task of rehousing someone already on the street. Among generic risk factors, poverty is the common denominator, but other circumstances have also been identified that increase the likelihood of homelessness: prior episodes of homelessness; divorce or separation among men, and single parenthood among women; leaving home or "aging out" of foster care among unattached youth; a history of institutional confinement in jails, prisons, or psychiatric hospitals; and weak or overdrawn support networks of family and friends.

We must focus more attention on individual risk factors and the underlying structural causes potentiating these factors if the cycle of homelessness is to be broken.

The previous report analyzed the relationship of the causes of homelessness to its widespread appearance in the nation. The following section analyzes the relationship of these causes to a form of homelessness rapidly emerging in the nation.

Why These Factors Translate into Homelessness

A number of analysts have suggested that the situation of households at risk of homelessness may be likened to a game of musical chairs. Too many people are competing for too few affordable housing units. In such a game, those troubled by severe mental illness, addiction, or potentially lethal infections, as well as those simply inexperienced in the delicate balancing act that running a household in hard times requires, are at a serious disadvantage.

Under such circumstances, the changes sketched above—in kinship, government support and work—greatly complicate the task of relocating people who have been displaced from their homes. Traditionally, as noted earlier, extended households were on hand as the recourse of last resort in difficult times. Those among the poor who were without family could make do in sections of central business districts where rooms were cheap and food could be had through the efforts of local charities. Even difficult behavioral problems could be accommodated: such people simply moved frequently, in effect spreading the burden throughout the marginal housing sector. For those still able, spot work opportunities provided a source of income.

But extended families are finding it difficult to make ends meet. The slack in cheap housing is gone. And studies suggest that what is left of the casual labor market prefers more compliant recruits.

Faced with these changes, Federal homelessness policy must be both preventive and remedial in scope. It must do more than merely relocate those who are currently homeless. It must also stabilize such housing placements once made, while securing the residences of those who are precariously housed. Government must seek, in effect, to do with deliberation and planning what the private market once accomplished: make housing work again. In today's environment, to make housing work will frequently require an infusion of fiscal resources and support services. Such services should be viewed, not as "add-on" frills, but as essential enabling ingredients—on a par with debt service, insurance or fire control measures—that are needed for some housing to be feasible at all.

The federal report proposed several solutions, which are outlined in the document that follows.

Building on What We Have Learned

Over a decade has passed since homelessness began its unprecedented postwar growth. During that time, social service agencies, advocates, and researchers acquired a wealth of experience in dealing with homelessness. This collective experience has taught us that homelessness is more complex and deeply rooted than some had originally forecast. Responsible policy must seek to address both the fundamental structures of poverty and the complicating risk factors specific to homelessness.

Solving homelessness will thus mean confronting the traditional sources of impoverishment: declining wages, lost jobs, poor schooling and persistent illiteracy, racial discrimination, public entitlements outpaced by inflation, chronically disabling health and mental health problems, the scarcity of affordable housing, and the increasingly concentrated nature of poverty. It will also mean confronting relatively new social phenomena that are adding to the costs of poverty: changes in family and household structures, the decline in traditional kin-based sources of support, and the proliferation of new drugs (such as crack cocaine) and socially-stigmatized infections, i.e., HIV and tuberculosis.

Accordingly, a comprehensive approach will have to mount initiatives on a number of fronts simultaneously. Homelessness will not be solved by simply outlawing the most visible evidence of its presence on the streets. Solving homelessness will require durable means of arresting the sources of residential instability—both structural and personal—that lie at its root. For virtually every homeless person, this will mean dealing with the affordability and availability of housing. For some, restoration of family ties and attention to the skills and resources needed to manage a household may be indicated. For others, appropriate treatment of mental illnesses and/or substance abuse problems will be essential if they are to be stably housed.

Accommodating the diversity and range of assistance needs among homeless persons will require the development of comprehensive, yet flexible, community-based continuums of care, much like those VA is working to develop through its Comprehensive Homeless Centers.

If we look further ahead, an even more ambitious agenda can be seen. This agenda will encompass long-term community and economic development, education, training and job opportunities, the reinstatement of support services as part of the "welfare" apparatus, and attention to such neighborhood facilities as health clinics and day care centers. But budgetary constraints require a transition to this larger agenda that fully addresses poverty and its accompanying ills. Welfare and health care reform should begin to address many of these ills. In the short run, we will need to direct resources to ensure that those who are currently homeless receive the appropriate range of services and housing as needed and that those poised on the brink of homelessness can be brought back from the edge (HUD, 1994).

Homelessness in Europe

This section introduces some of the initiatives in European countries, Canada, and Australian. In all of these settings national government has introduced new initiatives in the last decade to prevent and end homelessness. Each has had interaction with U.S. initiatives.

The emphasis of the European homelessness literature is on the provision of housing as the means to address the "social exclusion" resulting from homelessness. However, joblessness is the prominent theme of European analysis. Relative to U.S.

discussion and due to the differences in government safety net and social welfare programs, European resources make less mention of the role of chronic disability (including physical disability, mental illness, and substance abuse), and continuity in public systems of care, treatment, and custody (including child welfare, hospitals, prisons, treatment facilities). However, European, Canadian, and Australian strategies all address the various issues presented by the range of "historic" or First people, indigenous groups, Aboriginal people, immigrants, migrants, and the Roma and Traveler populations. More coverage of other nations is provided in chapter 3.

Homelessness in England

England's New Strategy on Street Homelessness

In 1999, British prime minister Tony Blair issued a new plan for addressing the needs of the country's "rough sleepers" or people living outside. The report was titled *Rough Sleeping: The Government's Strategy* and was issued by the country's Department of the Environment, Transport and the Regions.

The "rough sleepers" initiatives provided many key lessons for new U.S. efforts. Just one year after the U.S. Interagency Council on Homelessness was revitalized with the mission to end chronic homelessness, council-member federal agencies hosted a delegation led by Gordon Campbell, head of the Homelessness Directorate, and Louise Casey, former head of the "Rough Sleepers Unit." This meeting marked the first several annual bilateral and multilateral meetings to share national government strategies and results.

The British delegation identified several factors as being key to their success in achieving a reduction, including: (1) having a "single, clear target with top-level commitment to reduce rough sleeping by two thirds by 2002"; (2) creating a Rough Sleepers Unit as a "cross cutting office with an integrated budget" involving housing, drug, alcohol and mental health programs; (3) the use of repeated street counts "as a well tested, independent methodology" to establish a baseline and measure progress toward the target; (4) creating a data collection system to determine service demands and track outcomes; (5) establishing specific performance targets for providers and holding them accountable for meeting the targets; and (6) funding of multidisciplinary contact and assessment teams to carry out intensive street outreach efforts to help people "sleeping rough" to move into accommodation.

The rough sleepers populations was described as young (the majority of individuals were under age 25); overwhelmingly male; formerly in care (at least 25 percent had been in care); living with alcohol (50 percent) and drug (20 percent) issues; and living with mental health issues (30–50 percent) (SEU, 1999).

European Homeless Initiatives

FEANTSA developed a toolkit for the launch of the European "Ending Homelessness" campaign in 2010. FEANTSA's toolkit for developing an integrated strategy to tackle homelessness included 10 approaches to addressing homelessness. These included an evidence-based, comprehensive approach that is multidimensional and rights based as well as participatory. The strategic approach is statutory, seeking legislative authority for initiatives, designed as sustainable, and intended as needs-based for the individual. Approaches should be bottom up from the local level (FEANTSA, 2010).

Canada's National Partnership

The Homelessness Partnering Strategy (HPS) is Canada's national government model to address homelessness. HPS requires local communities to identify needs and develop solutions. HPS resources are invested in specific communities that have undertaken planning and support transitional programs and supportive housing. HOS also supports community efforts to prevent and end homelessness and seeks partnerships and collaborations between levels of government.

The 10 most affected communities were identified in 1999, and 51 additional communities were selected in 2000 in consultation with provinces and territories. Communities that are selected must have plans for long-term solutions to prevent and end homelessness. HPS's strategy includes pilot projects, development of an information system, and use of federal surplus property.

Australian Government Initiatives

In 2008, the new government of Australian prime minister Kevin Rudd launched a national government initiative to develop a new strategy on homelessness. More detail is provided in chapter 3, Worldwide Perspective.

The Rudd government's first green paper for "consultation" around the country was to be followed by a final "white paper" of a plan to 2020. The green paper identified several possible goals for Australia in addressing homelessness. They included decreasing the number of people moving from housing to emergency shelter, increasing housing stability for victims of domestic violence, decreasing the number of people who experience homelessness as children and again as adults, and increasing school stability for children experiencing homelessness.

The subsequent white paper, issued under Prime Minister Rudd, who is currently foreign secretary after a shift in government leadership, sought to answer several key questions. The white paper focused on goals, targets, best strategies, key research priorities, business involvement, community participation, and the role of philanthropy.

More information is provided in chapter 3. The Australian documents can be found at http://www.fahcsia.gov.au/sa/housing/progserv/homelessness/whitepaper/Pages/default.aspx.

References

FEANTSA (European Federation of National Organisations Working with the Homeless). Ending Homelessness: A Handbook for Policymakers, 2010. Available at http://www.feantsa.org/files/freshstart/Campaign_2010/background_docs/FEANTSA_handbook_EN_FINAL.pdf.

HUD (U.S. Department of Housing and Urban Development). *Priority Home! The Federal Plan to Break the Cycle of Homelessness*. Washington, D.C.: HUD, March 1994.

HUD (U.S. Department of Housing and Urban Development). Prepared Remarks for Secretary of Housing and Urban Development Shaun Donovan at the National Alliance to End Homelessness Annual Conference, July 30, 2009.

Mangano, Philip. The Business Case for Ending Homelessness. Remarks to the Vancouver Board of Trade. July 16, 2009.

SEU (Government of the United Kingdom Social Exclusion Unit). *Coming in from the Cold: The Government's Strategy on Rough Sleeping*. London, Crown copyright, December 1999.

USCM (U.S. Conference of Mayors). Resolution Endorsing 10 Year Planning Process to End Homelessness. 71st Annual Meeting, June 2003.

USICH (U.S. Interagency Council on Homelessness). "America's Road Home Statement of Principles and Actions." Washington, D.C.: USICH, 2009. Available at http://www.ich.gov/newsletter/Interactive_Statement_Action_Only.pdf.

7

Directory of Organizations, Associations, and Agencies

Introduction

This chapter provides a selected list of national organizations and federal, state, and local references for organizations and public agencies with a significant level of involvement in the issue of homelessness. Also include are national and local government entities for a few international resources as well as key nongovernmental organizations. These listings provide access points to much of the material described elsewhere.

Innovators whose work is being carried out under strategies for families and individuals for national and international replication are also included. Innovators highlighted here are in the areas of street engagement, housing, and employment. Innovations must be field tested and evidence based and operating in more than one location. Finally, there are listings for state and local 10-year-plans both in the United States and select countries, where the state or local plan is one often cited by practitioners as providing a results-oriented model for planning. The selected locations are generally referenced elsewhere in the book and represent a range of population and geography. These references include Web sites where the plan's results are being reported.

U.S. Government Agencies

Federal Agencies

U.S. Department of Agriculture (USDA)

Web site: http://www.usda.gov

USDA manages two mainstream federal investments that benefit people who are homeless: food and nutrition programs and rural housing and development. USDA's Food and Nutrition Service (FNS) administers 15 nutrition assistance programs, including the Supplemental Nutrition Assistance Program (SNAP) (formerly the Food Stamp Program), the National School Lunch and School Breakfast Programs, the Child and Adult Care Food Program, and the Special Supplemental Nutrition Program for Women, Infants, and Children (WIC). USDA rural development initiatives include the Single Family Housing program, the Community Facilities program, and disaster assistance provisions.

U.S. Department of Commerce

Web site: http://www.2010.census.gov

The Census Bureau in the Department of Commerce administers the decennial efforts to enumerate people who are homeless. In 2010, service-based enumerations of people who are homeless were conducted in shelters and meal programs.

U.S. Department of Defense (DOD)

Web site: http://www.oea.gov

The Base Realignment and Closure (BRAC) process requires local planners to address the needs of people who are homeless when planning the reuse of property from closure of military facilities. DOD also donates personal-property items (such as sleeping bags and blankets).

U.S. Department of Education (USED)

Web site: http://www2.ed.gov/programs/homeless/index.html

The McKinney Education for Homeless Children and Youth program provides allocation to states based on reported data on homeless children enrolled in school. The funds are used to support access and assist with services to benefit enrollment and the work of school liaisons in every district.

U.S. Department of Health and Human Services (HHS)

Web sites: http://www.hhs.gov/homeless and http://www.homeless.samhsa.gov/

HHS oversees the McKinney Act program to provide primary health care to homeless people through the Health Care for the Homeless Program, grants to provide access and increase services for mental health and addiction treatment, and programs for homeless and runaway youth. HHS operates the Medicaid and Medicare programs.

U.S. Department of Homeland Security/Federal Emergency Management Agency (FEMA)

Web site: http://www.efsp.unitedway.org/

FEMA's 25-year-old Emergency Food and Shelter Program (EFSP) allocates funds to every state and county for nondisaster uses including food, shelter, rent, mortgage and utility assistance. Local boards are chaired by the United Way. Local allocations are made based on population and unemployment and poverty levels at the national and local level.

U.S. Department of Housing and Urban Development (HUD)

Web sites: http://www.hud.gov and http://portal.hud.gov/poral/page/portal/HUD/topics/homelessness

HUD administers the McKinney homeless programs as well as the HEARTH Act programs passed in 2009 to reorganize federal housing funding. It publishes a variety of reports and research on housing and homelessness. Its Homelessness Resource Exchange houses all program materials, local reports and award information, and guidances.

U.S. Department of Justice (DOJ)

Web sites: http://www.ovw.usdoj.gov/ and http://www.reentry.gov/

DOJ's Office on Violence Against Women implements federal programs for financial and technical assistance to local communities across the country to address domestic violence, dating violence, sexual assault, and stalking. DOJ also provides funds and technical assistance for special courts, such as reentry courts and drug courts and the Second Chance prisoner reentry initiative.

U.S. Department of Labor (DOL)

Web site: http://www.dol.gov/dol/audience/aud-homeless.htm

DOL's homeless strategy emphasizes job readiness by addressing access to mainstream employment assistance and services and identifying skills that promote self-sufficiency. Its programs include the Homeless Veterans' Reintegration Program, the Veterans' Workforce Investment Program, Job Corps, and reentry initiatives.

U.S. Department of the Treasury/Internal Revenue Service (IRS)

Web site: http://www.eitc.irs.gov/central/main

IRS provides information and technical support for the Earned Income Tax Credit, a targeted antipoverty measure that allows lower-income working individuals and families to receive cash refunds based on income and family size, reducing their taxes.

U.S. Department of Veterans Affairs (VA)

Web site: http://www1.va.gov/homeless/

The VA, which announced a five-year plan to end veteran homelessness in 2009, is the largest federal investor in homelessness related spending. The VA operates veterans' reintegration program and the McKinney Act domiciliary care program to use surplus space in VA hospitals as shelter beds for homeless veterans and health care and transitional facilities.

Social Security Administration (SSA)

Web site: www.ssa.gov/homeless

SSA provides income support programs for elderly and disabled persons. The federal agency has focused its efforts on identifying and removing barriers that homeless individuals face in applying for SSDI or SSI benefits and developing and expanding SSDI/SSI outreach and application assistance through a Web site. SSA supported the application outreach program HOPE (Homeless Outreach Projects and Evaluation), the Department of Justice's "Going Home" project, which focuses on serious and violent offenders; the Department of Health and Human Services' project to provide training for case managers; and the Health Care for the Homeless programs.

U.S. Interagency Council on Homelessness (USICH)

Web site: http://www.usich.gov

The Interagency Council was reauthorized by the HEARTH Act in 2009 with substantially changed duties from its work during the last decade. The council has coordinated the development of the Federal Strategic Plan to Prevent and End Homelessness released in 2010. It provides local examples of strategies, information on federal funding, and other resources.

Grants.gov

Web site: http://www.grants.gov

The federal government operates an on-line system for learning about federal funding opportunities in homelessness, prevention, and mainstream programs. Grants.gov is available to any reader for searches by federal agency or other topic, including basic grant information and program highlights. Application links and background materials are generally included with site materials.

State, Provincial, and Local 10-Year Plans

This section contains listings for state and local 10-year plans both in the United States and in select countries, where the state or local plan is one often cited by practitioners as providing a results-oriented model for planning. The selected locations are generally referenced elsewhere in the book and represent a range of population and geography. These references include Web sites where the plan's results are being reported.

States

Kentucky

Web site: http://www.kyhousing.org/KICH/

The Commonwealth of Kentucky has undertaken to create a residential drug treatment program in every area of the state, based on needs identified through research for its Ten-Year Plan to End Homelessness.

Massachusetts

Web site: http://www.mass.gov

Massachusetts's joint executive-legislative commission made recommendations to the state's interagency council that have resulted in the development of eight regional networks to consolidate and reorganize the way homeless assistance and housing is delivered while reducing the need for shelter.

Michigan

Web site: http://www.thecampaigntoendhomelessness.org/

Michigan launched a statewide campaign to end homelessness with 10-year plans created for every part of the state.

North Dakota

Web site: http://www.ndhomelesscoalition.org/

North Dakota state leadership created incentives for 10 jurisdictions, including tribes, to develop 10-year plans.

Utah

Web site: http://housingworks.utah.gov/

Utah supported development of regional boards to create housing solutions to end homelessness.

Washington

Web site: http://www.commerce.wa.gov/site/478/default.aspx

State legislation required counties to develop 10-year plans and provides local communities with revenue from document recording fees to do so.

Cities and Counties

Asheville/Buncombe County, NC: *Looking Homeward: The 10-Year Plan to End Homelessness in Asheville and Buncombe County*

Web site: http://www.ashevillenc.gov/residents/housing/homeless/default.aspx?id=1584

Atlanta, GA: *Blueprint to End Homelessness in Atlanta in Ten Years*

http://www.unitedwayatlanta.org/OurWork/Homelessness/Pages/HOMELESSNESS.aspx

Boise, ID: *Boise's 10 Year Plan to Reduce and Prevent Chronic Homelessness*

Web site: http://www.cityofboise.org/Departments/Mayor/PDF/10-YearPlanFinal.07SP.pdf

Chicago, IL: *There's No Place Like a Home*

Web site: http://www.cityofchicago.org/city/en/depts/fss/supp_info/10_year_plan_to_endhomelessness.html

Denver, CO: *Denver's Road Home: Denver's Ten Year Plan to End Homelessness*

Web site: http://www.denversroadhome.org/

Fort Worth, TX: *Directions Home: Making Homelessness Rare, Short-Term and Non-Recurring in Fort Worth, Texas within Ten Years*

Web Site: http://www.fortworthgov.org/homelessness/

Indianapolis, IN: *Blueprint to End Homelessness*

Web site: http://www.chipindy.org/Blueprint.php

Minneapolis/St., Paul, MN: *Heading Home Hennepin: The Ten Year Plan to End Homelessness in Minneapolis and Hennepin County*

Web site: http://hennepin.us/headinghomehennepin

Norfolk, VA: *Blueprint to End Homelessness*

Web site: http://www.norfolk.gov/homelessness/

San Francisco, CA: *The San Francisco Plan to Abolish Chronic Homelessness*

Web site: http://www.ich.gov/slocal/plans/sanfrancisco.pdf

Sioux Falls, SD: *Blueprint: Ten-Year Plan to End Homelessness in Sioux Falls*

Web site: http://www.minnehahacounty.org/hab/docs/docs.aspx

Springfield, MA: *Homes within Reach*

Web site: http://www.springfieldcityhall.com/housing/homeless ness.0.html

Canada

Calgary, Alberta
Web sites: http://content.calgary.ca/CCA/City+Hall/Business+Units/Community+and+Neighbourhood+Services/Social+Research+Policy+and+Resources/Affordable+Housing+and+Homelessness and http://www.calgaryhomeless.com

Ottawa, Ontario
Web site: http://www.ottawa.ca/residents/housing/homeless ness/index_en.html

Vancouver, BC
Web site: http://www.streetohome.org/

Innovators

Common Ground

Web site: http://www.commonground.org

Common Ground pioneered a new model of permanent supportive housing that combines affordability, good management and design, and employment opportunity for people who are homeless. Development projects often restore properties to being neighborhood assets, and more than 4,000 individuals have been assisted to date. Projects are in New York City and State, Connecticut, and Australia. Common Ground conducts vulnerability index events in many communities.

Corporation for Supportive Housing

Web site: http://www.csh.org

CSH is a national organization focused on permanent supportive housing for people who are homeless, those with mental illness, and the reentry population. CSH works in 11 states and with local communities as an intermediary that combines research, best practices in development and operations, and resources for local partners.

The Doe Fund

Ready, Willing & Able
Web site: http://www.doe.org

"Work works" is the motto of the Ready, Willing, & Able employment, housing, and recovery program, which reaches single men in New York City and Philadelphia who have long histories of homelessness, addiction, and incarceration. Founder and President George McDonald describes the "men in blue" who enroll as those who are ready to work to succeed in a program of employment, counseling, recovery, and community. RWA has successfully graduated over 4,000 individuals to date with the key metrics of success measured as housing stability, employment, and sobriety.

Family Promise

Web site: http://www.familypromise.org/

Family Promise (Interfaith Hospitality Network) operates in partnership in communities in 40 states. The Family Promise models partners with local faith organizations to provide shelter, volunteers, social service support, and day programs to assist families in stabilizing and leaving homelessness.

Family and Senior Homeless Initiative of Denver

Web site: http://www.fshi.org

Denver's Road Home, the city's 10-year plan, and Denver Rescue Mission are the major partners with the local faith community. The mayor called on congregations to "embrace, befriend, and guide" 1,000 families experiencing homelessness over the course of the 10-year plan through mentoring teams from congregations who commit to provide a set of new relationships for families in need as they move from homelessness to stability. Teams also focus on financial management and self-sufficiency.

Pathways to Housing

Web site: http://www.pathwaystohousing.org

Pathways to Housing originated the Housing First innovation, which focuses on consumer preference for housing and access. Housing is provided first with the consumer choosing the services and the delivery of services. Pathways, named an evidence-based practice by HHS, has been replicated in New York, Philadelphia, and Washington, D.C., as well as in Canada and other countries.

Project Homeless Connect

Web site: http://www.projecthomelessconnect.com

Project Homeless Connect (PHC), a one-day event sponsored by mayors and other community leaders, mobilizes civic will to end homelessness and engages volunteers from all walks of life to meet, support, and assist people in accessing services and leaving the streets. Project Homeless Connect originated in San Francisco in 2004 and is designed to provide housing, services, and hospitality in a convenient one-day, one-stop model for people experiencing homelessness. More than 250 cities across the United States and globally have adopted the innovation. Project Homeless Connect is similar in spirit and substance to the successful volunteer one-stop service centers organized in communities across the country to assist Hurricane Katrina evacuees and to the service model provided by stand-downs.

National Organizations

American Bar Association (ABA)

Commission on Homelessness and Poverty
Web site: www.abanet.org/homeless

The ABA commission, established in 1991, consists of a staff attorney and 13 volunteer attorneys appointed by the ABA president to assist both the legal community and the general public in understanding and addressing legal and other problems of poor and homeless people through pro bono (volunteer) programs. These activities include training for lawyers and assistance in addressing local issues as well as work with state and federal government. The commission has created resources for attorneys on state and local programs to meet legal needs of homeless people, homeless "problem-solving" courts, education of homeless children, and issues affecting homeless youth.

American Round Table to Abolish Homelessness (ART)

Web site: http://www.abolitionistroundtable.com

The American Round Table is a national initiative to replicate innovative practices with state and local jurisdictional leaders implementing 10-year plans. ART provides expertise in building partnerships, knowledge of research, and peer-to-peer opportunities for leaders to learn about strategies.

Bazelon Center for Mental Health Law

Web site: http://www.bazelon.org

The Bazelon Center is a legal advocacy and public education organization for the rights of mentally disabled people including on fair housing issues. The center focuses its work on reform of public systems for people with mental disabilities, access to housing, health care, and support services, and protection against discrimination.

Catholic Charities USA

Web site: http://www.catholiccharitiesusa.org/NetCommunity/

Catholic Charities USA is a national federation of more than 600 private social services agencies, including many that traditional assist people facing hunger or homelessness. Catholic Charities is committed to reduce poverty in America by half by the year 2020, including measurable goals to reduce the number of families in emergency shelters and increase the number of affordable housing units available to low income people.

Center on Budget and Policy Priorities (CBPP)

Web site: www.cbpp.org

The center focuses on federal and state fiscal policy and programs for people of low and moderate income. CBPP publishes analysis of federal budget and tax initiatives at both the executive and legislative level and studies the impact of federal and state investment and state budget choices on populations of interest, including people living in poverty. Programs include Medicaid and the Children's Health Insurance Program, food stamps, Temporary Assistance to Needy Families, WIC and child nutrition, low-income housing programs, low-income tax credits, including the Earned Income Tax Credit (EITC) and the Child Tax Credit. The center conducts a national outreach campaign on EITC with more than 600 government and community-based partners.

Child Welfare League of America (CWLA)

Web site: http://www.cwla.org

CWLA is an association of more than 1,000 public and private nonprofit agencies that assist over 2.5 million abused and neglected children and their families each year with a wide range of services. CWLA works on issues of adolescent pregnancy and parenting, chemical dependency, parents in prison, foster care, health care, housing, and homelessness.

Children's Defense Fund (CDF)

Web site: http://www.childrensdefense.org/

CDF's goal is to educate policy makers about the needs of poor and minority children. It monitors federal and state policy and legislation on health, education, child welfare, mental health, teen pregnancy, and youth employment.

Funders Together to End Homelessness

Web site: http://funderstogether.org/

Funders Together to End Homelessness brings together foundations, corporate, and other investors focused on preventing and ending homelessness. The organization emphasizes research and collaboration and developed a statement of principles for funders.

Housing Assistance Council (HAC)

Web site: http://www.ruralhome.org

HAC has long been a voice on rural issues. The organization provides technical assistance, loans, research, and information on rural low-income housing development, especially Farmers Home Administration programs. It publishes regular reports on federal rural programs and trends in rural poverty and development.

International Downtown Association (IDA)

Web site: https://www.ida-downtown.org/eweb/

The International Downtown Association represents many business improvement districts and downtown associations, many of whom take part in initiatives to end homelessness. IDA provides technical assistance and case studies on best practice housing solutions and panhandling issues.

National Alliance to End Homelessness (NAEH)

Web site: httpo://www.naeh.org

The alliance is a coalition of corporations, service providers, and individuals that sponsors conferences and uses research and public education in its efforts to address homelessness.

National Alliance on Mental Illness (NAMI)

Web site: http://www.nami.org

This national advocacy and research organization for people with mental illness and their friends and families seeks to create a coordinated system of care. NAMI has been active in federal legislative initiatives on housing and health care for people with disabilities.

National Association for the Education of Homeless Children and Youth (NAEHCY)

Web site: http://www.naehcy.org

The organization provides support to state and local education officials on the federal education requirements for children who are homeless. It publishes awareness and best practice materials for ensuring children are enrolled, supported, and attend school.

National Association of Counties (NACo)

Web site: http://www.naco.org

NACo represents the nation's more than 3,000 counties. In some states, counties have responsibilities and resources for health and human services as well as social services and corrections. In its annual meetings, NACo has supported resolutions on ending homelessness.

National Center on Housing and Child Welfare (NCHCW)

Web site: http://www.nchcw.org/

The center focuses on housing policy solutions to improve the lives of families in the welfare system and youth. Key among these initiatives is support for the Family Unification Program (FUP), which provides housing vouchers to keep families together and children out of foster care.

National Center on Family Homelessness

Web site: http://www.familyhomelessness.org/

The center evolved from an early partnership with *Better Homes and Gardens* magazine. Its work focuses on homeless families and children.

National Coalition for the Homeless (NCH)

Web site: http://www.nationalhomeless.org/

NCH is a national network of homeless persons, activists, service providers, and others committed to addressing homelessness through public education, policy advocacy, grassroots organizing, and technical assistance. It focuses on civil rights and consumer involvement.

National Coalition for Homeless Veterans (NCHV)

Web site: www.nchv.org

NCHV serves as a liaison between branches of the federal government and community-based homeless veteran service providers. NCHV provides technical assistance on federal programs and funding for community organizations serving veterans in emergency, supportive services, and housing.

National Council of State Housing Agencies

Web site: http://www.ncsha.org/advocacy-issues/homeless-assistance

The council represents the state agencies where many federal housing resources combine with state investments.

National Governors Association (NGA)

Web site: http://www.nga.org

NGA represents the elected executive leadership of states. Its Center for Best Practices provides current information on evidence-based initiatives and offers expertise to states facing similar issues. NGA published a summary of state strategies for ending chronic homelessness.

National Health Care for the Homeless Council (NHCHC)

Web site: http://www.nhchc.org/

NHCHC represents more than 100 federal Health Care for the Homeless projects across the nation. The projects provide primary health care, mental health services, and drug and alcohol services, and the council coordinates their public policy initiatives. NHCHC publishes detailed bibliographies and manuals for practitioners and guidance on policy issues, such as health care reform and use of Medicaid.

National Law Center on Homelessness & Poverty (NLCHP)

Web site: http://www.nlchp.org

The National Law Center monitors federal agency action on several McKinney Act programs, including homeless children's education and federal surplus property and focuses on international human rights and civil rights for people who are homeless.

National League of Cities (NLC)

Web site: http://www.nlc.org

NLC represents over 190,000 smaller-sized towns and cities. It is a partner to municipal leagues in the states, which convene their cities and towns on a statewide basis. NLC provides elected officials with training, technical assistance, and models for local solutions.

National Low Income Housing Coalition (NLIHC)

Web site: http://www.nlihc.org

NLIHC is a national organization focused on education, public policy, and organizing for low-income housing. The coalition publishes resources on housing programs and policy as well as an annual report on housing affordability.

National Network for Youth (NN4Y)

Web site: http://www.nn4youth.org/

NN4Y supports community-based organizations and young people who are experiencing abuse, neglect, or homelessness. More than 1,000 local shelter agencies and state networks are members of this national network, which sponsors training, offers information on model programs, and sponsors a national telecommunications system for youth programs.

National Policy and Advocacy Coalition on Homelessness (NPACH)

Web site: http://www.npach.org/

NPACH is a national policy organization representing community providers on issues related to federal homelessness policy and investment.

National Student Campaign against Hunger & Homelessness

Web site: http://www.studentsagainsthunger.org

The student organization sponsors a national hunger and homelessness awareness week every year, to educate the campus community, increase community service, and build campus and community coalitions. Campuses and communities participate during the week before Thanksgiving each year by organizing education, service, and advocacy events.

United States Conference of Mayors (USCM)

Web site: http://www.usmayors.org

The United States Conference of Mayors is a national organization of the mayors of the cities in the United States over 30,000 in population. USCM provides support and partnership on the issue of homelessness and has passed numerous resolutions in support of key strategies to prevent and end homelessness. The Task Force on Hunger and Homelessness conducts an annual survey of member cities.

State and Local Homeless Organizations

Most states have at least one nonprofit organization focused on issues of homelessness and housing for homeless or low-income people. In addition, most large and medium-sized cities have at least one of these organizations. State coalitions can provide information on specific activities, such as state legislative action or initiatives on behalf of homeless people. Most of the state organizations as well as the local coalitions publish newsletters and actively seek volunteers and other resources. They can also provide referrals to organizations and services operated by homeless people for other homeless people.

Directories of state and local homeless organizations can be found at the Web site of the National Coalition for the Homeless at http://www.nationalhomeless.org/.

International Organizations

Comité Européen de Coordination de l'Habitat Social (CECODHAS) European Liaison Committee for Social Housing

Web site: http://www.cecodhas.org

CECODHAS is a nonprofit organization that promotes the work of 45 regional and national social housing organizations in the European Union. It fosters the exchange of ideas and experience among its members, provides an information service for its members, and promotes good practice through conferences, seminars, reports and other activities. CECODHAS monitors developments in European community law, provides its members with improved access to European funding, and campaigns for the right to a decent home for all Europeans.

European Anti-Poverty Network

Web site: http://www.eapn.org

EAPN brings together grassroots nongovernmental organizations representing people affected by social exclusion in all the member-states of the European Union. EAPN provides members with training, policy analysis, and representation.

European Federation of National Organizations Working with the Homeless (Fédération Européenne d'Associations Nationales Travaillant Avec Les Sans-Abri) (FEANTSA)

Web site: http://www.feantsa.org

FEANTSA is an international nongovernmental organization that brings together charitable and not-for-profit organizations that provide a wide range of vital services to homeless people in all the European Union member-states and also in other European countries. Its goal is to promote and support the work of nongovernmental organizations that provide services to meet the needs of homeless people. FEANTSA aims to raise public awareness about the situation of homeless people and of the need to recognize and realize the right to decent and affordable housing.

Habitact

Web site: http://www.habitact.eu/

Habitact is a new peer-to-peer initiative for policy exchange regarding local homeless strategies and was launched with FEANTSA's support. Habitact was a response to the need for best practice information and strategies from local authorities in Europe. A key feature of the EU's social inclusion strategy is the so-called Open Method of Coordination (OMC), which seeks to support comparisons across national boundaries. With similarities to the U.S. idea of seeing homelessness as a national problem with local solutions, Habitact was founded by cities to improve the exchange of ideas and results in initiatives to address homelessness.

International Network of Street Newspapers

Web site: http://www.streetnewsservice.org/

People who are homeless in a variety of countries contribute to and distribute "street newspapers," which offers a media voice to their stories and viewpoints. Volunteer news professionals and others support the work of street newspapers.

Sisters of Mercy

Web site: http://www.sistersofmercy.org

The international work of the Sisters of Mercy is focused on the housing needs of people, especially women, people who are homeless, and elders. Mercy Housing and the Mercy Foundation operate in North and South America, Australia, Great Britain, and Ireland, home of the order's founder, Catherine McCauley. In Australia, for example, the Mercy Foundation has been a leader in national initiatives to prevent and end homelessness.

United Nations Centre for Human Settlements (UNCHS)

Web site: http://www.unchs.org

UNCHS is the lead agency concerned with issues of housing and shelter. The United Nations Human Settlements Program, UN-HABITAT, promotes adequate shelter in all parts of the world. Key documents about the UN effort include the Vancouver Declaration on Human Settlements, the Habitat Agenda, the Istanbul Declaration on Human Settlements, and the Declaration on Cities and Other Human Settlements in the New Millennium. World Habitat Day is marked on the first Monday of every October.

England

Department of Communities and Local Government

Web site: http://www.communities.gov.uk/housing/homelessness

The department houses the homelessness initiatives of the national government as well as research and progress reports. Materials are available on the Rough Sleepers Initiative, youth homelessness, and the work of local government,

Shelter

Web site: www.shelter.org.uk

SHELTER is the largest homelessness charity in the United Kingdom and publishes a variety of fact sheets and self-help resources on homelessness. It maintains a national help line that tracks the demand for shelter. It publishes a variety of reports on policy, including Best Value and Homelessness.

Canada

Human Resources and Skills Development Canada (HRSDC)

Web site: http://www.hrsdc.gc.ca/eng/homelessness/

Human Resources and Skills Development Canada (HRSDC) is a department of the Government of Canada. Canada's Homelessness Partnering Strategy (HPS) is a responsibility of the department. HPS invests in Housing First, provides support to communities, and fosters partnership and collaboration.

Federation of Canadian Municipalities (FCM)

Web site: http://www.fcm.ca/English

FCM represents local government, including large, small, and rural jurisdictions. FCM's action plan on homelessness is focused on housing and chronic homelessness. Its Big City Mayors Caucus includes mayors who have developed local 10-year plans.

Australia

Department of Families Housing, Community Services, and Indigenous Affairs

Web site: http://www.fahcsia.gov.au/sa/housing/overview/Pages/default.aspx

The department oversees the national government's homeless initiative, launched with a white paper in 2008 and focuses on the three goals of prevention, improving services, and breaking the cycle of homelessness.

Homelessness Australia

Web site: http://www.homelessnessaustralia.org.au/site/index.php

Homelessness Australia is a key national nongovernmental organization that has been central to development of the country's national government white paper. The organization represents people who are homeless, their service providers, and other partners.

8

Resources

Introduction

This chapter covers general reference materials on homelessness. Literally thousands of books, research articles, news stories, and dissertations have been written on homelessness in the United States, though print coverage of all sorts diminished during the 1990s and then saw a resurgence as new national initiatives gained traction. In the last decade, daily headlines on homelessness and its solutions have once again become standard. Many resources related to homelessness now exist only as electronic tools.

While most of the resources included here are from the last decade, others are important print contributions that have stood the test of time and continue to offer insight into the roots of homelessness and the responses to it. The goal of this chapter is to identify key resources that are accessible and nontechnical and together offer a variety of views, including first-person accounts. Entries that offer an introduction or pathway to some of the numerous topics associated with individual and family homelessness are included, but resources that are hard to locate or highly technical have been kept to a minimum.

This list includes a few special issues of professional journals that have been devoted to the issue, but the chapter does not include the numerous articles published in mainstream media or academic journals or the useful, detailed reports issued by many of the organizations listed in chapter 7. Those organizations often publish regular newsletters and Web listings of the materials they distribute, and, increasingly, provide access to publications solely via their Web sites. The Web sites of major U.S. government agencies are included, recognizing that many agencies now make their reports and guides available electronically and that some agencies and organizations utilize Webcasts, Webinars, and audio conferences to disseminate information. A few agencies support free-standing electronic clearinghouses on homelessness resources.

General References

Barak, Gregg. ***Gimme Shelter: A Social History of Homelessness.*** **New York: Praeger, 1992.**

The author is a criminologist who analyzes homelessness as a crime against those who experience it. He also examines the history of advocacy efforts, both in public education and litigation.

Baumohl, Jim, editor. ***Homelessness in America.*** **Phoenix, AZ: Oryx Press, 1996.**

This collection of articles by advocates, researchers, providers, and academics focuses on causes, known data, and solutions for contemporary homelessness. Included are discussions of definition, rural homelessness, veterans, and children.

Baxter, Ellen, and Kim Hopper. ***Private Lives/Public Spaces: Homeless Adults on the Streets of New York City.*** **New York: Community Service Society, New York, 1981.**

This early study primarily reports on the causes of contemporary homelessness as they were first revealed in New York and other cities. It describes in detail the procedures and operations of the existing public and private shelters and the ways that homeless persons survive on the streets.

Blodgett, Lynn. ***Finding Grace: The Face of America's Homeless.*** **San Rafael, CA: Earth Aware Editions, 2007.**

Photographer Lynn Blodgett, also a businessman, has traveled across the United States both for his work and to raise funds for homeless programs. He began photographing people he met who were homeless. The results are combined here with narrative.

Bratt, Rachel G., Michael E. Stone, and Chester Hartman. ***A Right to Housing: Foundation for a New Social Agenda.*** **Philadelphia: Temple University Press, 2006.**

The authors are all academics with long-term involvement in housing policy and research. This volume of essays examines a broad range of housing issues and actors and the potential for universal access to housing.

Brickner, Philip, Linda Keen Scharer, Barbara Conanan, Alexander Elvy, Marianne Savarese, editors. ***Health Care of Homeless People.*** **New York: Springer Publishing Company, 1985.**

An overview of health issues for homeless people is presented, with special sections on medical disorders, mental health and illness, the organization of health services, and models of health care for homeless poor people. The offerings are by a total of 24 different authors or collaborators, with expertise on subjects ranging from infestations to alcoholism to nutrition.

Burt, Martha R., Laudan Y. Aron, Edgar Lee, and Jesse Valente, editors. ***Helping America's Homeless: Emergency Shelter or Affordable Housing.*** **Washington, D.C.: Urban Institute Press, 2001.**

The data from the National Survey of Homeless Assistance Providers and Clients (NSHAPC), is the basis of this book. Included in the content is an examination of the size of the homeless population, the distribution of the population, causes of their homelessness, and the duration of their homelessness. Homeless assistance programs are discussed in communities of various sizes.

Burt, Martha R. ***Over the Edge: The Growth of Homelessness in the 1980s.*** **Washington, D.C.: Urban Institute Press and Russell Sage Foundation, 1991.**

Persistent homelessness is related to structural changes in the nation, according to the author, who surveyed numerous cities and interviewed homeless people seeking services. She calls for increased low-rent housing production, more housing subsidies, restructured employment (including education and training), and more community-based care.

Burt, Martha, Laudan Aron, Toby Douglas, Jesse Valente, Edgar Lee, and Britta Iwen. ***Homelessness: Programs and the People They Serve. Findings of the National Survey of Homeless Assistance Providers and Clients (NSHAPC).*** **Washington, D.C.: The Urban Institute, 1999.**

The authors analyze the results of a 1996 survey of homeless programs and homeless people that was sponsored by 12 federal agencies.

Cisneros, Henry, Jack Kemp, Nicolas Retsinas, and Kent W. Colton. ***Our Communities, Our Homes: Pathways to Housing and Homeownership in America's Cities and States.*** **Cambridge, MA: Joint Center for Housing Studies at Harvard University, 2007.**

The authors are former HUD secretaries Cisneros and Kemp, Assistant Secretary Retsinas, and National Association of Homebuilders CEO Colton. Their wide-ranging knowledge and insight on housing issues includes an examination of successful strategies to end chronic homelessness.

Cisneros, Henry, Jack Kemp, Nicolas Retsinas, and Kent W. Colton. ***Opportunity and Progress: A Bipartisan Platform for National Housing Policy.*** **Cambridge, MA: Joint Center for Housing Studies at Harvard University, 2004.**

Innovation in solving housing problems in the nation can transcend partisan debate, according to the authors, who have been leaders in policy in federal and business positions. Housing must be a national priority based on partnership across the public and private sectors.

Coates, Robert C. ***A Street Is Not a Home: Solving America's Homeless Dilemma.*** **Amherst, NY: Prometheus Books, 1990.**

The author served for many years as a San Diego municipal court judge, giving him unique exposure to many of the issues related to homelessness. Coates's personal and professional experience add depth to considerable research on the myriad problems of America's homeless. Judge Coates supports solution-oriented strategies, including community support and resources to address mental illness.

Collins, Jim. ***Good to Great: Why Some Companies Make the Leap . . . and Others Don't.*** **New York: HarperBusiness, 2001.**

Collins is a business thinker and writer whose spent five years studying more than 1,400 companies that moved from good to great and those that didn't. He consulted with jurisdictional leaders at the first national summit convened by the federal Interagency Council on Homelessness to focus on his insights about "disciplined people, disciplined thought, disciplined action" and the importance of "the right people on the bus" for success.

Culhane, Dennis P., and Steven Hornburg, editors. ***Understanding Homelessness: New Policy and Research Perspectives.*** **Washington, D.C.: Fannie Mae Foundation, 1997.**

The three sections of this book represent the work of some of the key researchers who have studied the growth of homelessness and its characteristics. Here they examine means of defining homelessness, counting and tracking homeless people, the causes and prevention of homelessness, and possible policy and research initiatives.

Currie, Elliott. ***Reckoning: Drugs, the Cities, and the America Future.*** **New York: Hill and Wang, 1993.**

The epidemic of urban drug use is already known as a symptom of larger social ills, but the author dissects the documentation on when drug use occurs in poor families, especially immigrants, and how this plague has been increased by the destruction of poor communities through economic policy, housing loss, and other factors. He suggests ways that employment and redirected spending can end or prevent the resulting problems, including homelessness.

Day, Dorothy. ***The Long Loneliness: An Autobiography.*** **New York: Harper and Row, 1981.**

In the decades preceding the 1980s, there were two significant sources of help for homeless people: the traditional missions and Salvation Army establishments and the Catholic Worker Houses of Hospitality spread around the nation. This book, by the co-founder of the CW movement and its newspaper editor for over 30 years, tells the story of the Depression-era founding of the small shelters and soup lines that still exist today and the story of her longtime leadership on issues of social justice, peace, and racial equality.

Devine, Joel, Beth Rubin, and James Wright. *Beside the Golden Door: Policy Politics, and the Homeless.* New Brunswick, NJ: Aldine Transaction, 1998.

This book is written for a broad audience and covers issues ranging from poverty to the loss of housing affordable to those with little income, from enumeration issues to factors such as mental illness and substance abuse. Urban and rural issues are examined, and there is coverage of street homelessness among children in both North and Latin America.

Crowley, Sheila. *Out of Reach: Renters in the Great Recession, the Crisis.* National Low Income Housing Coalition, September 2010. Washington, D.C.: National Low Income Housing Coalition.

Detailed information is provided on the state-by-state basis of the gap between the cost of decent housing and what people can afford to pay as determined by HUD's annual fair market rent levels. Profiles are offered of the gap faced by persons earning the minimum wage in various housing markets as well as those renters who rely on public assistance for their income.

Ellen, Ingrid Gould, and Brendan O'Flaherty. *How to House the Homeless.* New York: Russell Sage Publications, 2010.

The authors examines pathways out of homelessness as well as prevention strategies. The housing market and the role of regulation are highlighted, and a section is devoted to "managing risk" that people necessarily face in life, or the role of "bad luck" in homelessness.

Gardner, Chris. *The Pursuit of Happyness.* New York: Amistead, 2006.

Chris Gardner tells his story of life as a homeless single father on the streets of San Francisco. With almost unrelenting optimism in his search for stability, Gardner studies at night and wins a prestigious internship in a financial firm while caring for his son between shelters, hotels, and the bus station.

Gladwell, Malcolm. ***The Tipping Point: How Little Things Can Make a Big Difference.*** **Boston: Back Bay Books, 2002.**

Gladwell's writing often focuses on unusual ideas or counterintuitive findings, and this book particularly influenced strategies on homelessness. For many working on the issue, the idea of reaching a "tipping point" that could produce new results was captured in this work. Gladwell particularly made the point that modest new resources had to be concentrated on the most visible part of a social problem to achieve the visible result that could lead to greater investment.

Hattery, Angela. ***Prisoner Re-entry and Social Capital: The Long Road to Reintegration.*** **Lanham, MD: Lexington Books, 2010.**

Reentry is a national issue impacting homelessness, as ex-prisoners need stable and legal housing, income, and necessary services to reintegrate successfully. Twenty-five men and women who were recently released from prison were interviewed for this book, which explores barriers as well as needs. The book also emphasizes social capital as a factor in reentry.

Hombs, Mary Ellen, and Mitch Snyder. ***Homelessness in America: A Forced March to Nowhere. 2nd ed.*** **Washington, D.C.: Community for Creative Non-Violence, 1983.**

This national survey of homelessness and its origins was first released in conjunction with the original 1982 congressional hearings of the same title. When it was subsequently updated the following year, it included the estimates of national homelessness that engendered national controversy.

Hopper, Kim. ***Reckoning with Homelessness.*** **Ithaca, NY: Cornell University Press, 2003.**

Hopper was one of two anthropologists talking to people on New York City's streets in the early 1980s. Here he combines 20 years of professional work with a long history of activism, to put homelessness into historical perspective and highlight the African American population generally overlooked in contemporary literature. Hopper includes individual stories of people living on the streets and finding refuge elsewhere.

Hubbard, Jim. ***Lives Turned Upside Down: Homeless Children in Their Own Words and Photographs.*** **Fullerton, CA: Aladdin, 2007.**

As a professional news photographer working across the world in a long career, Hubbard understood the power of pictures to tell stories and also the eye that children have for their own world. In starting the Shooting Back Media Center with professional volunteer photographers to mentor homeless young people, Hubbard provided a positive framework for children and their families to communicate their everyday life. This book is suitable for young readers.

Interagency Council on Homelessness. ***Priority Home! The Federal Plan to Break the Cycle of Homelessness.*** **Washington, D.C.: U.S. Department of Housing and Urban Development, 1994.**

This report was produced after a lengthy national process in response to the Executive Order on Homelessness signed by President Clinton at the beginning of his administration. This report combines data with the insights of provider and policymakers across the nation.

Jencks, Christopher. ***The Homeless.*** **Boston: Harvard University Press, 1995.**

The author focuses on the "visible homeless" and discusses the size of the population and possible solutions for their homelessness.

Joint Center for Housing Studies at Harvard University. ***The State of the Nation's Housing 2010.*** **Cambridge, MA: Joint Center for Housing Studies at Harvard University, 2010.**

The center annually looks at factors influencing housing costs, the housing market, and the nation's stock, especially of housing that is affordable. In this report with a background as the economy begins to add jobs and housing prices shift in the wake of foreclosures and short sales, the challenges in rental housing and homeownership are identified.

Joint Center for Housing Studies at Harvard University. ***America's Rental Housing: The Key to a Balanced National Policy.***

Cambridge, MA: Joint Center for Housing Studies at Harvard University, 2008.

Rental housing, whether assisted or not, will provide the housing solution for people experiencing homelessness or at risk of homelessness. This report looks at affordability, production, and demand for rental units in the nation.

Katz, Michael. ***In the Shadow of the Poorhouse: A Social History of Welfare in America.*** **New York: Basic Books, 1996.**

Katz is an historian at the University of Pennsylvania and examines the history of welfare programs in the United States. He focuses on the often competing goals of initiatives and the possibility of reform in the light of 200 years of history.

Kozol, Jonathan. ***Rachel and Her Children: Homeless Families in America.*** **New York: Three Rivers Press, 2006.**

This vivid account of life in the welfare hotels of New York City, first published in 1989, demonstrates not only the financial waste of this method for serving homeless families but also the damage done to young lives and struggling parents. Alongside the personal stories told by mothers, fathers, and children are the chilling statistics that explain how poverty works in daily life.

Kusmer, Kenneth L. ***Down and Out, on the Road: The Homeless in American History.*** **New York: Oxford University Press, 2003.**

Homelessness of the 19th and early 20th century is a focus in this book, which offers an historical perspective. Issues such as work and criminalization and events such as the Civil War and Great Depression provide context.

LeMieux, Richard. ***Breakfast at Sally's: One Homeless Man's Inspirational Journey.*** **New York: Skyhorse Publishing, 2009.**

Before a fall into homelessness precipitated by a failed business and family breakup, the author had his own publishing company and a home and possessions reflecting his success. After he was evicted, at age 60, he was homeless and eating breakfast at "Sally's" as the Salvation Army is often called. His writing was done on a typewriter and reflected his encounters and thoughts as he weathered the experience with a determined sprit.

Levinson, David. *Encyclopedia of Homelessness.* Thousand Oaks, CA: Sage Publishing, 2004.

This two-volume work with contributions by authors from every field related to homelessness includes detailed lists of a variety of resources, such as films, biographies, and street newspapers, as well as brief essays on hundreds of topic areas.

Levy, Jay S. *Homeless Narratives & Pretreatment Pathways: From Words to Housing.* Ann Arbor, MI: Loving Healing Press, 2010.

The author offers stories of individuals that convey the necessary elements of effective engagement on the streets with people with mental illness. The challenges and principles that accompany pretreatment work with mental illness, addiction, and health problems are addressed, as are case management and advocacy and integration of services and housing.

Liebow, Elliot. *Tell Them Who I Am.* New York: Penguin, 1995.

The author wrote the groundbreaking and widely hailed *Tally's Corner* in 1967 to describe the life of so-called street corner men in a black neighborhood of Washington, D.C. After years of volunteering, observing, and interviewing homeless women in shelters in the Maryland suburbs of Washington, D.C., he provides this picture of the women's individual stories as homeless persons as well as his own views of the broader economic, social, and political forces that cause and continue homelessness.

Lopez, Steve. *The Soloist.* New York: Berkley Trade, 2010.

Los Angeles Times columnist Steve Lopez happens on homeless cellist Nathaniel Ayres on the city's streets. Ayres was once a promising musician who was beset by schizophrenia and became homeless. When a bond forms as Lopez writes about Ayres, opportunities develop for housing and support, as well as family reconnection. This book represents the larger story related by Lopez in a series of columns and eventually seen in a feature film.

McNamee, John P. *Diary of a City Priest.* Kansas City: Sheed & Ward, 1993.

For more than 25 years, Father John McNamee was a priest in a poor parish in Philadelphia. Here he tells of the daily events at his door, as he meets and supports those who are his neighbors in need.

Miller, William. *Dorothy Day: A Biography*. New York: Harper and Row, 1982.

This biography of Catholic Worker co-founder Dorothy Day offers a candid portrait of her life and work in the social justice movement.

Murray, Liz. *Breaking Night: A Memoir of Forgiveness, Survival, and My Journey from Homeless to Harvard*. New York: Hyperion, 2010.

Liz Murray first came to the nation's attention when a made-for-TV movie told her story. Homeless at 15 and later enrolled in Harvard University, Murray became an example of personal determination and triumph. When Liz's mother, who suffers from schizophrenia and drug abuse, is institutionalized, Liz and her sister stay with their addicted father. When their mother returns, also diagnosed with AIDS, the family is torn apart by circumstances and eventually Liz becomes homeless. Determined to succeed, she focuses on school and wins a *New York Times* scholarship that allows her to attend Harvard.

National Academy of Science, Institute of Medicine. *Homelessness, Health and Human Needs*. Washington, D.C.: National Academy Press, 1988.

This controversial report had a congressional mandate to assess the provision of health care services to homeless people. The resulting work provides background data and recommendations on housing, income, employment, mental illness, and deinstitutionalization as these subjects relate to the problem. The document was debated on its release, when 10 of the 13 experts who contributed to it released a dissenting report, calling for national action on housing, wages, and benefits in order to fight homelessness.

Rader, Victoria. *Signal Through the Flames: Mitch Snyder and America's Homeless*. Kansas City, MO: Sheed & Ward, 1986.

The work of Washington, D.C.'s Community for Creative Non-Violence is explored here from a campaign viewpoint, with the development of the organization's various public efforts for peace and justice explored from inception to retrospective analysis. Significant insight into the workings of the community result from community members as well as the use of the group's extensive archives on its work.

Rossi, Peter. ***Without Shelter: Homelessness in the 1980s.*** **New York: Priority Press Publications, a Twentieth Century Fund paper, 1989.**

This volume examines some of the recent growth of homelessness, with a focus on research studies that have attempted to assess the problem.

Rowe, Michael. ***Crossing the Border: Encounters between Homeless People and Outreach.*** **Los Angeles: University of California Press, 1999.**

The first lengthy study of outreach work to the mentally ill homeless, this book depicts both a particular group of homeless people and their interactions with those who try to help them. The author was Director of the New Haven ACCESS outreach project.

Scott, Susan. ***All Our Sisters: Stories of Homeless Women in Canada.*** **Aurora, ON: Garamond Press, 2007.**

The author interviewed more than 60 women who represent the range of circumstances in which homelessness and risk is present. Among the situations addressed are poverty, domestic violence, addiction, abuse, and substandard housing.

Seider, Scott. ***Shelter: Where Harvard Meets the Homeless.*** **New York: Continuum, 2010.**

For more than 25 years, Harvard students have volunteered at the nation's only student-run night shelter. The effort unites two very disparate populations in Harvard Square.

Sheehan, Susan. ***Is There No Place on Earth for Me?*** **New York: Houghton Mifflin, 1982.**

This carefully detailed account of the repeated hospitalization and treatment of Sylvia Frumkin, a chronically mentally ill woman in New York, paints a careful portrait of the deficiencies of the public mental health system and the toll of mental illness on one family.

Shipler, David K. ***The Working Poor: Invisible in America.*** **New York: Knopf, 2004.**

Widely published as a reporter at major mainstream media, Shipler here offers insight into the lives of the working poor, those working on the margins of the U.S. economy, and the risk they face in struggling to survive. The book won a Pulitzer Prize.

Slesnick, Natasha. ***Our Runaway and Homeless Youth: A Guide to Understanding.*** **Santa Barbara, CA: Praeger, 2004.**

Young adults who are homeless, whether runaways, throwaways, or living outside families, are underserved with strategies and resources specific to their needs. The stories of four such young adults are used to describe the reasons for their homelessness and the realities of homeless life.

Tidwell, Mike. ***In the Shadow of the White House.*** **Rocklin, CA: Prima Publishing, 1992.**

Images of homeless single men as users of drugs and alcohol abound; for those who work to pull themselves out of addiction, the road is hard and unwelcoming: a daily struggle with recovery, no transportation, no resume, few chances at employment that pays enough to acquire housing or reunite a family. The author tells in gritty detail the efforts—frequently unsuccessful—of the men he encountered as a drug counselor in a transitional housing program in Washington, D.C.

Torrey, E. Fuller. ***Nowhere to Go: The Tragic Odyssey of the Homeless Mentally Ill.*** **New York: Harper & Row Publishers, 1988.**

The careless depopulation of public mental hospitals resulted in the creation of community mental health centers and a vast new federal government structure of ready financing. But the seriously mentally ill, whose plight was supposed to be bettered by these developments, instead were displaced by the "worried well" who sought treatment at these facilities, and they found themselves unable to reenter hospitals that had tightened admissions standards.

Tsemberis, Sam. ***Housing First: The Pathways Model to End Homelessness for People with Mental Illness and Addiction.*** **Center City, MN: Hazelden Publishing, 2010.**

A step-by-step manual and DVD on the policies, practices, and structure of a Housing First program that conforms to the Pathway to Housing model. The book includes client stories, information on structure for support teams, and useful lessons.

Wolf, Geralyn. ***Down and Out in Providence: Memoir of a Homeless Bishop.*** **New York: Crossroad Publishing Company, 2005.**

Bishop Geralyn Wolf was the first Episcopal female dean of a cathedral in the United States and is bishop of Rhode Island. Preparing for a sabbatical after 25 years of ministry, Wolf moves to the streets of Providence, RI, for a month, experiencing shelters and meal programs, winter weather, and friendship.

Wright, James. ***Address Unknown: The Homeless in America.*** **New Brunswick, NJ: Aldine Transaction, 2009.**

The author has published on homelessness since the mid-1980s, addressing many facets of the issue, including housing, mental addiction, and health care, as well as the populations of children, families, elders, veterans, and youth. Here he looks at the housing market role that he believes would render many poor people homeless absent any disability or challenge

Homelessness Policy and Research

Journals

Housing Policy Debate

This research and policy journal was published for most of the last 20 years by the Fannie Mae Foundation and then by the Metropolitan Institute at Virginia Tech (MI). The commercial publisher Routledge will begin issuing the journal for MI in 2010 as a print subscription and on-line download. *Housing Policy Debate* is peer reviewed and includes original research on key topics of U.S. policy on housing and homelessness.

Following are selected articles from the journal relevant to homelessness.

Franklin J. James, "Counting homeless persons with surveys of users of services for the homeless," Housing Policy Debate, 2152-050X, Volume 2, Issue 3 (1991): 733–753.

Kim Hopper, "Homelessness old and new: The matter of definition," Housing Policy Debate, 2152-050X, Volume 2, Issue 3 (1991): 755–813.

Deborah L. Dennis, Irene S. Levine, and Fred C. Osher, "The physical and mental health status of homeless adults," Housing Policy Debate, 2152-050X, Volume 2, Issue 3(1991): 815–835.

Barrett A. Lee, Bruce G. Link, and Paul A. Toro, "Images of the homeless: Public views and media messages," Housing Policy Debate, 2152-050X, Volume 2, Issue 3 (1991): 649–682.

Eleanor Chelimsky, "Politics, policy making, data, and the homeless," Housing Policy Debate, 2152-050X, Volume 2, Issue 3 (1991): 683–697.

Michael L. Dennis, "Changing the conventional rules: Surveying homeless people in nonconventional locations," Housing Policy Debate, 2152-050X, Volume 2, Issue 3 (1991): 699–732.

James Baumohl and Robert B. Huebner, "Alcohol and other drug problems among the homeless: Research, practice, and future directions," Housing Policy Debate, 2152-050X, Volume 2, Issue 3 (1991): 837–866.

Eric N. Lindblom, "Toward a comprehensive homelessness-prevention strategy," Housing Policy Debate, 2152-050X, Volume 2, Issue 3 (1991): 957–1025.

Peter H. Rossi, "Strategies for homeless research in the 1990s," Housing Policy Debate, 2152-050X, Volume 2, Issue 3 (1991): 1027–1055.

Cushing N. Dolbeare, "Federal homeless social policies for the 1990s," Housing Policy Debate, 2152-050X, Volume 2, Issue 3 (1991): 1057–1094.

Charles D. Cowan. "Estimating census and survey undercounts through multiple service contacts," Housing Policy Debate, 2152-050X, Volume 2, Issue 3 (1991): 867–882.

Douglas L. Anderton, "Using local longitudinal records to estimate transient and resident homeless populations," Housing Policy Debate, 2152-050X, Volume 2, Issue 3 (1991): 883–900.

James D. Wright and Beth A. Rubin, "Is homelessness a housing problem?" Housing Policy Debate, 2152-050X, Volume 2, Issue 3 (1991): 937–956.

Anna Kondratas, "Estimates and public policy: The politics of numbers," Housing Policy Debate, 2152-050X, Volume 2, Issue 3 (1991): 629–647.

Christopher Walker, "Federal homeless information needs and local practice," Housing Policy Debate, 2152-050X, Volume 2, Issue 3(1991), 617–627.

David S. Cordray and Georgine M. Pion, "What's behind the numbers? Definitional issues in counting the homeless," Housing Policy Debate, 2152-050X, Volume 2, Issue 3 (1991): 585–616.

Dennis P. Culhane, Edmund F. Dejowski, Julie Ibañez, Elizabeth Needham, Irene Macchia, "Public shelter admission rates in Philadelphia and New York City: The implications of turnover for sheltered population counts," Housing Policy Debate, 2152-050X, Volume 5, Issue 2 (1994): 107–140.

Leonard F. Heumann, "Assisted living in public housing: A case study of mixing frail elderly and younger persons with chronic mental illness and substance abuse histories," Housing Policy Debate, 2152-050X, Volume 7, Issue 3 (1996): 447–471.

Dennis P. Culhane, Chang-Moo Lee, and Susan M. Wachter, "Where the homeless come from: A study of the prior address distribution of families admitted to public shelters in New York City and Philadelphia," Housing Policy Debate, 2152-050X, Volume 7, Issue 2 (1996): 327–365.

Ellen L. Bassuk, Jennifer N. Perloff, and Ree Dawson, "Multiply homeless families: The insidious impact of violence," Housing Policy Debate, 2152-050X, Volume 12, Issue 2 (2001): 299–320.

Martha R. Burt, "Homeless families, singles, and others: Findings from the 1996 national survey of homeless assistance providers and clients," Housing Policy Debate, 2152-050X, Volume 12, Issue 4 (2001): 737–780.

Rae Bridgman, "Housing chronically homeless women: 'Inside' a safe haven," Housing Policy Debate, 2152-050X, Volume 13, Issue 1 (2002): 51–81.

Dennis P. Culhane, Stephen Metraux, and Trevor Hadley, "Public service reductions associated with placement of homeless persons with severe mental illness in supportive housing," Housing Policy Debate, 2152-050X, Volume 13, Issue 1 (2002): 107–163.

Lenore Monello Schloming and Skip Schloming, "Comment on Chester Hartman and David Robinson's 'Evictions: The hidden housing problem,'" Housing Policy Debate, 2152-050X, Volume 14, Issue 4 (2003): 529–540.

Ellen L. Bassuk and Stephanie Geller, "The role of housing and services in ending family homelessness," Housing Policy Debate, 2152-050X, Volume 17, Issue 4 (2006): 781–806.

Dennis P. Culhane, Stephen Metraux, Jung Min Park, Maryanne Schretzman, and Jesse Valente, "Testing a typology of family homelessness based on patterns of public shelter utilization in four U.S. jurisdictions: Implications for policy and program planning," Housing Policy Debate, 2152-050X, Volume 18, Issue 1 (2007): 1–28.

Martha R. Burt, "Comment on Dennis P. Culhane et al.'s 'Testing a typology of family homelessness based on patterns of public shelter utilization in four U.S. jurisdictions: Implications for policy and program planning,'" Housing Policy Debate, 2152-050X, Volume 18, Issue 1 (2007): 43–57.

Fred Karnas, "Comment on Dennis P. Culhane et al.'s 'Testing a typology of family homelessness based on patterns of public shelter utilization in four U.S. jurisdictions: Implications for policy and program planning,'" Housing Policy Debate, 2152-050X, Volume 18, Issue 1 (2007): 59–67.

Ellen L. Bassuk, "Comment on Dennis P. Culhane et al.'s 'Testing a typology of family homelessness based on patterns of public shelter utilization in four U.S. jurisdictions: Implications for policy and program planning,'" Housing Policy Debate, 2152-050X, Volume 18, Issue 1(2007): 29–41.

Hilary Botein; Andrea Hetling, "Permanent supportive housing for domestic violence victims: program theory and client perspectives," Housing Policy Debate, 2152-050X, Volume 20, Issue 2 (2010): 185–208.

Special Journal Issues

American Journal of Orthopsychiatry. Special section on homelessness and parenting. Vol. 79, No. 3 (2009): 291.

Journal of Behavioral Health Services & Research. Vol. 37, No. 2 (April 2010).

Special issue on the Federal Collaborative Initiative to End Chronic Homelessness. Publication of the National Council for Community Behavioral Healthcare.

Journal of Primary Prevention. Special Issue on Homelessness and Mental Illness (2007): 28.

The Open Health Services and Policy Journal (2010): 3, 53–70. Olivet, Jeffrey, Ellen Bassuk, Emily Elstad, Rachael Kenney, and Lauren Jassil, authors. Outreach and Engagement in Homeless Services: A Review of the Literature.

Nonprint Resources

Materials that are important reference sources for understanding homelessness are increasingly available through nonprint sources. Over the last decade, many sectors addressing homelessness have turned to purely electronic means of distribution. Some of the primary resources on DVDs and accessible through the Internet are included in this chapter.

DVDs

Several strong films on homelessness have emerged in the last several years, many starting as feature films depicting true stories. DVDs now make these and other works broadly available. While there are numerous local productions, the selected list included here focuses on some of the popular media with well-known names that allowed a range of people to be depicted: a homeless father, homeless youth, people with mental illness, and families.

Some of the issues associated with homelessness include addiction, mental illness, street life, family violence, and death. These can be challenging images for people of all ages and backgrounds. It is highly recommended that films and videos be screened before use in any group setting. Many distributors have additional on-line information about the films, and some productions routinely include discussion guides and advocacy material to assist viewers with understanding the material shown. Librarians can also provide assistance in locating appropriate viewing material for various audiences.

The Blind Side (2009)

Directed by John Lee Hancock, this is the true story of Michael Oher, homeless as a young adult in Memphis and depicted here by Quinton Aaron. Oher's mother used drugs and his father was in and out of prison. Sandra Bullock plays Leigh Anne Touhy, who offers a room to the young man and then adopts him. His new father enrolls him in high school football, and the film tells the story of his struggles. Oher succeeds to become a first-round draft pick for the Baltimore Ravens in the 2009 NFL draft.

Dark Days (2001)

Directed by Marc Singer, who also appears in the film, this story reveals the lives of people who are homeless and living in tunnels and underground spaces in New York City. Filmed over two years, it depicts some of the individuals transformed by their eventual move into housing of their own when forced out by sweeps of the area. The film won the Grand Jury prize for cinematography, the Freedom of Expression award, and an audience award at the 2000 Sundance Film Festival.

Empress Hotel (2009)

Directed by Irving Saraf and Allie Light, this film tells the story of individuals leaving homelessness and living in the Empress Hotel. The Empress is one of the San Francisco housing initiatives called Direct Access to Housing, which has innovated a model that succeeds for some of the longest term and mostly costly people experiencing homelessness.

Entertaining Angels (1996)

Directed by Michael Brindley, this is the feature film story of the life and work of Dorothy Day, young journalist and cofounder of the Catholic Worker. Featuring Moira Kelley as Day and Martin Sheen as Peter Maurin, her colleague, the film shows his vision for the work and his life of poverty.

Homeless: The Motel Kids of Orange County (2010)

Filmmaker Alexandra Pelosi made this documentary that explores the life of homeless children whose families are living in motels, playing in parking lots, and digging through dumpsters. Within walking distance of Disneyland, families tell their stories of economic struggle.

Homeless to Harvard (2003)

The true story of Liz Murray, who was homeless at 15 and later enrolled in Harvard University. When Liz's mother, who suffers from schizophrenia and drug abuse, is institutionalized, Liz and her sister stay with their addicted father. When their mother returns, also diagnosed with AIDS, the family is torn apart by circumstances and eventually Liz becomes homeless. Determined to succeed, she focuses on school and wins a *New York Times* scholarship that allows her to attend Harvard. The film, originally made for TV, was directed by Peter Levin.

Kicking It (2008)

This documentary of the annual Homeless World Cup follows six homeless players as they go to South Africa to play soccer.

Directed by Susan Koch and Jeff Werner and narrated by Colin Farrell, the film premiered at the Sundance Film Festival. The stories of Najib from Afghanistan; Alex from Kenya; Damien and Simon from Dublin, Ireland; Craig from Charlotte, North Carolina; Jesus from Madrid, Spain; and Slavan from St. Petersburg, Russia are told.

The Pursuit of Happyness (2006)

Will Smith and his son depict the true story of Chris Gardner, a homeless single father on the streets of San Francisco. Directed by Gabriele Muccino, the film shows Gardner's almost unrelenting optimism in his search for stability, as he studies at night and wins a prestigious internship in a financial firm while caring for his son between shelters, hotels, and the bus station.

The Soloist (2009)

Robert Downey, Jr. stars as *Los Angeles Times* columnist Steve Lopez, who happens on homeless cellist Nathaniel Ayres (played by Jamie Foxx) on the city's streets. Ayres was once a promising musician who was beset by schizophrenia and became homeless. When a bond forms as Lopez writes about Ayres, opportunities develop for housing and support. The film was directed by Joe Wright.

Where God Left His Shoes (2008)

Salvatore Stabile directs and John Leguizamo stars as Gulf War veteran and former prizefighter Frank Diaz, head of an evicted family in New York City. As Christmas approaches, Frank needs to have a steady job to secure an available apartment.

Databases

Census Data

http://www.census.gov/hhes/www/housing/ahs/ahs.html

The American Housing Survey (AHS) is the largest regular national housing sample survey in the United States. The U.S. Census Bureau conducts the AHS to obtain up-to-date housing statistics for the Department of Housing and Urban Development (HUD). Data includes housing types, family composition, income, housing and neighborhood quality, and housing costs. National data are collected every other year, from a fixed sample of about 50,000 homes.

Housing Cost and Income Data

U.S. Department of Housing and Urban Development—Fair Market Rents http://www.huduser.org/portal/datasets/fmr/fmrs/docsys.html&data=fmr11

Fair market rents are set annually by HUD to identify subsidy levels for every community.

Litigation

Sargent Shriver National Center for Poverty Law
www.povertylaw.org

A searchable database of poverty law cases is available, including civil rights, consumer law, criminal law, disability, economic development, education, employment, family law, food programs, health, housing, immigration, juveniles, mental health, prisons, rural issues, Social Security, veterans, and welfare.

Poverty Data

http://www.census.gov/hhes/www/poverty/poverty.html

Web Sites

Policy and Research

Center on Budget and Policy (CBPP)
http://www.cbpp.org

CBPP is a public policy research organization focuses on federal and state budget issues and provides concise analysis of programs. Many analyses and reports are distributed on-line, and some of the most relevant recent publications are listed here.

A Quick Guide to Food Stamp Eligibility And Benefits

The Earned Income Tax Credit

Food Stamps On-Line: A Review of State Government Food Stamp Websites

Introduction to the Federal Budget Process

Introduction to the Food Stamp Program

Introduction to Medicaid

Online information about key low-income benefit programs: links to policy manuals, descriptive information, and applications for state food stamps, TANF, child care, Medicaid, and SCHIP programs:

Pulling Apart: A State-By-State Analysis of Income Trends

State Earned Income Tax Credits

Streamlining and Coordinating Benefit Programs' Application Procedures

The ABCs of State Budgets

Dr. Dennis Culhane, University of Pennsylvania
http://works.bepress.com/dennis_culhane/subject_areas.html#Frequently Requested

Dr. Culhane has conducted important research on homelessness among families, individuals, and veterans during the last decade. His published work, including reports commissioned by governments and others, is consolidated on his Web site.

Dr. Sam Tsemberis, Pathways to Housing
http://works.bepress.com/sam_tsemberis/

Dr. Tsemberis is a clinical-community psychologist and the innovator of the Housing First strategy through Pathways to Housing. He serves on the faculty of the Department of Psychiatry at Columbia University Medical Center.

Media

San Francisco Chronicle
http://www.sfgate.com/homeless/

While local print news series focused on homelessness, cost studies, and 10-year plans that emerged during the last decade, the

San Francisco Chronicle published "Shame of the City," reflecting the experience of reporter Kevin Fagan and photographer Brant Ward, who spent four months on the streets and interviewing the health care workers, police, tourists, residents, business people, and commuters who encounter homelessness. The series has been maintained on the Web site with the paper's other coverage of the issue.

Federal Government Web Resources

As many federal agencies move to all-electronic documents, these Web sites, as well as the electronic clearinghouses that several agencies operate, provide a resource to identify funds, research, and publications.

U.S. Department of Agriculture (USDA)
http://www.usda.gov

USDA is responsible for the Supplemental Nutrition Assistance Program (SNAP), school breakfast and lunch programs, the WIC nutrition program, and rural housing programs.

U.S. Department of Commerce, Bureau of the Census
http://www.commerce.gov/category/news-type/economic-news?er=true

The decennial census and the American Housing Survey produce data related to housing and homelessness. Data is used in formulas that determine the distribution of federal funds to states and localities.

U.S. Department of Defense (DOD)
http://www.defense.gov/brac/

The Base Realignment and Closure process of 2005 resulted in plans addressing the needs of homeless people in communities across the nation. DOD also manages the surplus personal property that benefits people who are homeless.

U.S. Department of Education (USED)
http://www2.ed.gov/programs/homeless/index.html

The Department of Education is responsible for the state and local contacts who ensure the education rights of children who are homeless.

U.S. Department of Health and Human Services (HHS)
http://www.hhs.gov/homeless/

HHS has a homeless page that provides access to research, grants, and publications from the agency.

http://aspe.hhs.gov/hsp/09/HomelessnessDataHHS/

This research link examines how states collect data on homelessness and housing when they use HHS funds. Interviews were conducted with TANF and Medicaid directors in all 50 states and the District of Columbia, and there is also a review of data-collection practices in nine other HHS mainstream programs.

HHS Substance Abuse and Mental Health Administration
http://www.nrchmi.samhsa.gov/

HHS Substance and Mental Health Services Administration operates the Homelessness Resource Center as a one-stop on-line resource of resource materials, fact sheets, and training models.

U.S. Department of Homeland Security/Federal Emergency Management Agency (FEMA)
http://www.fema.gov/

FEMA administers the Emergency Food and Shelter Program (EFSP), which provides formula funds to states and counties for people who are homeless.

FEMA Emergency Food and Shelter Program (EFSP)
http://www.efsp.unitedway.org/

EFSP is a public-private partnership created in 1983 to support local organizations providing emergency services and food assistance. Local boards chaired by the United Way distribute the funds. Local allocations in historical tables are available.

U.S. Department of Housing and Urban Development (HUD)
http://portal.hud.gov/portal/page/portal/HUD/topics/homelessness

HUD provides web access to research, housing data, and homelessness program information.

Homelessness Resource Exchange (HRE)
http://www.hudhre.info/

HRS is the one-stop shop for homelessness-related guidance from HUD, funding information, local homeless data including federal funds, and archives of Webcasts and briefings. HUD awards homeless assistance grants through the Continuum of Care (CoC) and Emergency Shelter Grants (ESG). HRE provides information to locate CoCs around the country, find CoC contacts, find report data, and view CoC and ESG awardees since 2005.

HUD Neighborhood Stabilization Program (NSP)
http://www.hud.gov/offices/cpd/communitydevelopment/programs/neighborhoodspg/statelinks.cfm

NSP allocated recovery funds to states and local communities to purchase foreclosed housing. A percentage of funds had to be used for special needs housing opportunities.

U.S. Department of Justice (DOJ)
http://www.ojp.usdoj.gov/

DOJ's Office of Justice Programs provides federal, state, and local authorities with data, training, and resources to address and prevent crime. OJP works on reentry issues, mental health and substance abuse among offenders.

DOJ's National Institute of Justice (http://www.ojp.usdoj.gov/nij) provides research and information on evidence-based practices. DOJ oversees the federal Violence Against Women Act (VAWA).

U.S. Department of Labor (DOL)
http://www.dol.gov/dol/audience/aud-homeless.htm

DOL provides data on employment and jobs and grants for training, including for veterans and young adults.

U.S. Department of Veterans Affairs (VA)
http://www1.va.gov/HOMELESS/index.asp

VA maintains a site on homelessness among veterans that includes both the VA plan to end homelessness and locally developed data on homelessness.

U.S. Interagency Council on Homelessness (USICH)
http://www.usich.gov/

The Council released a 2010 strategy to end homelessness. A Web site offers an archive of weekly newsletters, tool kits for planning, and an index of cost studies.

Corporation for National and Community Service (CNS)
http://www.nationalservice.gov

The corporation provides support to the volunteer sector and operates the nation's formal volunteer initiatives, including Senior Corps, AmeriCorps, Learn and Serve America, and the Martin Luther King Day of Service.

General Services Administration (GSA)
http://www.gsa.gov/portal/content/105035

GSA oversees disposal of real estate and buildings in the federal inventory. Some of these properties are found suitable for use by homeless programs under provisions of the McKinney-Vento Act.

Government Accountability Office (GAO)
http://www.gao.gov/

The Government Accountability Office (GAO) performs fact-based reporting on federal programs and spending for the U.S. Congress. Many of the topics of its reports and testimonies result from requests by members of Congress or from direction in legislative language.

GAO reports offer background reading that provides useful information on the origin of programs, legislative history, and related GAO reports. Reports are issued electronically on a daily basis, and printed copies can be purchased. GAO offers a daily e-mail of new releases. Following is a selected list of recent reports concerning homelessness, grouped by subject matter.

Homelessness

Homelessness: A Common Vocabulary Could Help Agencies Collaborate and Collect More Consistent Data, GAO-10-702, June 30, 2010.

Homelessness: Information on Administrative Costs for HUD's Emergency Shelter Grants Program, GAO-10-491, May 20, 2010.

Homelessness: Improving Program Coordination and Client Access to Programs, GAO-02-485T, March 6, 2002.

Homelessness: HUD Funds Eligible Projects According to Communities' Priorities, RCED-00-191, July 24, 2000.

Homelessness: Barriers to Using Mainstream Programs, RCED-00-184, July 6, 2000.

Homelessness: Consolidating HUD's McKinney Programs, T-RCED-00-187, May 23, 2000.

Homelessness: Grant Applicants' Characteristics and Views on the Supportive Housing Program, RCED-99-239, August 12, 1999.

Homelessness: State and Local Efforts to Integrate and Evaluate Homeless Assistance Programs. RCED-99-178, June 29, 1999.

Homelessness: Overview of Current Issues and GAO Studies, T-RCED-99-125, March 23, 1999.

Homelessness: Coordination and Evaluation of Programs Are Essential, RCED-99-49, February 26, 1999.

Rural Homelessness: Better Collaboration by HHS and HUD Could Improve Delivery of Services in Rural Areas, GAO-10-724, July 20, 2010.

Youth and Children

Runaway and Homeless Youth Grants: Improvements Needed in the Grant Award Process, GAO-10-335, May 10, 2010.

Support for Low-Income Individuals and Families: A Review of Recent GAO Work, GAO-10-342R, February 22, 2010.

Foster Care: State Practices for Assessing Health Needs, Facilitating Service Delivery, and Monitoring Children's Care, GAO-09-26, February 6, 2009.

Young Adults With Serious Mental Illness: Some States and Federal Agencies Are Taking Steps to Address Their Transition Challenges, GAO-08-678, June 23, 2008.

Child Welfare: HHS Actions Would Help States Prepare Youth in the Foster Care System for Independent Living, GAO-07-1097T, July 12, 2007.

Youthbuild Program: Analysis of Outcome Data Needed to Determine Long-Term Benefits, GAO-07-82, February 28, 2007.

Foster Care: Effectiveness of Independent Living Services Unknown, HEHS-00-13, November 10, 1999.

Census

2010 Census: Operational Changes Made for 2010 Position the U.S. Census Bureau to More Accurately Classify and Identify Group Quarters, GAO-10-452T, February 22, 2010.

Decennial Census: Methods for Collecting and Reporting Data on the Homeless and Others without Conventional Housing Need Refinement, GAO-03-227, January 17, 2003.

Decennial Census: Overview of Historical Census Issues, GGD-98-103, May 1, 1998.

Decennial Census: 1995 Test Census Presents Opportunities to Evaluate New Census-Taking Methods, T-GGD-94-136, September 27, 1994.

TANF and Welfare Reform

Temporary Assistance for Needy Families: Implications of Caseload and Program Changes for Families and Program Monitoring, GAO-10-815T, September 21, 2010.

Temporary Assistance for Needy Families: Implications of Recent Legislative and Economic Changes for State Programs and Work Participation Rates, GAO-10-525, May 28, 2010.

Temporary Assistance for Needy Families: Implications of Changes in Participation Rates, GAO-10-495T, March 11, 2010.

Temporary Assistance for Needy Families: Fewer Eligible Families Have Received Cash Assistance Since the 1990s, and the Recession's Impact on Caseloads Varies by State, GAO-10-164, February 23, 2010.

Welfare Reform: Better Information Needed to Understand Trends in States' Uses of the TANF Block Grant, GAO-06-414, March 3, 2006.

Welfare Reform: More Information Needed to Assess Promising Strategies to Increase Parents' Incomes, GAO-06-108, December 2, 2005.

Child Care: Additional Information Is Needed on Working Families Receiving Subsidies, GAO-05-667, June 29, 2005.

TANF and SSI: Opportunities Exist to Help People with Impairments Become More Self-Sufficient, GAO-04-878, September 15, 2004.

Welfare Reform: Rural TANF Programs Have Developed Many Strategies to Address Rural Challenges, GAO-04-921, September 10, 2004.

Welfare Reform: Information on Changing Labor Market and State Fiscal Conditions, GAO-03-977, July 15, 2003.

Child Care: Recent State Policy Changes Affecting the Availability of Assistance for Low-Income Families, GAO-03-588, May 5, 2003.

Welfare Reform: Former TANF Recipients with Impairments Less Likely to Be Employed and More Likely to Receive Federal Supports, GAO-03-210, December 6, 2002.

Welfare Reform: With TANF Flexibility, States Vary in How They Implement Work Requirements and Time Limits, GAO-02-770, July 5, 2002.

Welfare Reform: States Provide TANF-Funded Work Support Services to Many Low-Income Families Who Do Not Receive Cash Assistance, GAO-02-615T, April 10, 2002.

Welfare Reform: States Provide TANF-Funded Services to Many Low-Income Families Who Do Not Receive Cash Assistance, GAO-02-564, April 5, 2002.

Workforce Investment Act: Coordination Between TANF Programs and One-Stop Centers Is Increasing, but Challenges Remain,GAO-02-500T, March 12, 2002.

Welfare Reform: States Are Using TANF Flexibility to Adapt Work Requirements and Time Limits to Meet State and Local Needs, GAO-02-501T, March 7, 2002.

Veterans

VA Faces Challenges in Providing Substance Use Disorder Services and Is Taking Steps to Improve These Services for Veterans, GAO-10-294R, March 10, 2010.

Formula Grants: Funding for the Largest Federal Assistance Programs Is Based on Census-Related Data and Other Factors, GAO-10-263, December 15, 2009.

VA Real Property: VA Emphasizes Enhanced-Use Leases to Manage Its Real Property Portfolio, GAO-09-776T, June 10, 2009.

Federal Real Property: Authorities and Actions Regarding Enhanced Use Leases and Sale of Unneeded Real Property, GAO-09-283R, February 17, 2009.

Rental Housing: Information on Low-Income Veterans' Housing Conditions and Participation in HUD's Programs, GAO-08-324T, December 5, 2007.

Homeless Veterans Programs: Bed Capacity, Service, and Communication Gaps Challenge the Grant and Per Diem Program, GAO-07-1265T, September 27, 2007.

Homeless Veterans Programs: Improved Communications and Follow-up Could Further Enhance the Grant and Per Diem Program, GAO-06-859, September 11, 2006.

Homeless Veterans: Job Retention Goal Under Development for DOL's Homeless Veterans' Reintegration Program, GAO-05-654T, May 4, 2005.

Veterans Affairs Homeless Programs: Implementation of the Transitional Housing Loan Guarantee Program, GAO-05-311R, March 16, 2005.

Homeless Veterans: VA Expands Partnerships, but Effectiveness of Homeless Programs Is Unclear, T-HEHS-99-150, June 24, 1999.

Homeless Veterans: VA Expands Partnerships, but Homeless Program Effectiveness Is Unclear, HEHS-99-53, April 1, 1999.

Other

Disaster Assistance: Federal Efforts to Assist Group Site Residents with Employment, Services for Families with Children, and Transportation, GAO-09-81, December 11, 2008.

Leveraging Federal Funds for Housing, Community, and Economic Development, GAO-07-768R, May 25, 2007.

Drug Offenders: Various Factors May Limit the Impacts of Federal Laws That Provide for Denial of Selected Benefits, GAO-05-238, September 26, 2005.

Food Stamp Program: States' Use of Options and Waivers to Improve Program Administration and Promote Access, GAO-02-409, February 22, 2002.

Workforce Investment Act: Coordination of TANF Services Through One-Stops Has Increased Despite Challenges, GAO-02-739T, May 16, 2002.

Department of Agriculture, Food and Nutrition Service: Food Stamp Program: Non-Discretionary Provisions of the Personal Responsibility and Work Opportunity Reconciliation Act of 1996, OGC-01-9, November 7, 2000.

Managing for Results: Barriers to Interagency Coordination, GGD-00-106, March 29, 2000.

Military Bases: Reuse Plans for Selected Bases Closed in 1988 and 1991, NSIAD-95-3, November 1, 1994.

Drug Abuse Treatment: Data Limitations Affect the Accuracy of National and State Estimates of Need, HEHS-98-229, September 15, 1998.

Grants.gov

This site provides access to federal agency announcements of funding opportunities; listings are updated daily.

Office of Management and Budget (OMB)

http://www.whitehouse.gov/omb/budget

The White House Office of Management and Budget (OMB) oversees all documentation of the federal budget, including agency spending. OMB's site contains an archive of federal budgets.

President's New Freedom Commission on Mental Health

http://www.mentalhealthcommission.gov/index.html

The President's New Freedom Commission on Mental Health was created in 2002 to address inequalities in everyday life for people with disabilities. The commission's report identifies federal, state and local government opportunities to maximize use of resources, improve treatment and service coordination, and promote successful community integration for adults with a serious mental illness and children with a serious emotional disturbance.

Social Security Administration (SSA)
http://www.socialsecurity.gov/homelessness

SSA's homeless site provides an overview of the agency's initiatives to reach homeless beneficiaries and persons who are institutionalized or incarcerated and to coordinate with key partners. Evaluation of its efforts is posted, along with annual reports.

U.S. Congress
thomas.loc.gov

The Library of Congress houses all legislative documents, including proposed legislation, enacted legislation, hearing records, and more.

Key State Government Sites

Council of State Governments, National Reentry Resource Center

http://www.nationalreentryresourcecenter.org/

National Association of State Alcohol and Drug Abuse Directors

http://www.nasadad.org/index.php?base_id=283

National Association of State Medicaid Directors

http://www.nasmd.org/links/state_medicaid_links.asp

National Association of State Mental Health Directors

http://www.nasmhpd.org/

State Housing Finance Agencies

http://www.ncsha.org/housing-help

Key Local Government Sites

National Association of Counties (NACo)

http://www.naco.org

NACo represents the nation's more than 3,000 counties. In some states, counties have responsibilities and resources for health and human services as well as social services and corrections. In its annual meetings, NACo has supported resolutions on ending homelessness. The Web site offers access to county sites and elected officials.

National League of Cities (NLC)

http://www.nlc.org

NLC represents over 190,000 smaller-size towns and cities. It is a partner to municipal leagues in the states, which convene their cities and towns on a statewide basis. NLC provides elected officials with training, technical assistance, and models for local solutions. The Web site offers research, analysis, and best practice information.

U.S. Conference of Mayors (USCM)

http://www.usmayors.org

The Conference of Mayors is a national organization of the mayors of the cities in the United States over 30,000 in population. USCM provides support and partnership on the issue of homelessness and has passed numerous resolutions in support of key strategies to prevent and end homelessness. The Task Force on Hunger and Homelessness conducts an annual survey of member cities. The Web site provides access to profiles of mayors, past reports from the Mayors Task Force on Hunger and Homelessness, and resolutions adopted by the mayors.

Nongovernmental Organizations

Boston Health Care for the Homeless

http://www.bhchp.org/BHCHP%20Manual/index.html

O'Connell, James K., MD, Stacy E. Swain, MPH, Christine Loeber Daniels, and Joslyn Strupp Allen, MSW, editors. *The Health Care of Homeless Persons: A Manual of Communicable Diseases & Common Problems in Shelters & on the Streets*. Boston: The Boston Health Care for the Homeless Program, 2004. The authors, all practitioners of health services for people who are homeless, have compiled the definitive work on the key issues facing the population. Heavily illustrated with graphic examples and detailed medical information, the manual offers treatment guidance, disease management information, and bilingual information.

National Alliance on Mental Illness (NAMI)

http://www.nami.org/gtsTemplate09.cfm?Section=Grading_the_States_2009

NAMI has numerous materials on evidence-based approaches and a state grading system on mental health services.

National Alliance to End Homelessness (NAEH)

http://www.endhomelessness.org/section/library/?type=34

The alliance is a coalition of corporations, service providers, and individuals, that sponsors conferences and uses research and public education in its efforts to address homelessness. It maintains an extensive on-line library of fact sheets, research briefs, conference presentations, and other electronic materials.

National Coalition for the Homeless (NCH)

http://www.nationalhomeless.org/index.html

NCH is a national network of homeless persons, activists, service providers, and others committed to addressing homelessness through public education, policy initiatives, grassroots organizing, and technical assistance. It focuses on civil rights and consumer involvement. On-line directories of national organizations, state and local policy groups, and homeless services are available.

National Law Center on Poverty and Homelessness (NLCHP)

http://wiki.nlchp.org/display/Manual/Homelessness+Advocacy+Manual

The National Law Center monitors federal agency action on several McKinney Act programs, including homeless children's education and federal surplus property. The center focuses on international human rights and civil rights for people who are homeless. The Homeless Advocacy Manual is a tool for attorneys to access information on the rights of homeless people and litigation strategies.

International Resources

Australia

http://www.fahcsia.gov.au/sa/housing/progserv/homelessness/Pages/default.aspx

The national government's on-line resources include both the green paper and white paper issued by the Rudd government in 2008 as well as research links and information on the Prime Minister's Council on Homelessness.

Mental Illness Fellowship of Australia (MIFA)

http://www.mifa.org.au/

MIFA has member organizations of families, friends, and mental health consumers in the states and territories and sponsors an annual awareness event across the country.

Canada National Homeless Hub

http://www.homelesshub.ca/Default.aspx

Canada launched its Homeless Hub as a national web-based research library and information center of the Canadian Homelessness Research Network (CHRN).

Homeless Partnering Strategy

http://www.hrsdc.gc.ca/eng/homelessness/index.shtml

The Homeless Partnering Strategy is the national government's initiative to prevent and end homelessness.

U.K. Department of Communities and Local Government

http://www.communities.gov.uk/housing/homelessness/

The lead agency for homeless initiatives maintains this site with current research, data, government reports and strategies, and publications.

European Commission on Employment, Social Affairs, and Equal Opportunities

http://ec.europa.eu/social/main.jsp?catId=751&langId=en

The European Commission's Directorate-General for Employment, Social Affairs and Equal Opportunities works for improved employment opportunity and social inclusion.

European Federation of National Organizations Working with the Homeless (Fédération Européenne d'Associations Nationales Travaillant avec les Sans-Abri) (FEANTSA)

http://www.feantsa.org

FEANTSA is a network of European organizations focused on homelessness. The Web site includes the FEANTSA magazine and newsletter and documents on the Ending Homelessness Campaign. Member organizations represent more than 30 countries.

Glossary

Any discussion of homelessness involves multiple systems and sectors, such as the housing market, government programs addressing addiction and child welfare, and policy and budget processes. Use of the Internet makes it easier to identify and understand the many government agency and program acronyms used in policy and budget discussion. The new terms that have entered the language used to discuss homelessness and its solutions over the last decade are provided in this chapter.

AHAR (Annual Homeless Assessment Report) HUD submits an annual report to Congress documenting the nature and extent of homelessness. Included are yearly homelessness counts from localities, demographics, trends, and service use. AHAR compares prior year data to identify if homelessness in increasing or decreasing.

Affordable housing Housing costs are considered affordable if a household will pay no more than 30 percent of income for housing.

Appropriations Funding provided for a program or budget line item in a given year. Language in a budget document sometimes sets the terms under which funds may be spent.

Assertive Community Treatment (ACT) Teams ACT's multidisciplinary teams are key to the success of Housing First. ACT teams include case managers, formerly homeless people, and specialists in mental health and addiction, social work, nursing, and vocational rehabilitation. The work of teams uses an assertive approach that supports client choice and delivers services where individuals are, either at home or on the streets.

Authorization Legislation that establishes or continues a federal program or agency, specifies its general goals and conduct, and usually sets a ceiling on the amount of money that can be appropriated for it.

Block Grants Funding allocations from the federal government to states that can be used for a variety of purposes. Block grants are usually allocated by formula to provide considerable flexibility to governors for delivering the services outlined in the block grant.

Case management Coordination of an individual's use of social and other services, often by a consistent individual case manager who assists with access to health and mental health services, substance use services, and training and employment.

Chronic homelessness A definition of chronic homelessness was developed as a result of research that demonstrated that just 10 percent of homeless adults use 50 percent of homeless resources, because of their disability and length of stay in homelessness. When the federal HEARTH Act became effective in 2010, chronic homelessness was expanded to include families as well as individuals where the person(s) involved have been living on the streets or in shelter continuously for at least one year or on at least four separate occasions in the last three years and there is an adult head of household (or a minor head of household if no adult is present in the household) with one or more disabilities. A person who currently lives or resides in an institutional care facility, including a jail, substance abuse or mental health treatment facility, hospital, or other similar facility and has resided there for fewer than 90 days is considered chronically homeless if such person meets all of the other requirements.

Continuum of care A concept of the U.S. Department of Housing and Urban Development used to define the relation of homeless programs and services in a community. The continuum was introduced as a linear organizing principle for programs and services, beginning with outreach and emergency services, moving to transitional programs, and becoming "housing ready" for permanent housing. A continuum is also the group of local service providers who convene to seek federal funding.

Criminalization The act of attaching criminal charges and penalties to common outdoor activities of homeless people, such as sleeping in public places (parks, etc.). Some jurisdictions have passed such punitive laws as well as laws against sleeping or camping for extended periods in parks or on beaches with little effect in solving homelessness.

Couch surfing Homeless and runaway youth often live in temporary situations where they rely on couches or spare bedrooms of friends or family members as an alternative to the streets or shelters.

Day labor Usually manual labor jobs are available to homeless and poor workers on a temporary basis. Workers are paid very low wages, are charged for their equipment (such as gloves, brooms, etc.), and are not protected from unsafe conditions or practices. Workers wait at designated locations or go to hiring halls to seek jobs.

Deinstitutionalization Officially defined by the National Institute of Mental Health (NIMH) as the prevention of inappropriate mental hospital admissions through the provision of community alternatives for treatment, the release to the community of all institutionalized patients who have been given adequate preparation for such discharge, and the establishment and maintenance of community support systems for noninstitutionalized people receiving mental health services in the community.

Disability A person is determined to have a disability if an individual has a physical, mental, or emotional impairment that is expected to be of continued and indefinite duration, substantially impedes his or her ability to live independently, and is of such a nature that the ability could be improved by more suitable housing conditions; or has a developmental disability.

Discharge planning The practice of preparing a person in an institution or system of care or custody for release and successful integration into the community upon entry into the institution or system.

Domestic violence Verbal, emotional, financial, and sexual abuse may be present in personal relationships of all kinds. The abusive person or partner is usually referred to as a batterer and may be a spouse, live-in partner, significant other, boyfriend/girlfriend, or an ex-spouse or past partner.

Doubled up An accommodation to housing need in which one or more households share housing with family or friends.

Drop-in center Usually a daytime service for homeless clients that includes meals, clothing and laundry facilities, showers, support groups, and service referrals but does not provide overnight accommodations.

Dual diagnosis Sometimes referred to as co-occurring disorders and usually defined as the presence of both a substance abuse and mental health problem.

Emergency shelter Facilities that provide a temporary place to stay, usually only at night. Some shelters operate on a first-come, first-served basis where shelter residents must leave in the morning and have no guaranteed bed for the next night. Some programs have a definite length of stay and only offer a specific number of nights to each person. Some programs serve only one group (domestic violence, youth, veterans) and some operate only during winter months. Access to shelter in some communities is through a single point of entry or intake.

Entitlement Program mandating the payment of benefits to any person meeting eligibility requirements established by statute. Entitlement programs include Social Security, Medicare, TANF, and Medicaid.

Extremely low income A household income below 30 percent of area median income, as defined by HUD.

Fair Market Rent (FMR) HUD's annual estimate of the market rent for a specific size housing unit in a given area. Fair market rents are then used to calculate payments for low income tenants using assisted housing programs, where HUD will pay the difference between 30 percent of the person's income and the FMR.

Family unification or reunification Efforts or resources to return adults or children to the home or to the city of origin through the provision of travel funds, adequate housing, or other measures than prevents or ends separation and homelessness.

Fiscal year (FY) The federal government's accounting period, which begins October 1 and ends September 30. States and localities often use July 1 fiscal-year accounting.

Food bank A nonprofit clearinghouse for surplus or salvaged food that is usually redistributed to soup kitchens, meal programs, food pantries, and shelters.

Homeless Management Information System (HMIS) An HMIS is a computerized data collection system to collect information on the characteristics and needs of men, women, and children experiencing homelessness. An HMIS may cover a statewide or regional area.

Homeless person The McKinney Homeless Assistance Act, first passed in 1987, defined a homeless person as "1) an individual who lacks a fixed, regular, and adequate nighttime residence that is a) a supervised publicly or privately operated shelter designed to provide temporary living accommodations (including welfare hotels, congregate shelters, and transitional housing for the mentally ill); b) an institution that provides a temporary residence for individuals intended to be institutionalized; or c) a public or private place not designed for, or ordinarily used as, a regular sleeping accommodation for human beings." With the implementation of the new federal HEARTH Act at HUD in 2011, a homeless individual will be defined by a newly expanded set of factors that will include people who are living in defined situations of unstable housing as well as those considered homeless under other federal agency definitions.

Homelessness prevention Activities including use of short-term subsidies for rent and utility payments for families with eviction or utility-termination notices; security deposits or first month's rent so that a homeless family can move into its own housing; mediation programs for landlord-tenant disputes; legal services programs for eviction proceedings; and payments to prevent foreclosure.

Homeless, runaway, and throwaway youth There is no single definition for this population, which includes youth with unstable or inadequate housing who stay at least one night in a place not their home because they could not stay at home, ran away from home, did not have a home, were asked to leave home, and/or stayed at a shelter, outdoors, or in a temporary arrangement with another person (couch surfing). This group may also include current and former foster youth and youth with mental health or other issues.

Housing First Housing First is one of the field-tested, evidence-based innovations of the last decade that has successfully moved thousands of people experiencing chronic homelessness to permanent supportive housing. Housing First, pioneered by Dr. Sam Tsemberis at Pathways to Housing in New York City, places people who are homeless and living with disabilities, and most often living on the streets, directly into permanent supportive housing.

McKinney-Vento A general term for the set of federal programs created by the Stewart B. McKinney Homeless Assistance Act in 1987.

Medicaid Medical benefits for eligible low-income and disabled people provided under guidelines established by the federal government, with program requirements created by each state. Medicaid is funded through state and federal funds. Coverage will be expanded by new federal health care reform.

NIMBY (Not In My Back Yard) The resistance of neighborhoods to the siting or location of any facility or residence identified as undesirable; in this case, programs or housing for people who are leaving homelessness or living with special needs, such as mental health issues or addiction recovery issues, or reentry from prison.

NOFA (Notice of Funding Availability) The means by which several federal government agencies announce the availability of funds, publish applications and other information, and distribute funds through competitive processes. Called a Solicitation for Grant Applications (SGA) in other agencies.

Outreach Usually street-based engagement activities programs that contact homeless clients to offer food, blankets, or other necessities to support individuals in moving off the streets and into housing or services.

Permanent supportive housing Permanent affordable housing with support services designed to help tenants who are homeless, very low income, or have disabilities or other chronic health conditions to maintain their housing and achieve maximum independence.

PIT (Point in Time) A count of homelessness on a single night or 24-hour period.

Poverty line An official government measure produced by the U.S. Department of Health and Human Services to define the income needed to provide basic necessities.

Safe Haven A "low-demand" program intended to help engage mentally ill homeless people who might be wary of traditional shelters or other settings.

Safety net A general term for the array of benefits and assistance available to meet basic needs, such as food, housing, income, and health care.

Section 8 The chief federal rent subsidy program that provides monthly rental assistance to low-income individuals residing in privately owned units.

Skid Row A general term for an impoverished urban area where people who are homeless are living and where cheap housing, day labor, and other marginal businesses could be found. Many Skid Row areas have been wiped out by gentrification.

SNAP (Special Nutrition Assistance Program) Formerly known as food stamps, SNAP is a national program to improve the ability of poor families to purchase food by providing monthly benefits for a specific dollar amount to be used in most grocery stores.

Soup kitchen A food program that includes soup kitchens, food lines, and programs distributing prepared breakfasts, lunches, or dinners.

SRO (single-room occupancy) Inexpensive rental units in hotel settings, where tenants share bath and kitchens facilities if available.

Stand Down A local or regional event with a variety of social and other services provided to homeless veterans, created to offer a welcoming environment, a safe gathering place, and easy access. Stand-downs are derived from the military practice of 'standing down" from customary activity or the front line.

Supplemental Security Income (SSI) A federally administered income assistance program providing monthly cash payments for the needy aged, blind, and disabled.

Supportive services Programs providing job training, alcohol or drug treatment services, case management assistance, educational services, and the like. Services may be provided in conjunction with housing or shelter or in a different site.

Temporary Assistance For Needy Families (TANF) Block grant to states created by federal welfare reform under the Personal Responsibility and Work Opportunity Reconciliation Act of 1996, which established a new welfare system. The TANF block grant replaced Aid to Families with Dependent Children (AFDC).

Transitional programs Residential programs that provide a placement for persons before moving to permanent housing. A program may have a specific target population, such as persons with mental illnesses, runaway youths, victims of domestic violence, homeless veterans, and so on.

Index

About the Author

MARY ELLEN HOMBS served as deputy director of the U.S. Interagency Council on Homelessness from 2003 to 2009. Prior to joining the council, Ms. Hombs was executive director of the Massachusetts Housing and Shelter Alliance, a statewide alliance of 85 agencies that operate over 250 housing and emergency services programs for homeless people. Beginning in 1995 she was the alliance's director of special projects and coordinated statewide technical assistance initiatives in the areas of housing development, homeless programs, and discharge planning.

Ms. Hombs has more than 25 years of public policy, direct service, and technical assistance experience in homeless advocacy and programs at the local, state, and national level. She is the author of several books and numerous articles on homelessness, including "American Homelessness." She holds a BA in political economy and public affairs from George Washington University and a master's degree in city planning from Howard University.